A FIELD GUIDE TO
Retirement

A FIELD GUIDE TO
Retirement

14 LIFESTYLE OPPORTUNITIES

AND OPTIONS FOR A

SUCCESSFUL RETIREMENT

Alice and Fred Lee

DOUBLEDAY

NEW YORK LONDON

TORONTO SYDNEY AUCKLAND

PUBLISHED BY DOUBLEDAY
a division of Bantam Doubleday Dell Publishing Group, Inc.
666 Fifth Avenue, New York, New York 10103

DOUBLEDAY and the portrayal of an anchor with a dolphin are trademarks
of Doubleday, a division of Bantam Doubleday Dell Publishing Group, Inc.

Library of Congress Cataloging-in-Publication Data

Lee, Alice, 1923–
    A field guide to retirement : 14 lifestyle opportunities and options
for a successful retirement / Alice and Fred Lee. — 1st ed.
        p.   cm.
    1. Retirement—United States. 2. Lifestyle—United States.
  I. Lee, Fred, 1922– . II. Title.
HQ1063.2.U6L44 1991
646.7'9—dc20   90-48378
                                                                  CIP

BOOK DESIGN BY BARBARA M. BACHMAN

ISBN 0-385-41472-2

Copyright © 1991 by Alice and Fred Lee

ACKNOWLEDGMENTS

Hundreds of wonderful people throughout the United States have assisted us in researching and writing this book. Needless to say, we can't list them all, but we would be remiss in not acknowledging the following:

Our pastor, Dr. Don F. Renshaw, senior pastor, Spring Valley United Methodist Church, Dallas, Texas, who through his gerontological competence gave us insights into the makeup of the entire book.

The Seekers, our Sunday school class, who from the very inception of our idea ten years ago patiently listened and critiqued our thoughts and concepts.

Russ and Francine Manning, our backdoor neighbors, the recipients of a barrage of ideas as they prepared for retirement. Their decisions provided us with a laboratory for testing the validity of our "helpful hints."

Our literary agent, Denise Marcil, for her doggedness in finding us a publisher.

Arabella Meyer, our editor, who guided us in a very professional manner through the intricacies of publishing; and copy editor Estelle Laurence, who kept us on the straight and narrow.

Our two sons, Larry and Gary, and Gary's wife Becky, who provided constant encouragement to pursue our dream.

Our loving parents, the Lees and the Margots, three of whom are gone and Alice's ninety-one-year-old mother, who through their parenting instilled in us the old-fashioned concept of "can do." Putting together a book has its highs and lows. "Can do" took us through the lows.

Thanks, y'all!

Alice and Fred Lee

Description, mention, or inclusion of any area, community, retirement facility, residence, or association/society does not constitute endorsement or recommendation by the writers or publisher.

To communicate with Alice and Fred Lee for more information about Lifestyle Seminars, contact:

Fred E. Lee & Associates, Inc.
P. O. Box 5503
Richardson, TX 75080
214/783-8981

CONTENTS

. . .

PREFACE xiii

1. FIVE KEY QUESTIONS 1

2. FREEDOM TIME IS OPPORTUNITY TIME 10

3. SEVENTY-FIVE ACTIVITY IDEA GENERATORS 21

4. STAY PUT OR MOVE
   Lifestyle Option #1, Stay Put in the Community 46

5. SNOWBIRDS
   Lifestyle Option #2, Winter Resident 56

6. NOMADING—FULL OR PART TIME
   Lifestyle Option #3, RV'ing 73

7. RETIREMENT AREAS
   Lifestyle Option #4, Retirement Area Living 89

8. CLUB/RESORT/VACATION COMMUNITY
   Lifestyle Option #5, Leisure/Social-centered Living 122

9. LARGE RETIREMENT VILLAGE/CITY
   Lifestyle Option #6, Total Retiree-dominated Living 134

10. TOTAL PLANNED COMMUNITY
    Lifestyle Option #7, Planned Intergenerational Living 148

11. SMALL RETIREMENT COMMUNITY
Lifestyle Option #8, Partial Retiree-dominated Living 157

12. PAU HANA IN HAWAII
Lifestyle Option #9, Hawaiian Living 172

13. FOREIGN RETIREMENT
Lifestyle Option #10, Foreign Living 187

14. SPECIAL INTERESTS
Lifestyle Option #11, Optimum Fulfillment 201

15. ENTERING PHASE TWO RETIREMENT 217

16. RETIREMENT RESIDENCE
Lifestyle Option #12, Phase Two Carefree Living 228

17. RETIREMENT COMPLEX—AVAILABLE HEALTH CARE
Lifestyle Option #13, Phase Two Health Care When
Needed 236

18. CONTINUING CARE/LIFE CARE COMMUNITY (CC/LCC)
Lifestyle Option #14, Phase Two Care for Life Security . . 247

19. YOUR LIFESTYLE PREFERENCE 277

20. YOU ARE UNIQUE—YOUR PLAN IS UNIQUE 282

EPILOGUE
Our Mission Statement 288

APPENDIX
Where to Write 289

PREFACE

. . .

Our Great American Dream was disintegrating—going up in smoke! Our dream? The same one that many corporate people have. Leave the rat race and join the faculty of a university—in our case, Fred to teach and Alice to become a faculty wife. Both to become engrossed in student activities.

We achieved our dream in September 1970, when we moved from North Stamford, Connecticut, to Dallas, Texas. Fred was appointed Professor of Business Administration and Director of Management Development Programs in the School of Business at Southern Methodist University.

The goal of the business school was to build an exciting, innovative, creative program. One that would really turn on our students. We were making progress. But then a major change took place. C. Jackson Grayson, Jr., dean of the school, went to Washington to become the price czar. This was in October 1971. Our dynamic leadership was gone! Traditionalism started its slow creep back into the curriculum.

In the mid-seventies, we were in our mid-fifties. Our sons, Larry and Gary, were on their own. Our only debt was a small mortgage on a large house. It was at this time that we decided to strike out on our own. We set up a management consulting company.

The question of our eventual retirement was a major concern. We did a great deal of research and put together a one-day Retirement Planning Seminar. Did some advertising and presented our program. Both as a public seminar and an in-company workshop. A newspaper article, civic club speeches, and radio interview resulted from this endeavor.

Although we felt we were satisfying a need, there was a problem with our one-day program. It was too compact. Not enough detail.

About this same time some three-day preretirement planning programs were being offered. We let our one-day program fade away.

However, a deep interest in the subject remained. We attended some three-day programs. One subject was treated very lightly. Lifestyle. What to do with 2,500 hours of newfound time. Where? What about preparing for the time when age takes its toll? Are there alternatives? What are they?

From the spring of 1983 to the summer of 1985, when we started writing this book, we did in-depth research on the subject of retirement lifestyles. We continued researching and writing through 1990.

We have traveled the states searching out alternative lifestyles:

Down the East Coast through Connecticut, New York, New Jersey, Pennsylvania, D.C., the Virginias, the Carolinas, and both coasts of Florida.

The cold country of Minnesota and Wisconsin and along the Great Lakes through Illinois, Indiana, Michigan, and Ohio.

From the Pacific Northwest to Southern California, with a stop in Hawaii.

The high country of Colorado, the Deep South, and the Sunbelt states of Arkansas, Texas, New Mexico, and Arizona.

We learned a lot and would like to share our findings with you.

THE PURPOSE OF OUR BOOK
■   ■   ■

From hundreds of on-site visits, personal experiences, and observations, information obtained through interviews and extensive research, we want to help you—
To:

Be prepared for the happy freedom years—
Know what's ahead in retirement—
Understand and handle the changes—
Minimize the effects of stress—
Determine the most effective use of 2,500 newfound hours each
    year—
Understand/evaluate 14 Lifestyle Options—
Be aware of the changes in old old age—
Know how to prepare for old old age—

Surface self/spouse retirement expectations—
Understand the applicability for singles—
Develop your unique retirement plan and take action.

**HAVE A GREAT RETIREMENT
BY LIVING YOUR TOTAL LIFE
TO THE FULLEST!**

Alice and Fred Lee

A FIELD GUIDE TO
Retirement

1

FIVE KEY
QUESTIONS

∎   ∎   ∎

Retirement: it's the time of your life to have the time of your life. Why? Because it's opportunity time! The chance of a lifetime to have a new beginning. To be pro-active. To make things happen. To make your dreams come true. You move:

FROM	TO
Time regimentation	2,500+ new free hours per year
Daily routine	Self-determined schedule
Meeting deadlines	No deadlines
Imposed schedule	I'll do as I wish
Accountability to boss	No boss (spouse excluded)
The rat race	Freedom of choice
Corporate career path	A new self-made path

Opportunities abound!

Today's retiree is younger, more liberated, and more affluent than those in any earlier generation. The Social Security Administration reports that age sixty-two has replaced sixty-five as the retirement age and there are indications that it is going lower.

Life expectancy has increased:

MALE	WHITE	ALL OTHERS	FEMALE	WHITE	ALL OTHERS
At 60 live to	78.2	77.0	At 60	82.6	81.2
At 65 live to	79.8	79.1	At 65	83.7	82.7
At 70 live to	81.7	81.5	At 70	85.1	84.5

Source: HUD, National Center for Health Statistics.

Women of this generation are more self-confident, have a greater self-awareness, and are more involved than ever before. Many are single and career-oriented. They are increasingly rejecting the past gender role of just following their husbands.

Today's retirees are more affluent due to Social Security cost-of-living increases, private pension plans (in which 56 percent of Americans participate), real estate ownership, personal investments, and an increasing number of two-income families. This has created a window of opportunity. There is a high probability of ten to twenty years of active contribution before physical impairments cause cutbacks in activity.

THE SENIOR LIFESTYLE REVOLUTION
■ ■ ■

Gone is the old stereotype retirement: buying a small house in Florida, fishing from the city pier, and then rocking away watching the sunset. Today retirees have numerous options which offer many opportunities to experience years of satisfaction—living one's life to the fullest.

Great retirements don't just happen, they are planned. They require making choices and developing plans. Where a spouse is concerned the plan has to be for two and requires give and take as decisions are made. Your feelings, opinions, and preparations need to be identified and clarified before examining specific lifestyle options.

Ask yourself these five questions. Your answers, and when applicable those of your spouse, will be the cornerstone of your retirement plan.

1. Do you know what your retirement income will be?
2. Are you going to retire or change jobs?
Assuming Retirement:
3. How great a change do you want to make to your lifestyle?

4. How much provision for "old age" (when there are health impairments) do you want to include?

5. What will you do with your free time?

There are no right or wrong answers—except for the first question. Each person will have his/her own likes, dislikes, and biases. These differences, in the case of a husband and wife, need to be worked out.

■ 1. DO YOU KNOW WHAT YOUR RE-TIREMENT INCOME WILL BE? IS IT A GUESS OR IS IT BASED ON FACT?

If you answered this with "I don't know" or "I think it's about "X" number of dollars—that's a wrong answer. You need to take immediate action.

In order to decide on a lifestyle, you need to know what you have to work with. After all, you must be able to afford what you want to do.

When estimating your potential income, some figures will be educated guesses. For example, you can only guess what the future interest rate on your CD's or the future dividends on your stock will be. Get as much past information as you can. Then set a conservative amount. If you have a complicated situation, get help from a financial planner, banker, or accountant, doing a thorough check, including client references, before putting your financial resources in someone else's hands.

Company pension and benefits are one of the major sources of retirement income. Make sure your projected pension benefits take into consideration the various options you are offered. Also, be certain you know well in advance what life, medical, and dental insurance carries over into retirement.

A recently retired couple told us of their dilemma when they planned for retirement. They used the pension figures sent out in their company's yearly summary of benefits statement. However, when it came time to retire they found themselves with four options concerning guaranteed payments to the wife if her husband predeceased her. The option they chose resulted in a reduction of his retirement benefits by $2,600 a year.

Social Security is another major source of retirement income. Applying for Social Security benefits can be very confusing. If you apply for Social Security three months prior to the time you hope to receive benefits, you don't leave much time to fix whatever errors there may be in your records. To prevent any potential problems, obtain form SSA 7004-PC-OPI, "Request for Earning and Benefit Estimate Statement," from your local Social Security office, fill it out, and send it in. If you have ever used another name or number, include that information. In a few months you will receive a listing of your yearly contributions and an estimate of the amount that is available to you on your retirement. There is no charge for this service. Check your account against your records and check that there are no differences between your records and those of the Social Security office. The closer you get to retirement, the more often you ought to do this.

Financial security is a major concern for those approaching retirement. In general retirement income is lower than preretirement income. In addition there are outside influences that can affect your future income.

A few years ago soaring inflation worried many retirees; they had some bitter comments concerning their predicament. These people blamed everyone except themselves when basically they had not done a good job of preparing for their retirement.

If you have a few years before retirement, start thinking. A few thousand earning interest now will come in handy during those golden years. This is easier said than done, but for many savings are possible. Most people have finished paying their kids' college tuition and living costs. If you hold on to your car for two or three extra years you can save on new car payments. Vacations can be simplified.

It's a matter of choices. If you put extra money away before retirement, there is greater security after retirement. If you live it up now, you could find yourself doing without later.

Another factor to consider is that you or your spouse may live until your mid-eighties. Will you be financially secure?

Dr. Richard Suzman, Health Science Administrator of the National Institute on Aging, reported that there is almost double the rate of poverty over the age of eighty-five compared with those over sixty-five.

■ 2. ARE YOU GOING TO RETIRE OR CHANGE JOBS? IF YOU CHANGE JOBS, WILL IT BE FULL TIME OR PART TIME? HOW LONG WILL YOU KEEP WORKING?

Your answer may be dictated by financial need. However, we will assume you have a choice. The key element is whether you want freedom. Any full-time job takes away your ability to come and go as you wish. A part-time job provides some degree of freedom, although there is still a schedule to meet.

Why would a retiree from one job want another full-time job, other than because of financial needs?

- To fill the time.

- To fulfill the need to belong.

- To fulfill the need for recognition and rewards.

- To help others.

- To try something different.

- To build a second career.

A decision to take on full-time responsibilities, bridging the gap between formal company retirement and actual retirement, is not easy. Many have decided to continue working because they didn't plan their retirement.

Mr. R.V., a middle-level executive, retired early. It wasn't exactly a golden handshake, but each party was more than ready for a parting of the ways. The only plans he made involved using a small cabin cruiser extensively and dabbling in silver and other rare coins. He had always been very aggressive and traveled widely. Then he and his wife were together twenty-four hours a day. Mrs. R.V. confided in us that she was having a terrible time adjusting, and a few months later she had a severe nervous breakdown. He went back to work as a traveling executive and she fully recovered.

What's right for you? Will you be ready for full retirement? Will your spouse be ready? Open discussion about possible areas of conflict is essential.

■ 3. ASSUMING RETIREMENT, HOW GREAT A CHANGE DO YOU WANT TO MAKE TO YOUR LIFESTYLE? HOW MUCH CHANGE CAN YOU, AND YOUR SPOUSE, HANDLE?

Retirement will bring change, the question is how much. Many of the options open to a retiree involve considerable change. Many people move to a smaller house or a new city, state, or country. Others are full-time travelers, driving a motor home or pulling a trailer, essentially becoming nomads.

How much change do you want?

Consider the following questions. You and your spouse should answer each separately and then share your answers. Be honest and focus on what you are rather than what you might like to be.

1. **Are you an adventurous person?** (A) Yes (B) Sometimes (C) Rarely (D) No
2. **Are you daring?** (A) Yes (B) Sometimes (C) Rarely (D) No
3. **Do you do exciting things?** (A) Yes (B) Sometimes (C) Rarely (D) No
4. **Do you like variety and change in your life?** (A) A lot (B) Some (C) Little (D) Never
5. **Do you like challenging assignments?** (A) Yes (B) Sometimes (C) Rarely (D) Never
6. **Do you like new situations?** (A) Yes (B) Sometimes (C) Rarely (D) Never
7. **Do you consider yourself an extrovert?** (A) Yes (B) Somewhat (C) A little (D) Not much
8. **Are you a self-confident person?** (A) Yes (B) Somewhat (C) A little (D) Not much

9. **Do you feel in control of your life?** (A) Always (B) Sometimes (C) Rarely (D) Seldom
10. **Do you consider retirement the last major change in your life?** (A) No (B) Maybe (C) Probably (D) Yes

There are no right or wrong answers. If you have a majority of *C* and *D* category answers you may have a greater problem than many making major changes. You could find moving or nomading very upsetting. Take this into consideration when putting together your retirement plan.

However, it is possible that your job and family responsibilities have kept you or your spouse bottled up. Maybe you're just itching to try something new. Retirement offers you the opportunity to be adventuresome, daring, and different.

We recently talked to a couple just past their mid-fifties about their personal retirement objectives. The wife feels that full-time traveling in an RV would be the ultimate experience. Her husband is in the throes of job burnout after spending twenty-seven years with the same company. He turned down a promotion to headquarters years ago and has been shelved ever since. He has a very negative outlook. His fulfillment comes from involvement with the symphony chorus, where he heads up the bass section. He is also an avid golfer, participating in seniors tournaments at local country clubs. What will they do in retirement? Their needs and objectives are far apart. Now is the time for retirement discussions, particularly since he is a prime candidate for a golden handshake.

■ 4. HOW MUCH PROVISION FOR "OLD AGE" (WHEN THERE ARE HEALTH IMPAIRMENTS) DO YOU WANT TO INCLUDE?

Today it may be difficult to visualize a time when you will be in need of help. However, there is a high probability that in the future you will require some assistance. Who will help? Will your mate always be there? Can you count on your kids? Do you want to be dependent on your children?

The concept of life care or continuing care has recently emerged as a means of ensuring help for seniors when it's needed. Fraternal organizations have been around for a long time. Many have had homes for their aged members and spouses for years. Basically you sign over all your assets and in return you have a room in the home, meals, activities, and health care. They give you a small monthly allowance for personal needs. These homes are available for organization members only and don't involve a large number of people.

In the late sixties and early seventies a new version of life care emerged, mostly in the form of church-related communities. You didn't have to sign over all of your assets, only provide an entrance endowment and monthly fee. Now a for-profit service industry has emerged and a variety of financial arrangements are possible.

One approach is to consider an option of this nature as phase two of your plan. You can plan to move into a life care village when the burdens of a household become too overwhelming. However, all of these facilities require that you are self-sufficient when you move in and many have three- and four-year waiting lists.

■ 5. WHAT WILL YOU DO WITH YOUR FREE TIME?

This is undoubtedly the toughest question that a retiree faces. But you have been asked this same question before. As a youngster approaching high school graduation how many times did your parents say, "What are you going to do?" College was an easy reply for some. That only delayed an answer. Soon parents and counselors asked, "What's your major? What are you going to do?" As your kids approached graduation, how many times did you ask them, "What are you going to do?" It's possible that you may have asked your grandchildren, "What are you going to do?" Now this question has gone full circle.

Your thoughts may be going in different directions at this time. The question, "What are some retirement options?" may be foremost in your thinking. Along with, "What are these different lifestyles like?" "What's involved?" "Where?"

The following chapters will help you sort through a variety of lifestyles. We will not give any recommendations or endorsements. Our purpose is to explain our findings and feelings and to list advantages and concerns. This will provide you with a data base to help you reach your own conclusions. The prices mentioned throughout are those effective in 1990. An asterisk (*) following a facility, area, or town indicates an address is available in the Appendix.

2

FREEDOM TIME IS OPPORTUNITY TIME

■   ■   ■

How much freedom time?

For those who don't retire but just change jobs there is no additional freedom time. True, people may retire from one company or job but if they take another full-time job they have not entered retirement.

Part-time work equals part-time retirement. The schedule that must be followed, whether it is a few hours, a day or two, or three days a week, inhibits the use of the free time available. There is a work schedule that dictates time allocation, which overrides the use of time for personal activities.

Is this bad? Of course not. It's just a choice that has been made. A continuum of a routine imposed by others vs. the freedom of full retirement. This doesn't mean that in retiring there cannot be routine or a schedule. Many activity choices are structured. The key element is that it is the retiree's choice whether a routine is accepted or followed.

FULL RETIREMENT
■   ■   ■

Captain R.B. and Captain C.C., both pilots for a major airline, faced retirement at about the same time. Captain R.B. and his wife made their retirement decision many years in advance of retirement day. Because of his high seniority he was able to choose San Francisco as a base. They moved from the East Coast to the outskirts of Reno, Nevada. He commuted to San Francisco when he was scheduled to fly. They fulfilled their dream by purchasing a mini-ranch. It's a beautiful spread, large enough to have a few horses. They go out the back gate and are soon riding in some desolate hill country. They have invested in some houses which they rent out, so they have a mini-business. He is very active in the Civilian Air Patrol. They participate in local parades as a part of the horse brigade. They take many trips. All in all they have a very happy retirement.

Captain C.C. did nothing to prepare for retirement. His wife was very anxious and wanted to make some plans. She confided in us about her fear that he would have nothing to do—that he would be around the house all the time. He evaded our queries about his retirement plans. His usual answer was, "I'll probably set up a woodworking shop in the garage." Nothing was done. Today he openly admits he is not happy in retirement—he has nothing constructive to do. His words are, "I'm bored." He said he misses the "command" and respect he had when he was a captain. They have traveled a lot but they say you can only visit old friends just so often. He has thought of taking some real estate courses, but he's "still thinking about it." Another friend urged him to join the Lions Club. He's gone every Friday for lunch. His wife remains active in her clubs, which get her out of the house quite a bit. They both take it day by day, just filling in time.

DECISIVENESS
■ ■ ■

What can be learned from these two captains? The main thing is to accept what will eventually happen—retirement—and do something about it. Be decisive! Both of these men had to be decisive as pilots. Decisions involving human life were made by each of them on a daily basis. But when it came to a personal decision one of them copped out.

Mr. K.M. got fed up and left a senior executive position at age sixty-one. He accepted another senior position in Seattle and he and his wife moved across the country.

After three years he decided to retire. He bought a luxury cruiser in order to explore Puget Sound. After a while he felt a lack of fulfillment. He told us, "I'm not making a contribution." Then he received a phone call from a previous employer. He was asked by the widow of the founder of the company to be her financial consultant.

He became a new man. His voice radiated excitement—he was back in the mainstream. But not full time. There will still be plenty of free time for his boat, golf, and the grandchildren. Now he had a meaningful purpose—he will be making a contribution.

Wives bear the brunt of the indecisiveness of many men. While using a laundromat during one of our trips, Alice became engaged in conversation with a couple of snowbirds. The gist of the conversation centered around one woman's attempt to get her recently retired husband into woodworking. She never mentioned her husband's interest in this hobby. This woman and her son felt it would be good for him and they were trying to force him into adding a workshop onto their house. It was evident that the wrong people were being decisive.

WHAT ARE YOU GOING TO RETIRE TO —NOT FROM?
■   ■   ■

Doctors Thomas H. Holmes and Richard Rahe have done considerable research on the subject of stress and its effect on an individual's health. They have made up a life event change chart, rating from 1 to 43 the stress of each change on an individual. The severest change, number 1, is the death of a spouse. They rate this at 100 on their scale of impact. They rate retirement at number 10 and give it a 45 on their scale of impact. Further proof of the traumatic effect of retirement. Accepting the reality of forthcoming retirement and doing something about it will ease its impact.

Everyone doesn't fear retirement. There are thousands, perhaps millions, who can't wait to get out of their routine. Retirement offers an escape for those who have been forced into a rut, usually via the golden handcuffs—i.e., very good benefit programs.

Mr. K.S., from a very small town in northern Ohio, could not wait for retirement. His duties as a foreman were causing him all kinds of stomach problems. He took an early retirement and today enjoys his leisure in the small town where he has lived for more than fifty years. A daily walk to the coffee shop for morning coffee with "the good ole boys" is the highlight of each day. Twice a week he and one of the "boys" drive to a nearby town to watch the animal auction.

Could you be satisfied with such inactivity? If your answer is "no" or "I don't think so" or "probably not," then you need to do some very serious thinking and decision making about what you are retiring to.

WHAT TO DO IN RETIREMENT
■　■　■

No one can give you the answer to this question. There are a lot of references to use but when push comes to shove it's a personal decision. It should be compatible with your spouse's views on the subject. If it isn't, the first thing to do is work it out together, finding something both of you can be happy with.

When you have come to a decision start searching for a new set of purposes. To prepare for your search, consider the following:

■ Make sure there is meaningful purpose to what you choose to do, not just busyness to fill time.

■ You will need both mental and physical stimulation.

■ Find at least one activity that is not a husband and wife activity.

■ Recognize the seasonal limitations of some activities.

■ Have an inside and an outside activity.

■ Don't become involved in something because it's the current fad.

■ Don't withdraw from circulation.

■ Let the child loose—do what you've always wanted to do.

Does "let the child loose" include the following? We think so.

Mr. J.D. of Cleveland, Ohio, a retired executive, earned his pilot's license at sixty-four. He bought a single-engine Cessna 182 and after fifteen flights to the West Coast, two to Alaska, one to Europe, he made a solo 25,000-mile flight to Australia and back. He took his latest trip at age seventy-one. When you talk with him, he exudes optimism and is determined to have fun.

Before beginning your search for "what to do in retirement," take an inventory. What are your answers to the following:

- Is there a secret desire that I have always had? What?

- Do I have a pent-up need to achieve a certain goal? What?

- What have I always wanted to do but couldn't find the time?

- What did I really love to do before I had to make money?

- Have I been envious of someone and said, "I wish I could do that" ?

- I've always wanted to build _____.

- I'd love to be able to create a sculpture, a painting, a _____.

- I'd like to become an expert in _____.

- As a kid I thought I'd like to be _____.

Unless you know at the onset what you want to do, don't figure on making up your mind overnight. It will take time. It will probably not be a clear-cut "I know without a shadow of a doubt" decision. You may have some false starts. Keep at it and the spotlight will eventually focus on an answer.

Many of the lifestyles we will identify will have a great impact on how you use your time. In some cases a lifestyle will provide numerous interesting activity opportunities. But having a golf course in your backyard, a weaving loom nearby, or a swimming pool down the street will not be the complete answer to this important question of how to use your time.

I'LL FIND SOMETHING TO DO
■ ■ ■

Our files have hundreds of articles concerning the need to retire to something, not retire from something. Time and time again we have seen the distressing results of "I'll think of something to do." Undoubtedly this person will find something to do, mostly busy work. Nonchallenging ways to fill up the time. Soon he/she becomes bored with what he/she is doing, hence becomes a boring person. Boring people don't find satisfaction and they become irritable. Then they become irritable boring people.

Some folks, very few in our opinion, can just sit and idle away the time. Most of us need the stimulation of accomplishment. We need to feel that we are doing something worthwhile.

What's worthwhile?

There's no set answer. It's like—what is beautiful? It's in the eye of the beholder. What's worthwhile is in the mind of the doer. That's why it doesn't work to get involved in some activity merely because someone else likes it, or because it seems to be the thing to do.

"IN" ACTIVITIES
■ ■ ■

Not so long ago macramé was the "in" thing. Everywhere you went there were twine wall hangings and long colorful hanging plant holders. Because others find tying knots interesting is no guarantee that you will also find satisfaction in being a knot tier.

MULTIPLE ACTIVITIES
■ ■ ■

You will need more than one activity. You need different interests at different times. What do golfers do when the shoulder gives out or there is a prolonged rainy spell? Some head for the clubhouse and spend the day at the nineteenth hole! That's dangerous. We all know that serious problems can result from using the bar as a means of escape from boredom. There's a need for stimulating activities which can be fitted in when health conditions intervene or when there's a change in plans.

THE OLD-TIMER
■   ■   ■

Why is it that the retiree golfer doesn't always get invited to play in the regular foursome? In a lot of cases it's because the retiree can't join in on the conversation that takes place at the tee-off, on the green, or while riding in the golf cart.

If the retiree isn't into stimulating activities there's not much to talk about. There are two old standby conversations to which the retiree can contribute. "I remember when" and "Lately I've been having a lot more problems with my ulcer and my allergy is acting up, and my doctor says . . ."

The logical reaction, by others in the foursome, is to find a way to ease the "old-timer" out. They get tired of constantly hearing about the past and aches and pains. It is unfortunate but true.

People like to be around those who are stimulating and interesting— those who can contribute in a positive way to the discussion.

IMMERSION IN THE JOB
■   ■   ■

Unfortunately, a lot of men, and lately more and more women, have let their lives evolve completely around their work. It's become the center of their lives. Many of their outside activities emanate from their workplace. For example, working on the company picnic or being a part of the bowling league. Or being appointed the company representative to the United Way or to a civic or professional association. In addition, friendly little groups emerge at the workplace—the Tuesday lunch group, the Thursday lunchtime shopping group, or the gang that gets together after work for a beer and a quick game of pool or darts.

For those with responsibility and authority—i.e., managerial positions —there are always many places to go and places to be seen. It goes with the territory. Many managers complain about these command performances. But there's also a great deal of satisfaction being seen with those who are also there to be seen. Much of the complaining is surface in nature.

Many social invitations are extended to those in positions of power, just because they do have power. These are duty calls but many times a good time can be had by all. These business and social affairs become an integral part of a family's social life. A retired CEO of a large Eastern public utility company and his wife told us that they lost practically all of their social life upon retirement. They had not realized how intertwined their social life and their business responsibilities had become. When he was no longer in a position of power they found themselves on the outside.

THE CUT-OFF
■ ■ ■

Retirement very abruptly cuts off involvement. Meaningful substitutes are needed. The difficulty is that now the retiree must initiate the action, must be creative. In the past involvement was easy. The company, the job, and co-workers existed. A person just had to meld into what was already there. A new challenge emerges when this built-in group partici-pation is severed. What will take its place?

Normally retirement brings with it a lower income. It's possible that the money may not be there to continue the country club membership, the yearly subscription to the symphony, or the local little theater group.

Most people will not be in a poverty situation. However, if the cut-backs required free up more time, activity substitutes are needed to fill these additional hours.

SOMETHING TO RETIRE FOR
■ ■ ■

Christopher Hallowell hits the nail on the head with his article "Something to Retire For," which appeared in the October 8, 1985 issue of the *Houston Chronicle.* His opening statement concerns a sad mem-ory of his father who retired in his mid-sixties while still in good health. He described his father's way of spending time. First, he read, in great detail, the morning paper and the mail, mostly junk mail. He examined each coupon carefully before throwing it away. A nap followed lunch and then it was time to go grocery shopping. He spent hours in the supermar-ket reading the fine print on labels, comparing prices, and examining new products. Late afternoon and evenings he spent watching television.

Retirement, to the author's father, was time that had to be endured rather than used. He died five years after retirement.

Mr. Hallowell feels that his father's shrinking from life is very typical.

His research brings out one emotion that seems to predominate all others —*the fear of empty time.*

One of his research interviewees was Jesse, a seventy-year old woman, whom he met in a senior citizens center. She was filling a figurine mold with plaster. When asked if she had made many of these she replied that she had made about a dozen and could do it in her sleep. She called it fill-up time that someone concocted for old folks to do. Her parting words were, "I get so bored."

The author's main premise is that we don't regard retirement as an opportunity.

He favors doing away with mandatory retirement at seventy, but recognizes that for many people that will only postpone the hollow days that retirement brings. Society does a disservice to retirees by casting them off. People must be made aware, long before they retire, that they have to retire to something.

YOUR CHALLENGE
■   ■   ■

Becoming involved in meaningful pursuits is a challenge. There's no magic dust that will all of a sudden provide the answer. There is no way we can tell you what you should do in retirement. We can give you examples, give you points to consider, and raise questions. But you have to make the decision. That's the challenge.

It's not our intent to suggest that you become completely wrapped up in activities to the point that you haven't any free time. If your pursuit causes worry and anxiety, then you might just as well be back at work.

What's needed is a happy medium. This balance will emerge if you carefully think through this key element of retirement and take some action steps.

The easy way is for a person to say, "I'll find something to do." As a matter of fact, you will find things to do. It will be your choice, busy work or meaningful purposeful activity, that causes that warm feeling of accomplishment.

SINGLES APPLICABILITY
■ ■ ■

In all probability single people will have less problem with the usage of time than married folks. Singles are used to taking initiatives, to making decisions, and taking action on their own. They have many hours by themselves to fill and have been used to initiating activities.

A widow of many years came to Dallas to be married. Unfortunately the wedding never materialized, but she had sold her house and was now a Dallasite. In a matter of a few months she had a full daily calendar of activities. She took the wedding setback in stride and went forward.

Undoubtedly her years of widowhood gave her the ability to cope with setbacks. Today she has a happy social life centering around her church, AARP tours, and her positive outlook on life.

Being single comes about in many ways.

The need for complete freedom causes many to choose a single life-style. We all start out single and some people choose to continue that way.

Having tried the nuptials route, a divorce converts a person to the singles classification.

In The Younger Years
At this time in one's life there is still time to build a career and become self-sufficient.

In The Later Years—The Overdependent Wife
Devastation is the only way to describe the case of Mr. and Mrs. D.B., an upper-middle-class-income couple who retired to Florida having originally come from New Jersey. After a short time they moved to the husband's hometown in Tennessee. A very small town where he felt he could feel secure being among his few remaining relatives.

His wife, a classic example of the "overdependent wife," went along with the move. Her dependency was extreme. Over the years she expressed to us her constant fear—"I don't know what I'd do if he went before me."

Neither one had any meaningful activities. They just used to pass time. They befriended a recent widow. In a short time a romance blossomed between the widow and the overdependent wife's husband.

In a small town there are no secrets. The gossip caused many violent arguments. Excessive drinking resulted in broken furniture, tears, and her daily diary of his transgressions written in the wee hours of the morning.

After over forty years of marriage, they divorced. Her naïveté resulted in her getting a pittance of a settlement.

She moved back to Florida with a poverty-level income. After forty years of motherly and wifely duties she had no skills that could be utilized to augment her income. It took years of adjustment and study until she was finally able to reenter the work force.

Even if terminal illness precedes death, there is no way anyone can prepare for the departure of a spouse. Yet all couples face this inevitable loss. To many this will transpire after retirement. The deeper the love and the longer the commitment the harder the adjustment will be. At our age we see this happening to quite a few of our friends. But life must go on. The loss results in a person once again entering the ranks of the singles.

EQUAL APPLICABILITY
■   ■   ■

All of the lifestyles we will discuss are equally applicable to single and married. Until much later in life—old, old age—most activities are geared to husband and wife. Our research brings this out since traditional married couples predominate in the lifestyles.

3

SEVENTY-FIVE ACTIVITY IDEA GENERATORS

· · ·

Most people in corporate or business life have not been creative in terms of their own personal life. Creative in terms of job performance, yes, but not in their personal activity. In many cases business life and personal life become very intertwined. This is equally applicable to single and married persons.

Retirement, therefore, puts many people in a quandry and sometimes in a very stressful situation. It's not easy for someone who has worked five days or more a week for years and years and who has not prepared for retirement. If this person, upon retirement, decides to improve his wife's kitchen in terms of efficiency and quality control, he will naturally create a lot of stress. From what we've learned this sort of thing has happened many times.

Our research and travels have uncovered many opportunities for participation in activities in which a person may find the key to meaningful purpose. The following are some general interest categories and organizations within each category that may be of interest to you. A postcard, letter, or phone call to an organization will bring a wealth of information.

ASSOCIATIONS—RETIREES

■   ■   ■

By any yardstick, one association stands out far and above as the leader in retiree services.

American Association of Retired Persons (AARP)*

In 1958 Dr. Ethel Percy Andrus, principal of Lincoln High School in Los Angeles and founder of the National Retired Teachers Association, launched a new organization open to all older Americans—AARP. According to *The Wall Street Journal* (December 27, 1989), there are now 32 million members fifty years of age or older. AARP's 1988 operating results showed membership dues of $89,800,000 and total operating revenues of $262,020,000.

William F. Buckley, Jr., refers to an approaching "gerontocracy" when older people will exercise decisive political power. AARP is very influential in determining the course that this "gerontocracy" takes. They have a Washington lobbying staff of eighteen persons and a nation-wide legislative advertising program. The politicians *have* to respond. An organization with a membership that has a high voting rate can get things done.

The other side of AARP is the services it offers its members. Dues are $5.00 a year.

■ Purchase privileges program—discounts on car rentals, hotels, and motels

■ Pharmacy service

■ Investment program

■ Travel service

■ Motoring plan

■ Group health insurance

- Auto/homeowners insurance

- *Modern Maturity* magazine and bi-monthly news bulletin

- Books and special reports

There are 3,700 AARP chapters throughout the United States. The national headquarters provides chapter guidance and material on a great number of subjects of interest to the retiree. You can help others as a tax aide, widowed persons volunteer, or teacher of defensive driving.

We have been AARP members for years, have been to the national headquarters in Washington, and attended the 1984 National Bi-annual Convention in St. Louis. Within the AARP structure, starting at the local chapter level, up through the nine geographic regions and the national office there are unlimited opportunities for involvement in meaningful activities. All it takes is a little personal initiative.

Mature Outlook*

This organization is a member of the Sears family of companies. We became members of this organization when the 270,000-member National Association of Mature People (Montgomery Ward-sponsored), became a part of Mature Outlook.

Annual dues are $9.95 and you must be at least fifty years old to join. Benefits include discounts on Sears services/products, hotels, and car rentals. There is a mail order pharmacy and some other miscellaneous services. They regularly mail out booklets, a magazine, and a newsletter.

National Council of Senior Citizens (NCSC)*

This organization was formed in 1961 and according to an endorsement by President Johnson, "without the NCSC there would have been no Medicare." The group also has the endorsement of the AFL-CIO; Mr. Jacob Clayman, former head of the Industrial Union Department AFL-CIO, is listed as president emeritus.

The NCSC is an advocacy organization headquartered in Washington. There are over 5,000 senior citizens clubs and the total membership is four and a half million.

Their activities have included demonstrations against the big oil companies and building many low-income housing units for the elderly and handicapped—funded under HUD's Section 22, Direct Loan Program. This is an action-oriented group.

Dues are $12 a year, and entitle members to buy medicare supplemental insurance, prescription drugs by mail, and travel services. Also available are hotel and car rental discounts and a monthly news publication. This can best be described as a "grass roots" organization.

National Association of Partners in Education, Inc. (NAPE)*
The mission of the National Association of Partners in Education is to help establish and strengthen education partnership programs throughout the nation. There are two classifications of membership—corporate and individual/professional; dues are $60 a year.

NAPE sponsors a national conference on volunteering, sends out legislative and media alerts and a newsletter. Mrs. George Bush is honorary chairperson.

ORGANIZATIONS—POLITICAL
■ ■ ■

One of Fred's former bosses waged a full-scale campaign for the Ohio state legislature when he retired. He was elected for two terms. If you have deep-rooted political convictions, work with the party of your choice. Dedicated campaign workers are always welcome. Of course, you have to be able to understand and accept the wheeling and dealing that goes on. Everyone will not fit into the inner working structure of political parties.

ORGANIZATIONS—FRATERNAL
■ ■ ■

Many people carry membership cards of fraternal groups but have never had the time to become really involved. Many had a sincere interest in the workings and teachings of a particular organization, but never had the time to study and progress through the chairs.

Retirement takes away the "no time" excuse, opening the door for in-depth study and understanding. A deep sense of satisfaction from accomplishment and the camaraderie of others who share the same values can provide a great deal of meaningful purpose.

ORGANIZATIONS—CIVIC/SERVICE
▪ ▪ ▪

Besides the good-natured meeting banter and the luncheon speaker, all civic/service organizations have a project or cause that they support. This combination of good will, learning, and contribution offers an opportunity for a well-rounded activity.

Leadership positions can be had by those with time, energy, and vision. Finding the right civic/service group requires some initiation and evaluation.

EDUCATION
▪ ▪ ▪

You're never too old to learn, as the saying goes. If you haven't been in a formal classroom for a good many years, you will probably be somewhat apprehensive, that's only natural. Going after a degree requires courses that tax anyone's mental ability. But if you have the qualifications to be accepted as a degree candidate, you can survive. The time to study is available, all that's needed is the resolve to win.

If you're not interested in the academic laurels that go with degree certification, there are other ways to learn. Many colleges have special rates for auditing a course.

Elderhostel*

We have attended three Elderhostel programs and our experiences have been terrific! In the United States the courses are one week in length, abroad they are three weeks. In the United States, registration is on Sunday afternoon and departure is the next Saturday morning. Classes are normally held on campus and are taught by faculty members. At Clemson University we stayed in a dormitory and ate with the students in the cafeteria. At the other two programs we were housed at a motel.

This nonprofit organization was started in 1975 and their growth has been phenomenal. In 1988 there was a total enrollment of 162,000. Of the total, 110,000 were in U.S. programs, 9,000 in Canada, and 43,000 in international programs. Enrollment in 1990 is expected to be 195,000. There are 1,200 host campuses.

Each one-week program has three courses which meet one and one-half hours a day. The following are some of the courses from the programs we attended: Tales of the Superstition Mountains, Journal Writing, the Power of the Positive, Sex in the Eighties, and Desert Flora and Fauna.

There are activities such as tours to local places of interest and field trips. Evening activities include student performances, concerts, and game nights. Every day and evening was completely filled. Being with a group of forty retirees from all parts of the country and with diverse backgrounds is very stimulating.

Tuition in 1990 averaged about $250 a week. That is all-inclusive except for your transportation to and from the university. Unfortunately, the programs are so popular there is a problem of excessive registration. We tried for a 1990 program but were wait-listed.

The best endorsement comes from the number of individuals who have attended programs over the years. In one of our programs a couple in their eighties said, "This is our fifty-seventh Elderhostel program!"

Interhostel*

The University of New Hampshire has an international educational program for those fifty years of age and older—Interhostel. This university was the original sponsor of the Elderhostel program. Their international program was started in 1980. Each two-week program is designed in cooperation with a local institution that serves as a host. This is not a tour program. There is no time set aside for shopping or side trips to visit friends.

Each program centers around a city. The host university is responsible for program scheduling, planning, and day-to-day implementation. A representative of the University of New Hampshire accompanies each group. Normal group size is forty participants. Accommodations are usually in multi-unit residential halls with shared bath and most meals are served in dining facilities on campus. Social and cultural activities are designed to acquaint participants with the country, people, and customs.

The Spring 1990 catalogue lists: Christchurch, New Zealand; San Juan, Puerto Rico; Lisbon, Portugal; San José, Costa Rica; Bamberg, West Germany; Athens, Greece; Florence, Italy; The Hague, Holland; Toledo, Spain; Vienna, Austria; and a new two-week cruise to Alaska.

Per person costs (double occupancy) vary from New Zealand at $1,750 to $1,095 for Costa Rica, plus air fare.

Grace Graham Vacation College*

In Eugene, Oregon, the University of Oregon has a one-week program for seniors. Started in 1964 by Professor Grace Graham, Grace Graham Vacation College engages each participant in an atmosphere conducive to intellectual and cultural renewal and growth.

The August 13–19, 1989, program was Creativity and Criticism— Tasting and Judging the Lively and Literary Arts.

Accommodations are in the high-rise University Inn. Each room has a private bath and there are gourmet meals along with wine each evening —all of which indicate a first-class experience. The cost is $400 per person double occupancy.

The Chautauqua Institution*

For nine weeks every summer the Victorian community of Chautauqua in southwestern New York is full of visitors. Ten thousand people come to enjoy themselves and improve their minds.

The Chautauqua Institution was founded in 1874. Originally it was a summer tent colony for Sunday School teachers. Since then, it has expanded to include classes and lectures on government and current events. Almost all U.S. presidents have spoken there at one time or another.

The last week of the nine weeks has special provisions for older adults. In 1989 this was the week of August 20–27, during which seniors participated in the regular programs, lectures, music, recreation, drama, and group fellowship. The Center for Older Adults also programs "55 Plus" weekends. One focused on Central America, the other on the Bicentennial of Congress.

The fee is $255, including lodging, breakfast, dinner, and a gate pass to most of the programs including evening entertainment. The weekend fee is $92.

Undoubtedly there are many more unique educational experiences available to the more mature adults. Check at your local library.

VOLUNTEERING

■   ■   ■

Unlimited is the only word to describe volunteer opportunities. "When you give you get much more back in return." What's the return? That warm feeling when you can say, "I helped."

How would you like to help? There are so many ways that you can take your choice.

Here's a two-step process:

1. What will give you a warm feeling? One approach is figure what will not. That rules out certain things automatically. For example, Fred can't take hospitals or health-related problems. Sorrow, depression, pain, and physical agony get him down. His volunteering in a hospital or nursing home just would not make any sense. Make a list of the kinds of organizations or causes that are of interest to you. Would you like to help the poor—the infirm—young people—minorities—refugees—unwed mothers—elderly—disabled—those with a terminal illness? The list could go on and on.

2. After you have thought through your preferences, shop around. Search out those organizations or institutions that have a need in an area that is of interest to you. Then work out an arrangement that will be helpful but will fit your schedule.

Unfortunately many people do things because others have found a particular activity interesting. We have been tracking a retiree for the last five years. A physical ailment has caused a change in his routine. His statement to us was: "If you hear of something interesting to do let me know." He may end up with some busy work. From that he can say, "I gave them a hand." That's not the same as having a warm feeling and enthusiastically saying, "I helped."

On a local basis, there are volunteer coordinating or referral services. In Dallas the morning paper has an "Opportunity for Volunteers" column. Here are some representative listings:

■ Help Cambodian refugees adapt to a new life in Dallas.

■ Garland Nursing Home welcomes visitation to talk with residents who have no family or friends.

■ Tutor children between ten and sixteen who live in a counseling center for runaway teens.

■ Present Texas history programs to children in their classrooms.

■ Educate tenants about their Fair Housing Rights.

■ Teach your specialty at the YMCA-based programs for those fifty-five and older.

■ Write the "Opportunity for Volunteers" column.

One of the TV stations promotes its volunteer connection, which is a coordinating function for volunteers. Most likely there are similar volunteer-coordinating agencies in your town.

Action
This is the U.S. Government's national volunteer agency and is made up of many diverse programs designed to assist others: (Phone book, listed under "Government Offices—U.S.")

VISTA—Volunteers in Service to America
FGP—Foster Grandparent Program
RSVP—Retired Senior Volunteer Program
SCP—Senior Companion Program
NCSL—National Center for Service Learning
OVL—Office of Volunteer Liaison
OPP—Office of Policy and Planning
YVA—Young Volunteers in ACTION
VVLP—Vietnam Veterans Leadership Program
ADUPP—Action Drug Use Prevention Program

There are two volunteer programs that offer international assignments. The Peace Corps and the International Executive Service Corps.

*Peace Corps**

There was a time when there wasn't much push to interest older people in the Peace Corps. Today there are special brochures aimed at recruiting retirees. Here are some actual retiree assignments:

Barbados—Plan Irrigation Systems
Paraguay—Design Buildings and Flood-Control Facilities
Nepal—Teach Math and Science
Honduras—Teacher/Counselor to 69 Girls Living in a Group Center
Mali, West Africa—Improving Nutrition and Hygiene
Sierra Leone—Design and Construction—147 Classrooms

There is no upper age limit. U.S. citizenship is required and there are some basic medical and legal criteria. Married couples are encouraged to apply if both can work and wish to be volunteers.

Transportation to and from Peace Corps assignments is provided. Training is extensive including language, cross cultural, and technical, and usually takes between eight and sixteen weeks.

A monthly living allowance is provided. It is designed to allow volunteers to live at the level of the people with whom they work. Medical personnel are assigned to countries to attend to the health needs of the volunteers. Each volunteer earns two days' vacation for each month of service, which can be accrued. In addition to the monthly allowance, a readjustment allowance is paid for each month's service at the conclusion of a twenty-four to twenty-seven-month assignment. One of the brochures says: "The toughest job you'll ever love"—we would assume that's a true statement.

*International Executive Service Corps (IESC)**

This is a not-for-profit corporation run by American businessmen. It is dedicated to serving developing countries around the world. Assignments are usually short term (two or three months) and are for those with managerial, technical, or administration talents. Individuals and singles can participate.

IESC provides a briefing on the country, the assignment for the husband and wife, round-trip air transportation, a per diem allowance that permits comfortable living, but no salary.

The organization was founded in 1964. More than 18,000 projects have been completed in eighty countries around the world.

We interviewed Mr. and Mrs. H.D., formerly of Cleveland, Ohio, and now in Florida. They had many assignments in Kuwait. Mr. D. was vice president of personnel of a major company and the assignments were all "people-oriented." They were extremely high on the entire experience— the way IESC is run, the courtesies extended to them by their host company, and the fulfillment they experienced by being able to help.

Following are some other national programs that might be of interest:

Service Corps of Retired Executives (SCORE)*
Sponsored by the U.S. Small Business Administration, this organization is made up of 13,000 retired executives who provide free management assistance advice to small businessmen. There are 400 chapters throughout the United States. SCORE volunteers receive no compensation but are reimbursed for out-of-pocket travel expenses.

U.S. Information Agency*
Their American participant program offers opportunities for Americans traveling abroad to meet with groups and fellow professionals interested in their specialty. Some expenses are paid and in some cases a modest honorarium is paid.

Volunteers in Parks*
A program administered by the National Park Service of the Department of the Interior. Volunteers are assigned work in such areas as interpretation—helping visitors understand the natural and human history of the area, arts and crafts—demonstrating craft skills, resource management—assisting a park ranger in duties of resource management. No salary is paid. Some parks reimburse volunteers for incidental expenses such as local transportation costs, uniforms, and meals.

Department of Veterans Affairs*
There are 30 million veterans and their families. Offering services to those who have served our nation is the responsibility of the Department of Veterans Affairs (DVA), formerly called the Veterans Administration.

The DVA is the nation's largest single health care system with 200 medical centers and other health care facilities throughout the country.

There are over 100,000 patients in their hospitals and nursing homes. Each week 250,000 veterans will visit DVA outpatient clinics.

They have been organizing volunteer activities since 1946. There is a program for the involvement of an organization and another for individual volunteering. Help is needed for veterans in hospitals, nursing homes, community residential homes, and group living facilities as well as for those living in their own homes.

To help you get your own plan underway, here are seventy-five ideas from the personal experiences of people around the country. Some we have read about in newspapers or magazines and others we have discovered by talking with people. Hopefully one of these will strike a chord and an interest will emerge.

Have fun planning your retirement activities!

(1) TRAINING GUIDE DOGS. Additional help is always needed. Retired people have the time and patience to give to this needy project. If you care to raise a puppy, turning it into an enjoyable pet, and then give it up, you can provide a service to your nearest guide dog training school. Contact the Guide Dog Foundation for the Blind, Inc.*

(2) VOLUNTEER TUTOR—ADOPT-A-SCHOOL PROGRAM. This program helps teachers give remedial instruction to students. For example, eighth-graders learn math from a retired postmaster, English from a local newspaper columnist, and science from a former engineer. It's not necessary to have been a teacher. No college degree is required.

This kind of involvement would give much satisfaction to the retiree who gets his/her rewards from seeing students improve as a result of the extra attention they receive. Check with your local school board.

(3) SAIL (SENIORS ACTIVE IN LIFE). SAIL programs are planned by the Dallas Parks and Recreation Department for older adults. Schedules are made up with a wide variety of activities such as exercise classes, painting, and a drama group. Is there a SAIL program in your town? If not, why not start one?

(4) FUND RAISING WITH CANS. A group of just under 900 people in Macon County, North Carolina, collected enough aluminum cans in one year to raise money for a portable respirator for the hospital. Two objectives were accomplished. They cleaned up the county and raised money for the hospital.

(5) CRAFTS FOR CASH. There is an Elder Craftsman Shop in New York that sells handiwork of older people from around the country. The handcrafter receives 65 percent of the purchase price, the remaining 35 percent helps pay overhead costs. Other cities around the country have adopted similar plans.

(6) BUILDER TURNED COUNTY JUDGE. A sixty-one-year-old retired home builder who takes on many civic responsibilities served out the term of a county judge who died while in office. He was reelected to a full term. Have you always wanted to be a politician?

(7) GRUBBY LOT BECOMES GARDEN SPOT. A retired minister and his wife received a great deal of praise for turning an unsightly area near their apartment into a spot of springtime beauty. In addition to beautification, the plan prevented soil erosion.

(8) RETIREE GUARDIAN ANGELS. A concern about safety prompted senior citizens to help the Guardian Angels prevent robberies and other crimes in a Dallas suburb. A similar group in Jacksonville, Florida, was organized with the average age of seventy-five! Another group of retirees in Cleveland, Ohio, formed patrols to combat high crime. They carry walkie-talkies and patrol in pairs, reporting suspicious activity to the police.

(9) CAREER VOLUNTEER TO PAID POSITION. Numerous volunteer jobs held throughout a lifetime can provide excellent qualifications for a paid position. Hundreds of skills are transferable to paid positions. Many cities give assistance through programs such as Involvement Corps, Inc., in Los Angeles, California. They show employers how to evaluate volunteer experience. A great way to help those reentering the work force.

(10) HOUSE SITTING FOR PAY. Home Sitting Service, Inc., of Denver, Colorado, provides people on Social Security with a house sitting job while the owners are away. From as little as two days at a time to as long as two months, sitters receive a modest payment for their services. This Denver-based company has offices in other cities around the country. A great way to earn some money while helping alleviate worries about vandalism for those on a trip.

(11) SORORITY/FRATERNITY HOUSEMOTHER. A Midwestern college provides an apartment and meals. In return the housemother offers a listening ear to the students and shares in their experiences. She would not trade her job for anything. A great opportunity to remain young in heart and be an active part of the mainstream of life!

(12) PH.D. AT NINETY-THREE. A gentleman in Florida has completed work on his doctoral dissertation in history. He is one of the oldest students to receive a doctorate.

(13) RETIREES—25 PERCENT OF SALES FORCE. At a very large, unique hardware store retirees working on a part-time basis give advice to homeowners. A customer said, "Since I can't ask my dad, I come to Elliott's." A six-acre site has been purchased for a second store. The chief financial officer said ". . . and the nearby retirement community will supply a goldmine of part-time workers."

(14) MAKING MONEY IN COMMODITIES. A retired international offshore oil-rig superintendent has a computer on which he tracks five commodities every day. His goal is to make $200 a day. Whenever the market is open he takes no phone calls. His five acres on a lake provide him with exercise as he works the land after the market closes.

(15) SPRY—SLIM—SIERRA CLUB* MEMBER. Leading 200 hikers through Iron Canyon near Chico, California, is an eighty-year-old. During the eight-hour strenuous hike some of the hikers pant and puff, but not Mrs. H.E.B.

(16) RETIRED DOCTOR OPENS FREE CLINIC. At seventy years of age a retired practitioner is fulfilling his lifelong dream—running a free

clinic in Aurora, Illinois. He treats 80 to 100 patients a day. From his own funds he pays an RN and receptionist. Could you use your specialty to help others?

(17) SPORTS FOR THE BLIND. A seventy-two-year-old retired airline pilot founded BOLD—Blind Outdoor Leisure Development program. He is assisted by his wife. They tour the country and give clinics for ski instructors in techniques of teaching the blind.

(18) SENIOR ACHIEVEMENT. He ran *Junior* Achievement on the West Coast for many years. Now he teaches retirees how to turn their skills, interests, and hobbies into profitable businesses.

(19) SEVENTY-FOUR-YEAR-OLD—TEACHER/VOLUNTEER. Mr. M.M. retired from a twenty-three-year engineering career. Then his world came "crashing down" when his wife of fifty-one years died. Now he is very enthusiastic about his twice-a-week volunteer teaching of gifted children. Thousands of volunteers around the country donate many hours of time, saving school districts lots of money. The reward is the affection and appreciation that tie the two generations together.

(20) VOLUNTEER SERVICE CREDIT. Florida's State Department of Health and Rehabilitation Services has set up a Volunteer Service Credit Program. Records are kept of volunteer hours. When needed, credits can be redeemed for services. This could work in any organization.

(21) ELDERLY ACTIVISTS. In Cannon City, Colorado, 150 seniors conducted a traffic survey which saved the city thousands of dollars and helped the city fathers block a railroad's plan to close some railroad crossings. They initiated other programs such as cut-rate taxis for the elderly and a postal alert for shut-ins. The AARP chapter was the rallying point.

(22) TENNIS FOR EIGHTY-YEAR-OLDS. The finalists in the Annual North American Tennis Tournament for eighty-year-olds were from Ohio and New Jersey. Their one and three-quarter hours of play should be an inspiration to all seniors.

(23) ADOPT-A-GRANDPARENT. This Santa Monica, California, program started in 1976 for people in their seventies and eighties and youngsters twelve through seventeen. Students get school credit for meeting once a week with their adopted grandparents. The program gives the young an opportunity to observe that old age is part of the continuum of life.

(24) PEER COUNSELING FOR THE ELDERLY (PEP). Developed in 1974 at the Leonard Davis School of Gerontology, USC, PEP offers individual and group help to the elderly by trained paraprofessionals who range in age from fifty-five to eighty-one. A two-month training program for counselors covers aging, depression management, suicide, human sexuality, memory dysfunction, and crisis intervention. Counselors help bring people to an emotional level where they can take advantage of what's going on in the community. The program has a high rate of success.

(25) FOOD CO-OPS. There is a common goal—to provide quality food at low cost to co-op members. Why not start one in your neighborhood? Check at your local library for "How to" information about co-ops.

(26) SENIOR CITIZENS LEARN POLITICS AS LEGISLATIVE IN-TERNS. The congressional Senior Citizen's Internship Program operates at the state and national level. Interns have passes to Senate and House Chambers where they hear debates about programs for senior citizens. Then they have seminars and learn how the political system works. Why not write your legislature about your interest in this program?

(27) HIKING AT SIXTY-SEVEN . . . AND COUNTING THE MILES. R.E. *began* hiking at age fifty-five. This was during the time he was planning his retirement. He believed that boredom contributed to a high suicide rate, along with alcoholism, and he didn't want to be threatened by uselessness. Now that he has retired, he plans to hike 2,600 miles. This is the length of the Pacific Crest National Scenic Trail from Mexico to Canada. When he is not on the trail, he will teach backpacking.

(28) SPICE . . . PROGRAM MATCHES RETIREES WITH LOCAL VOLUNTEER GROUPS. *Senior People Investing Career Expertise.* In the Minneapolis–St. Paul area Cargill, Inc., has organized a program to assist company retirees who want involvement in community activities.

(29) SWINGING AT SEVENTY-FIVE—KIDS & KUBS SOFTBALL TEAMS. The Three-quarter Century Club of St. Petersburg, Florida, is made up of softball players seventy-five and over. In 1985 one player celebrated his one-hundredth birthday. Several are ninety-plus—you're never too old to play.

(30) SUNDAY CYCLING CLUB. One hundred Dallas-area bicyclists— the oldest is seventy-four—bike in all kinds of weather. They go varying distances to suit the interest of the group and they always include a lunch stop.

(31) USING FOOD, NOT THROWING IT AWAY. Food stores dispose of dated food. A group of retirees collect this food on the critical expiration date and take it to their church. Charitable organizations then pick up the food and distribute it. Food stores are very willing to cooperate. Within the group there is great camaraderie while being of service.

(32) PROUD OF YOUR AREA? If so, write the history of your town. An AARP chapter in Arizona published the history of Cottonwood, Clarkdale, and Cornville. The same concept applies to your club or association.

(33) CLOWNING AROUND. Clowns give people a reason to smile, especially at hospitals and nursing homes, and this lightens the day for shut-ins. Some churches have a clown ministry.

(34) YOUNG AND OLD TOGETHER IN HIGH SCHOOL. Harbor Springs, Michigan, senior citizens and high school students go to school together. Several hundred elderly in the school district blend into high school facilities. No one forces togetherness, but facilities and equipment are available to all. Older people can study for fun or for credit. Teachers call on the elderly for lectures and to share their knowledge.

(35) SAN FRANCISCO GAME FIELD—NEW WAY TO KEEP FIT. The San Francisco Heart Association and the San Francisco Senior Center backed the installation of a game field. This is a one-mile trail with fifteen exercise games along the way which can be done in groups or individually. It is aimed at developing physical strength and cardiovascular fitness as well as reducing stiffness problems. Note: We have seen the game field at many retirement communities around the country; it's a great idea.

(36) SENIOR CUB SCOUT LEADER. His interest began when his foster child was invited to join the Cub Scouts. The seventy-year age difference didn't matter. He holds weekly meetings in his home. Because of his success he urges others his age to give their time to this good cause.

(37) GRUMMAN RETIREES DEDICATED TO RESTORATION. They restore everything from World War II fighter planes to lunar modules. Their first undertaking is on display at the Smithsonian in Washington, D.C.—an F-4-F Wildcat. One lunar module they've restored is at the Franklin Institute in Philadelphia.

(38) WRITING CAREER IN RETIREMENT. It's never too late to write about your particular interest or area of expertise. Don't worry about competition, just write *your* very best. But don't continue to mull over ideas forever; it does not sell articles. Your local library will have many resources that will help you get started.

(39) NEW BREED OF ELDERS. Maggie Kuhn was forced to retire at sixty-five. At seventy-six she founded the Gray Panthers* to refute the stereotypes of aging and to gain respect for older people. Through the Gray Panther chapter network in most states the organization initiates local action on social issues affecting seniors. Maggie Kuhn says, "Aging is the term for a continuous process of growth through life."

(40) RETIRED FOOTBALL COACH—TO R.E. SALESMAN. Retired at sixty-three from coaching at DePauw University, this former coach is now studying for his real estate license. The school has a preretirement

sabbatical. He can take a semester at full pay to get ready for retirement. A good way to plan out a great retirement.

(41) ADVENTURER/PHOTOGRAPHER. A retired army major, this gentleman now is in his seventies and travels 50,000 miles per year. He films while skiing, hot-air ballooning, or camel riding. He does his own editing and commentary, accompanied by appropriate music, and presents his travelogues for clubs and groups around the country.

(42) BICYCLE MINISTRY/KIDS BICYCLE FIX-IT MAN. A small-town retiree repairs bikes in his garage at no charge. He also takes old bikes, fixes them up, and gives them to kids who don't have a bike.

(43) SENIOR TUTORS FOR YOUTH IN DETENTION. To be helpful, residents from Rossmoor in Walnut Creek, a retirement complex in California, journey to San Francisco's Youth Guidance Center. There they spend two hours with youths who are in trouble. These caring seniors have had a positive effect on the young people.

(44) CENTENARIAN PAINTER WHO STARTED PAINTING AT EIGHTY. His chess partner didn't show up and he was disconsolate. A young volunteer at the Golden Age Club urged him to *try* painting. Now he has one-man shows. His paintings "tell a story" about his early life in an East European village. This man's first six years of retirement were the most miserable of his life, because he was bored. Now that he is engaged in activities he says he was brought back to life! He is following in Grandma Moses footsteps—he's still painting at 101.

(45) GENEALOGY. Tape record information about your family history. This can be passed along to all in the family tree. Attend genealogy workshops, subscribe to genealogical magazines, and then find a quiet corner and write about your findings.

(46) HUSBAND/WIFE INNKEEPERS. This couple, retired school-teachers, are part of LaQuinta Motor Inn's aggressive program to hire retirees. They feel being innkeepers is fun and the company feels the program is an unqualified success.

*(47) TREASURE HUNTING/HOBBY FOR SURE—MAYBE BUSI-
NESS SOMEDAY.* They sold their motel business and bought a motor
home and boat. The summer finds them in the Upper Peninsula of
Michigan. In October they head south and eventually end up in Florida.
Then it's back home to Michigan in late spring. What do they do?
Explore dump sites, lakes, abandoned copper mines, ghost towns,
beaches, with the help of a metal detector. They have found thousands
of coins, rings, etc., over the years. If they make a profit in two of the
first five years, their hobby will have turned into a business. Then they
can deduct expenses. Check with your CPA on writing off expenses.

(48) THE LIVING LIBRARY CONSULTING SERVICE. In Rich-
mond, Virginia, a group of fifty retired executives, technicians, and professionals give advice to small businesses and local governments. They
charge modest fees.

(49) RARE TEACHING EXPERIENCE. A retired grocery store owner
in Wyoming teaches fifty high school students how to process domestic
and wild meat—buffalo, antelope, elk, bear, etc., as well as hogs, cattle,
etc. The teacher and students earn money selling their products.

(50) STILL EXPLORING IN HIS SEVENTIES. Thor Heyerdahl was
twenty-three when he first headed to a remote Polynesian area and he
has spent a lifetime exploring and writing on his findings. He would find
a life of luxury very boring. He needs to use his mind and body in
projects that allow him to lead a life "worth living."

*(51) HOBBY SHOP OWNER—FORTY-FIVE YEARS AND COUNT-
ING.* A successful salesman for model airplane kits, he used his products
and won many contests. He served as president of the Academy of
Model Aeronautics. In the forties he opened his own hobby shop. At
seventy-two he is especially interested in helping retirees fill a void in
their lives through model building. He says he gives those who enter his
shop 50 percent expertise, 50 percent museum, and 50 percent bull!

(52) CALL FOR CUDDLERS. The Volunteer Center in Houston sent
out a plea for child care volunteers to help care for children in temporary
group foster homes. All of the children are under five years of age and

many are babies. Three hours a week are needed to provide much needed loving.

(53) RETIRED TEACHER TURNED ENVIRONMENTALIST. In Delaware a need was met for both the volunteer and the project. A former teacher helped nurse twenty-eight oil-soaked birds back to good health. Then she and others helped lobby legislators for a grant for the Tri-State Bird Resource and Research Center.

(54) FROM PHARMACIST TO COUNSELOR. A retired pharmacist provides *free* service to older citizens. He answers questions regarding side effects, when to take medications, and foods to avoid when taking certain medicines. To publicize his services he leaves fliers at pharmacies.

(55) RESEARCH EXPEDITION. The University of California at Berkeley has a research program centering around fact-finding excursions. Included are digging for rock art in Arizona, observing penguins in Australia, collecting marine life in a South Pacific lagoon, and studying the impact of tourists on a Sherpa village at the foot of Mount Everest. The only cost is for travel, food, and accommodations. Sometimes travel expenses are tax deductible.

(56) FROM LIBRARIAN TO READING TEACHER. A widow teaches adults to read and write. She has two students for two hours a week. One student is a cowboy. He started with dog/cat books and after a year and a half he can read several paragraphs. There is a feeling of satisfaction/accomplishment for teacher and student. Check with your local school system.

(57) SENIOR CITIZENS ADOPT HOSPITAL CHILDREN. Disabled children and senior citizens give love to each other through an adoption program. The Texas Scottish Rite Hospital for Crippled Children and senior citizens of the C. C. Young Memorial Home work together to help the disabled children. Some of the children are at the hospital without their parents. The senior citizens become surrogate parents or grandparents—everyone benefits.

(58) THE HAWAIIAN ICE CREAM MAN. Walter Lappert had vacationed on the island of Kauai for three decades. Upon retirement he moved there but soon became restless. He opened a little ice cream parlor. His business has grown. Now there are stores on the other islands and in several states on the mainland. He has seventy flavors and expects to expand to 100.

(59) WIDOW, SIXTY-THREE, STUDIES TO BECOME MINISTER. Following college graduation she was "a homemaker." At sixty-three she decided she had time for one more major task. Her husband, an oil company executive, died of a heart attack. Her daughter had thyroid cancer, she also had cancer, and both have been cured. All of these factors contributed to her decision to go into the ministry.

(60) NEIGHBORHOOD REFERRAL SERVICE. A seventy-two-year-old retiree started a unique service. He sought out service people, checked their references, inspected their work, checked with the Better Business Bureau, etc. From his findings he developed a list of people with expertise in all areas of home repair. This satisfied his need to be of service to others, satisfied the users, and satisfied the people performing the service.

(61) LOVER OF HARD-SHELLED FRIENDS. A retiree wanted something to do so he wouldn't become a "fuddy duddy." He loves turtles so he built a complex of pools and raises turtles. Now he has several hundred.

(62) SEVENTY-EIGHT-YEAR-OLD FORMER STATE ATTORNEY GENERAL. After ten years of retirement he is now an assistant county district attorney. He gets great satisfaction in helping people and feels there are a lot of folks who need help.

(63) CARE OF VERY INFANT MONKEYS. They are small enough to fit into a person's hand. When they get bigger they will go to Albert Einstein College for training to help disabled persons. They will eventually assist in grooming, opening and closing doors, etc. This is a special breed of monkey that is very docile. When not performing a task it will

sit on a person's lap for hours. This program is utilized by the Department of Veterans Affairs.

(64) REQUEST FOR VOLUNTEERS. A community center in San Antonio was given a barracks building by Lackland Air Force Base. But it had to be in working order six months after it was moved. They sent out a plea for carpenters, painters, plumbers. There was plenty of space where mobile homes could be parked while their owners helped with the repair work. A very worthwhile project of service to others and a different approach to finding volunteers.

(65) GRANNY TAPS HER WAY TO MS. SENIOR AMERICA. Her first date with her husband of forty-plus years had been to a movie at Radio City Music Hall. She always dreamed of being a Rockette but was too shy and too short. At sixty-four she had the courage to try out for the Ms. Senior America Pageant. She took dancing lessons, sewed her own evening gown, and won the local contest, state contest, and ultimately the national contest.

(66) SENIOR OLYMPICS. To promote health, fitness, and friendship a committee made up of representatives from sports clubs in the Dallas area organized the first senior olympics. These events are also held in other cities around the country—Houston, Albuquerque, Las Vegas, etc. Help organize one in your area.

(67) EMERITUS EXECS. A large percentage of executives return to income-producing jobs within two years after retirement, many working on a free-lance or consulting basis in their area of expertise. It's a chance to try out your entrepreneurial talents.

(68) A BIG GREEN THUMB. He buys 15,000 blooming annuals—about $1,000 worth. This is the yearly purchase Sundal Shadi needs to plant his 150 × 125-foot hillside slope overlooking San Francisco Bay. He puts in twelve-hour days during the blooming season and gives something back to the community.

(69) TEXAS'S SILVER-HAIRED LEGISLATURE. The first mock senior legislature in which senior citizens elect their own legislature to draft laws they want passed during the upcoming Texas legislature was held in 1986. In the other twenty-eight states that have senior legislatures 70 to 80 percent of all recommendations eventually become state laws. Contact your local state representative to see if your state has such a program.

(70) **RETIREES OFFER CAREER ADVICE TO HIGH SCHOOL STUDENTS.** At a Career Fair in Colorado valuable advice was given by senior citizens to junior and senior high students. They gave practical answers to students' questions. Would your local high school be interested?

(71) **WORKING GOLFERS.** In Toledo, Ohio, a fifty-year-old golf course was closed by the city because it was a money loser. Sixty older golfers negotiated a lease for the course at $1.00 a year. A revitalized 3,400-yard, nine-hole course was ready 4,500 man-hours later. The greens fee was $1.50. It's managed and staffed by volunteers and is truly a golfer's paradise.

(72) **PROJECT FOR MEN INTERESTED IN WOODWORKING.** A group of seniors provides therapeutic activity for nursing home residents. They design, cut, and assemble small wooden articles. These are taken to a nursing home where patients do the sanding and painting. Then they're sold for the home's benefit.

(73) **SEAMSTRESS FOR THE POOR.** At eighty-one years of age a lady in Sun City, Arizona, still sews over 1,000 outfits a year for poor and underprivileged children. All materials are donated. She gives her time because she believes "every little girl" needs a new dress.

(74) **"KILLER" . . . KOREAN KARATE.** Known as "Killer," an eighty-nine-year-old Illinois woman earned the black belt ranking in Tae Kwon Do. She is believed to be the oldest person to have earned it.

(75) **FULFILLING A CHILDHOOD FANTASY.** A St. Paul, Minnesota, retiree has realized her lifelong ambition to be a nun, bag-lady, and a murderess—on stage of course. Not until retirement, after thirty-three years of teaching music, could she fantasize on the amateur stage, and on

film. She has appeared in industrial films and a local McDonald's commercial. A fantasy come true because she wanted it and worked to make it happen. What's your fantasy?

THE SPARK
▪   ▪   ▪

In summary, activity of mind and body does not halt at any given age. As the saying goes, "Use it or lose it." Keep active as long as you can keep going. Jacques Yves Cousteau said at seventy-six, "I feel as if I'm fifty—why should I stop?"

But no one can tell you what is the best activity for you. Books and seminars will give you ideas but *you* must determine what your interests are. It requires thinking and trial and error to zero in on *your* choice of activities.

If there is a small activity spark smoldering in the back of your mind— let it out. Let it increase in intensity.

Forget what anyone else might think. It's your freedom time; your time to do your thing. The personal satisfaction that you will receive will make it all worthwhile.

4

STAY PUT OR MOVE

. . .

LIFESTYLE OPTION #1, STAY PUT IN THE COMMUNITY

"Where's a good place to retire?" We can't remember the number of times we have been asked that question. It has to be in the hundreds. Our immediate answer is, "What are you going to do when you retire? Determine the activity first and then consider whether or not a move makes sense."

This question shows that many people consider moving when they retire. It's quite natural to think of new places when a change in lifestyle is imminent. For some people, a move will be required. We talked to a retired couple who moved to Jupiter, Florida. Theirs was a forced move. They originally lived in Ossining, New York, and could not afford the high taxes and winter utility bills. Another retiree, a policeman from Garden City, Long Island, couldn't afford the taxes and moved to Dayton, Ohio, his old hometown, with his wife. Things weren't the way they used to be, so they moved to a retirement community in Florida.

Key Question 1. (see Chapter 1) Do you know what your retirement income will be? This question becomes extremely important at this time. Can you live on a reduced income? An honest, practical analysis of projected income versus current expenses will give answers. You may not like the answers but you have to deal with the facts.

Key Question 2. (see Chapter 1) Are you going to retire or change jobs? This question may be automatically answered. Financial considerations may require another job.

SUBSIDIZED HOUSING
■   ■   ■

There are other options available if there is a money crunch. For example, in the Seattle, Washington, area—King County—there are dozens of housing projects built with federal subsidies from the Department of Housing and Urban Development. You will find these all around the country.

In Wickcliffe, Ohio, we surveyed a retirement community that has a HUD program high-rise adjacent to the community center. This is an exception. Most units that we have seen are in areas zoned for apartments.

This is commonly referred to as HUD's Rent Subsidy Program for low-to-moderate-income elderly and handicapped. To be eligible there are limits on income, and rental payments are based on a percentage of monthly income. Rent cannot exceed 30 percent of income.

We have not made an in-depth investigation of this type of program. It entails government regulations, politics, and red tape. There are many, many different subsidy programs available. One point is continuously brought out—there are long waiting lists.

If you're going to need this kind of assistance, start your own investigation as soon as possible. Don't wait. Begin with your local office of the Department of Housing and Urban Development or the Farmers Home Administration of the Department of Agriculture.

To find other possibilities, check with your local

Senior center
Church or synagogue administration office
American Association of Retired Persons
National Council of Senior Citizens
Mayor's office—in Seattle it is the Mayor's Office for Senior Citizens
State, county, city agency on aging

Don't be discouraged by the bureaucracy; persist, ask questions. There are a lot of additional aid possibilities. It will take some investigative work but they can be found.

We will assume from here on that there is not a major money crunch. This doesn't mean we will concentrate on opportunities for the wealthy.

We will present a broad spectrum of alternatives available to preretirees and retirees with moderate to above-average financial capabilities.

For those who want to remain in the same locality there are many different lifestyles that can be combined so that someone can retire and still stay put; life can go on in its normal fashion at the family homestead. Staying put represents a minimal change retirement situation. But the work change—from work to leisure—presents a problem. How do you use this newly found leisure time?

Key Question 3. How great a change do you want to make to your lifestyle? How did you answer that question and the other questions dealing with change? Did you and your spouse come to agreement on this?

Are you single? The question is still relevant—but you have to answer it alone.

If you feel you can't handle much change, then a move to another residence should be one of the last things you consider. If financial considerations require a move, then you have a serious problem. Professional financial counseling may help. See your CPA or local banker.

We'll assume you have a reasonable tolerance for change and want to consider a move. Your question might well be: "What are some of the things we need to know if we want to consider a move?"

TEN QUESTIONS
■   ■   ■

Here are some questions that will help in your discussion of whether to move or stay put. You and your spouse should consider these options separately, compare your results, and resolve any differences.

1. Will your present house and location allow you to pursue your retirement activities? For both of you?
2. Is your city or village growing? How? In a desirable or undesirable manner? What will be the effect on house values? Future taxes?
3. Is your neighborhood getting better? Stable? Or going down? What's the prognosis for the future?
4. How's the traffic? Will future plans make it worse?
5. How's the crime rate? Going up or down? Do you feel secure?

6. What's the condition of your house? In good shape or are there constant irritating repairs?
7. Are the house and yard too big? Will they interfere with planned retirement activities?
8. If there are steps, would a house with one floor be better?
9. Is there adequate space for each person to have a private retreat area?
10. Is the climate okay? If not, what would you like? Is this preference so strong it may dictate a decision to move?

What are your needs? What's it like around your house? If you require, or are used to, a bustling household with the phone ringing all the time and many people stopping by, keep in mind it will take a long time to build that kind of activity in a new community. Do you need to have a small group of friends with whom you exchange intimate soul-searching thoughts? These kinds of friendships don't come easily or in a short time. Are you still recognized as "someone" in your community? Is basking in the glory of past achievements extremely important to you? In a new community one has to start from the beginning, in competition with many others.

These and many more "deep" feelings need to be considered by you and your spouse.

Yet, retirement offers a chance for new challenges, new undertakings, new friendships—a new beginning. A move could be a great rejuvenator. A way of putting some new spice in your life. This represents an excellent opportunity for singles to meet new and interesting people. A move to a community with planned activities provides a common meeting place for those with like interests to become acquainted.

All moves don't have to be across the country. Many opportunities can be explored on a local basis.

A SMALLER PLACE
■ ■ ■

We will draw on our personal experience here. Our large house, with a big lawn which required constant scheduled care, and the unused rooms that needed cleaning and upkeep, encouraged us to build a smaller place.

We moved from the large house to a much smaller patio/zero lot line house—on one side the house is built right on the lot line. Traumatic? You bet! We had to dispose of a lot of furniture, keepsakes, and things in the attic that we always said, "We might need someday." We had a very large garage sale.

This process is not as easy as it sounds. We were both raised on such sayings as "Waste not, want not" and "Prepare for a rainy day." This translated into a strong feeling of not being able to throw things away. Sound familiar? A retired couple who moved south still has a large mini-storage rental full of things "they just can't get rid of"—this is after two years!

Besides a lot of unnecessary things, we had items that were associated with "memories of the past." That little table that was Grandmother's— our first kitchen table and chairs—worn but comfortable stationary rocker that helped calm down sick children—and boxes of clothes, still good, out of style, but full of memories of special occasions.

We are very satisfied with our small home. We have no lawn. Just plantings of shrubs and small trees encircled with ground cover and interspersed among decorative rocks. Our house has a redwood deck around a spa. A sprinkler system allows us to lock up the place and take off so we can "smell the roses." We have an agreement with the retirees across the street who watch the front of our house and a similar arrangement with the retirees across the back alley. Our agreements also include transportation to and from the airport. It's really great to see a friendly smiling face when you depart from the plane.

Finding a smaller single-family residence isn't always easy. In most cases the smaller homes are in the "first home" neighborhoods—sometimes referred to as "the pregnant acres subdivision."

Mr. and Mrs. V.V., who moved from Iowa to the Sunbelt, chose this type of neighborhood. They like being around the youngsters and all the neighborhood kids call them Grandma and Grandpa. Incidentally, Mr. V. has an interesting retirement activity. He bought a car kit and has built a fancy two-seater car. He'll sell it and probably start over.

We chose a zero lot line concept with one very small side yard and an equally small front and backyard. It's not very conducive to raising a family and our neighborhood is primarily made up of young professionals and retirees. This type of home requires down zoning so there are some drawbacks. A business park built nearby causes a little extra traffic but it's basically a very quiet neighborhood.

We had some retirement home amenities built into our house:

No steps inside or to the front sidewalk or alley.
Lever-type door handles rather than knobs.
Energy efficient—extra insulation—double glass windows.
Plenty of ceiling lighting.
Phone outlets in every room.
Our own offices/private space for each of us.
Sliding doors in the master bathroom (swing-in doors could be
    blocked).
Wax-free vinyl tile in the kitchen.
Carpeting—no slippery rugs—no shag rug to snare a cane.
Nonskid bathtubs.
Public transportation available within a couple of blocks.

We have read that an outside view is extremely important for older
people. Studies have shown that as people age they are particularly eager
to see what is going on around them. We were lucky in this aspect. Our
kitchen is in the front of the house and the kitchen table looks onto a big
bay window.

We interviewed Joan Maehr*—an interior designer specializing in the
field of seniors' home design. She is a member of the American Society
of Interior Designers. It was fascinating listening to her explain the need
for lower countertops, reducing glare, strong color contrast rather than
pastels, lever faucets not twist, and lights that operate by sound. She says,
"There is a great need for this rapidly growing specialty."

Town Home

If you want to downsize your living space, own your own place, but be
relatively maintenance free, then a town house might meet your needs.
Town houses are units with common walls, usually with no other unit
above or below.

Ownership includes the unit and land beneath it. The community as a
whole owns the common elements. Costs for the pool, recreation center,
tennis courts, etc., outside maintenance and repair of each unit, plus
overall grounds maintenance is assessed by a homeowner's association.

One can putter around the outside shrubbery but no changes can be made. This assures a well-maintained community. You don't have the problem of someone in the neighborhood who doesn't keep up the yard or the exterior of the house. But there are rules which we will cover later.

Condominium

Similar to a town house, but usually with units above, below, and on each side. Ownership is always interior airspace only. Walls and other common elements are owned with the other residents. As with a town house, there are rules.

Co-op Apartment

Ownership is through the acquiring of shares of stock in the building. The co-op corporation board of directors (elected by the shareholders) controls such things as who can buy in, whether subletting is allowable, and upkeep of the building and grounds. And there are rules.

Rules, Rules, Rules

In most cases the rules governing a community will be beneficial. That is, until they inhibit what a person wants to do. Knowing what you are getting into is just common sense. But it would be easy to become enamored with the unit and the amenities and not investigate the rules. These are the covenants and restrictions that you agree to live by. They should be completely understood.

Rules may govern a wide range of things. For example:

Firewood in the carport
Outside TV antenna
Parking a fishing boat
Exterior Christmas lights
Pool parties and personal parties
Doggie walking and stopping
· House guests
Vegetable gardens

Other regulations can be more personal. A single-parent condo owner was robbed three times so she had a burglar alarm installed. This included a revolving light and siren on the roof of her unit. It was against the rules and after much battling with the association she was forced to remove the light and siren.

NBC's "Today" show featured an interview with the president of the homeowners' association of an adult community in Florida and a resident husband, wife, and one-year-old child. During the interview the family acknowledged that the rules of the community prohibited children. They further acknowledged that the youngster was unplanned. They had tried to sell their condo for twenty-three months but were unable to find a buyer. The homeowners' association has filed suit to force them out.

Besides the rules there are:

Assessments:

Keeping up the unit exterior, the amenities, and the common grounds require money. Through a democratic process an elected board administers rules, regulations, and the assessment and distribution of funds.

An owner has a vote but decisions come from others. Disputes arising from interpretation of rules and determination of costs will understandably arise. Each individual has to go with the decision of the duly elected officials, whether or not they agree.

If you're investigating a facility, ask to see minutes of some of the meetings of the members and of the board of directors. You will learn much about the operation of the complex and the problems that are encountered.

One condo owner said, "I own everything inside the door. Everything outside the door is owned by everybody!"

This "everybody" involvement can also have many advantages. It is the perfect environment for meeting new people, especially if it is an adult community complex. There are many people with similar needs.

We did an in-depth investigation of this kind of living when we made the decision to cut down on the size of our house. Needless to say, we didn't chose a condo. Our independence told us we would be better off with full control of our house and land. We recognized that this carried with it property upkeep, but a little of this is okay as far as we are concerned.

WHAT SIZE?
■   ■   ■

When is small too small? If the present house is too big, what size would be just right? Personal choice will dictate. In making a house-size decision try and think ahead. Go ahead ten years. Visualize a person who has slowed down to some degree. We're not suggesting you visualize a tottering decrepit person. But it is an irrevocable fact of life that through years of usage certain body parts are going to show some wear and tear. There will be a slow down. What will housing needs be ten years down the line? We should not dwell on this unnecessarily. But keep it in mind as you wrestle with the question of what is the right size home for you.

Time and time again we have been told by retirees that each person needs his or her personal space. This doesn't mean the chair in the living room. Ideally it's a separate area; preferably a small room that's personal space. A room that is decorated and arranged the way that person prefers. Not to please others. Just himself or herself.

Room Considerations

Separate bedrooms and baths? This could be the personal space area if you desire.

If there are to be joint hobbies or activities, a small area for this should be included.

Consider whether you need a dining room. Ask yourself how often it will be used.

Do you need a den and a living room? A TV room? Would one large family room make more sense?

Is a guest room necessary or would a sofa bed suffice?

A small laundry room should be adequate.

Consideration should be given to a small work area in the garage.

Two people together, nearly constantly, will spend a great deal of time in the kitchen. The kitchen table is a natural place for conversation. Make sure this room is large enough. We have found that a small TV set to watch the noon news while having lunch is enjoyable.

Scaling down is a delicate act of balancing. It involves what we are used to, what is needed in the new retirement environment, and what is needed when aging is taken into consideration.

EMOTIONAL ATTACHMENT
■ ■ ■

Many years, perhaps fifteen, twenty, thirty, or more, of living under the same roof causes a very strong emotional tie that resists a move. Talk of a smaller home will bring resistance on the part of the kids. This is to be expected. They too have sentimental ties to the house, to their old room, to the old kitchen table where many a problem was worked out.

Those away from home might well raise the question, "Where will we all sleep when we come home?" "What about Christmas or Thanksgiving dinner, where will we all sit?"

One retired couple very nicely solved the "when we come home" problem. When family gatherings are planned with out-of-the-city kids, the parents move to a motel for a few days. This leaves the brothers, sisters, and grandchildren some additional space and time to talk. The parents come home for meals and family time and go back to the motel when it seems appropriate. There's no question that the peace and quiet of the motel have many advantages over the noise of many grandchildren trying to upstage each other.

If you determine that a move would be best, severing emotional ties will be traumatic. After a few tears, the advantages will far outweigh the disadvantages. There must be resolve to not live in the past, but to attack the future aggressively.

5

SNOWBIRDS

■ ■ ■

LIFESTYLE OPTION #2, WINTER RESIDENT

STAY PUT AND MOVE!
■ ■ ■

Contradictory? Not if you want to keep your old home yet get away for the winter. The geese aren't the only ones that go south for the winter and north for the summer. Their fly-a-way parallels the concrete fly-a-ways used by snowbirds and Winter Texans.

Our travels indicate that Florida draws part-time residents from the Northeast and Lower Great Lakes. The Texas Lower Rio Grande Valley attracts people from heartland America. Arizona/New Mexico get a number of visitors from the heartland and the Pacific northwest. Southern California serves the West Coast winter escapee. Hawaii has a true fly-a-way used by those from the Northwest and Canada.

Getting away during the gray days of winter isn't exclusively for those from the far north. Although we live in the Sunbelt, our plans call for going farther south in January and February. We feel we can do without our occasional ice storm and chilling winds.

WHEN AND WHERE?
■ ■ ■

The greater the number of winter months at home, the longer time people want to spend basking in the sun. Most of the migration to the South takes place right after Christmas. Logically so. Having come from the North, we cherish our memories of Christmas in New York and Connecticut. On Christmas Day a new-fallen snow, family, old friends, and a roaring fire in the fireplace are hard to beat.

We have talked to winter escapees throughout the South. When asked, "How did you choose this location?" the most common answer is,

"One of our neighbors came down here and said it was nice so we gave it a try and have come back ever since." As a result, one location continues to attract more and more people from one part of the country.

FLY TO THE WARMTH AND
RENT A CAR
■   ■   ■

If the expense of a rental car is prohibitive, stores and activities need to be within walking distance. We found this to be the case in Honolulu. Thousands of rental units are within four or five blocks of Waikiki Beach and grocery stores.

Every morning there is a westward procession of bathers carrying their reed mats, coolers, shopping bags full of towels, paperbacks, and sunscreen. They are en route to Waikiki Beach. They go back to their studio apartments for lunch, then back to the beach. At 5 P.M. on the return trip to their condos they stop at the grocery store. Some stay at the beach until the sun dips into the Pacific in a beautiful Hawaiian sunset.

We attended a condo owner's Monday night cocktail party. This place had become a haven for Canadians. There was much laughter and camaraderie. One couple used to winter in the San Diego area but they said you couldn't count on the weather. They felt the Waikiki area was just right for them. Since they come from Vancouver, British Columbia, they spend about four months of every year in Honolulu.

The grocery stores aren't cheap, but compared with the charge for a rental car, the premium paid at a downtown supermarket seems acceptable.

DRIVE AND RENT AN APARTMENT,
TRAILER, HOME, ETC.
■   ■   ■

This offers the ease of driving your car on the long trip south and then having it constantly available. You also end up with a lot of rent receipts.

DRIVE AND PULL
YOUR OWN TRAILER
■   ■   ■

The aggravation of towing a trailer during the trip must be considered. But taking it slow and easy can lessen the irritation. There are no motel expenses en route but there is a rental cost for a trailer site. Once positioned, you're set up for the duration of your stay and have the car or pickup truck available for daily usage.

DRIVE YOUR OWN MOTOR HOME
■   ■   ■

En route there are no motel receipts and there's a great deal of comfort; however, gasoline bills are heavy—you are getting only eight to ten miles a gallon. And once set up and leveled, you're without wheels. Fastening a couple of bikes to the rear could give you some mobility but you're still restricted.

You can drive the motor home around but each time you move you have to repack breakables, disengage hoses, and then hook up and relevel each time you come back. This could get pretty old.

The selection of a site would be extremely important with this kind of a setup. A larger complex with recreational facilities, a laundromat, and a store would be a real advantage.

DRIVE A MOTOR HOME AND SPOUSE
DRIVE THE FAMILY CAR
■   ■   ■

It's a double gas bill but gives you freedom when you arrive. But another hassle is two people having to drive without the help of a relief driver. Equipping both vehicles with a CB would be a tremendous help.

DRIVE YOUR MOTOR HOME AND
PULL A CAR
■   ■   ■

Other than having a trailer attached to the rear of the motor home during the trip this would give you a great deal of flexibility. At an RV show we saw a two-tiered trailer. On the top was a rack for a small boat and beneath it there was room for a subcompact car. No mileage on the odometer of the small car during the long trip south with this kind of rig. Plus, the availability of a boat and trailer.

STORAGE
■   ■   ■

Another choice is to leave your motor home or trailer on site, or in a protected storage area, so you don't have to haul it back and forth. This builds up more rental receipts but it is a lot more convenient. However, summer camping trips aren't possible when the trailer is down south.

EARLY DECISION
■   ■   ■

An ideal situation would be to determine a snowbird lifestyle as early as possible and purchase a condo in the Sunbelt. If a decision of this nature could be made when a person is in his/her fifties a great deal of use could be made of the condo. It could be used for vacations and later as a winter retreat. Renting it out could also provide income. From a straight dollars and cents standpoint this would be very attractive. Check with a CPA concerning depreciation, handling of rental income, travel expenses, etc.

But there are some other drawbacks. Mr. and Mrs. J.O. did this. They purchased a condo in Florida many years before they retired. They used it for winter vacations. In retirement it was to be their snowbird retreat. However, a problem has emerged. They purchased a condo in a new unit, when the other people in the condo were new retirees, many in their early sixties. Although they were younger than the other owners there was always something going on. It was an active, buzzing place.

Now it has aged. The original people are in their mid-seventies. Mr. O. told us that it's now an old folks' place. Canes and walkers are all that you see. All that you hear is the comparison of each person's aches, pains, and complaints. Mr. & Mrs. O. now rent out their condo and go to Hawaii instead.

Another drawback is that you will probably be tied down to one location. Going back to the same place year after year might get boring.

Although it would give you an opportunity to build up a group of "winter friends."

Finding a "snowbird roost" that is just right for you is limited only by your pocketbook and the time and energy you're willing to put into searching out your version of Shangri-la.

Wherever you go in the Sunbelt, from the Atlantic Coast of Florida to the Pacific Coast of California, and the islands of Hawaii, you will find an abundance of possibilities. These will vary from specialty facilities such as the Tennis Club of Palm Beach, Florida,* which is tailor-made for tennis enthusiasts—to Villa Ocotillo,* a retirement residence in the heart of Scottsdale, Arizona, that invites winter residents. Or, if you prefer, the West Coast Château La Jolla,* La Jolla, California, has winter rates with maid service, twenty-four-hour security, complimentary chauffered limo service, a social director, and a health supervisor. Clerbrook RV Resort* in Clermont, Florida, is built around an eighteen-hole executive golf course and Sunflower Resort,* a travel-trailer community in Surprise, Arizona, has a 42,000-square-foot life enrichment center.

We have had a great deal of fun searching out various retirement opportunities. You too can experience this same excitement as you get ready for this new dimension in your life. There will be frustrations. More than once, in fact many times, we have gotten lost trying to find a complex. But that's all part of the fun of exploring new opportunities.

Probably the least expensive way to be a true snowbird is to have your own motor home or trailer. Far south Texas has a large area in which there is an abundance of facilities for the RV or trailer owner.

WINTER TEXANS
■   ■   ■

We have been to the Lower Rio Grande Valley in Texas many times. We've traveled the main roads and the side roads extensively searching out the big and the little retirement-living accommodations.

Brownsville* is the southernmost town in Texas. It's near the point where the Rio Grande River sweeps into the Gulf of Mexico. Across the river is Matamoros, Tamaulipas, Mexico. In a northeasterly direction, about twenty-five miles, is Port Isabel* and the resort town of South Padre Island.* Here there are great beaches and your choice of deep sea fishing in the gulf, or bay fishing in the Laguna Madre.

About thirty miles to the northwest of Brownsville is Harlingen,*
Texas, home of the Confederate Air Force. Out of Harlingen is what is
known as the longest main street in America. Due west for about forty-
three miles, Route 83 connects LaFeria,* Mercedes,* Weslaco,*
Donna,* Alamo,* San Juan,* Pharr,* McAllen,* and Mission.* A slight
jog north from McAllen is Edinburg.* This is what's known as the
Lower Rio Grande Valley. A subtropical climate with an average yearly
temperature of 74° F. and an annual rainfall of slightly over twenty-six
inches. The city of Pharr is on the twenty-sixth parallel, the same as
Miami, Florida.

This area is due south of Fargo, North Dakota. Interstate 29 from
Fargo and Interstate 35 from Duluth, Minnesota, join up at Kansas City.
From there it's Interstate 35 to San Antonio, Texas. From San Antonio
to Brownsville it's about half interstate and half divided highway. As best
we can figure, it's about 1,700 miles from Fargo, North Dakota, to
Brownsville, Texas.

Heartland America has a straight route south to escape subzero temperatures and enjoy tropical breezes.

All along Route 83 and its many side roads are hundreds of trailer and
motor home parks. A 1990 directory for this general area lists 513 parks
with 65,999 sites!

SNOWBIRD PROFILE
▪   ▪   ▪

Each year Professors Vincent and De los Santos of the University of
Texas-Pan American in Edinburg survey Winter Texans. During the
1988–89 season they found:

▪ There were 81,000 Winter Texans—a 30-percent increase from the
previous year.

▪ Typical Winter Texan—sixty-seven years of age, married, retired.

▪ Spend $914 per month, up from $790 the previous year.

▪ 78 percent plan to return next year, 8 percent will not return.

■ 70 percent come from Midwestern states—Minnesota and Iowa 14 percent, followed by Illinois, Michigan, Wisconsin, Missouri, Kansas, Indiana, Ohio, and a representation from thirty-three other states and Canada.

■ 82 percent were influenced to come to the valley by friends.

■ Their concerns were the same as last year, locals who spoke Spanish in their presence, car theft, poor quality of drinking water.

The survey randomly sampled 101 of the 513 RV mobile home parks.

Many community activities are geared to the Winter Texan: Pharr, a growing city of 35,000, bills itself as the "RV Park Capital of Texas"; Brownsville, with a population of 107,000, features Charro Days, a week-long celebration of friendship held each January on both sides of the border; in South Padre Island, a Winter Texan fishing tournament is held the last week in February; a Seafest is held Labor Day weekend in Port Isabel, featuring the world's largest shrimp boil; in March, Harlingen has a three-day Riofest, an international celebration of music, drama, dance, and the visual arts; an easy way to pick up a lot of information about the valley is to visit the Texas State Tourist Bureau located in Harlingen; the International Rio Grande Valley Music Festival is held in the McAllen-Mission area. This is two weeks of musical events which surround the opera held the first week in March; Mercedes has an annual Rio Grande Valley Livestock Show in mid-March.

In fact, if you want to travel outside the valley to other parts of Texas, there's always a festival or cook-off taking place somewhere. For example, there's a: Rattlesnake Roundup; Possum Fair; Lamb Blast; Mule Day; Crappiethon (fishing for crappies); Rocky Mountain Oyster Fry; Shrimporee; Hushpuppy Olympics; Spam-O-Rama; One-Arm Dove Hunt; Prairie Dog Chili Cook-Off; and the World Championship Pickled Quail Egg Eating Contest. These and many other gastronomical events prompted a Dallas columnist, Dick Hitt, to say, "One of the great uniquenesses of Texas is that it is possible to spend every weekend of the year with a different kind of indigestion!"

Individual businesses also solicit the Winter Texans' attention. The Brownsville Medical Center has a Winter Health Care Plan. This is basically a registration form to be kept on file which would simplify the process of admission should a person require the services of the center.

One of the banks in Weslaco sponsors the Mid-Valley Winter Olympics. Each area trailer park sends its winners to compete in playoffs in shuffleboard, fishing, golf, tennis, bowling, horseshoes, and card games. This bank also sends out a summer newsletter and offers free personalized checks.

Another bank in Harlingen has a Golden Club. For those over sixty it offers many free banking services and monthly meetings featuring guest speakers. It also has guided trips to places outside of Texas and social events such as Octoberfest, masquerade balls, dances, and picnics.

A Fun and Fitness Sports Palace in Harlingen has a large ad showing male and female seniors working out on the equipment.

A special edition of the valley magazine written by the editors of the *Valley Morning Star* is published and sent to subscribers in August. It features articles on what's happened in the valley while Winter Texans were back home.

All of the major towns along the longest main street in America (Route 83) have Winter Texan activities: Spanish classes; weekly card parties; winter residents' chorus; many state picnics; Polish American Club of the Rio Grande Valley; fish fries; cribbage tournaments; bridge parties; shuffleboard scrambles; pot-luck luncheons; Caterpillar Tractor Company retirees dinner meeting; Honeywell retirees annual picnic; and Hormel retirees reunion. Each RV/trailer park seems to be the primary center of activities. Some of them are big—really big. A few have golf courses, and many of them have large dance halls.

Dancing is the popular activity in the valley. In a February 1990 issue of the Sunday *Valley Morning Star*, we counted fifty-three dances listed to take place the following week. Most of these were square dances to be held at various RV resorts along the main street. About half were association or club group dances; most had a small admission charge.

The Magic Valley Square and Round Dance Directory (thirty-nine pages) covering January through March 1990 lists 287 individual classes and dances each week! The square dance definitions column has seven levels of square dance proficiency—from basic to extended challenge. A good way to get your exercise, meet new people, and have fun.

The *Herald*, a Brownsville paper, had an article in which a couple from the Magic Valley Association Square Dance Club was interviewed.

They felt strongly about the friendliness of dances—"a square dancer never knows a stranger, other dancers are just friends he hasn't met yet."

There are also many options for singles in the paper including:

Dance-Trophy Gardens, Alamo 8–11 P.M. Chet Short and his Texas Swing Band. No smoking area. Singles welcome. BYOB.

Dance-Tradewinds RV Park 7:30–10:30 P.M. Music by the Texas Rhythm Rangers. Singles welcome. No smoking, no alcohol. Homemade cookies served.

Another attraction is the pancake breakfast or supper. There are nine of these listed in the paper. We had breakfast at one of the RV resorts. For $2.00 it's all you can eat—pancakes, sausage, and coffee. In addition, there was good conversation with some fine people.

As we have traveled from park to park we have met some great, down-to-earth people. RV or trailer living is a good equalizer. Most rigs are comparable, there's not much showing off one's affluence with extra-fancy accoutrements. A portable TV dish was the only extra that we noticed. Some rigs are longer than others, but that's just accepted as something nice, not showing off.

Everyone dresses very casually. Blue jeans, a shirt or blouse and jacket with the name of the facility on the back are standard. Caps are also predominant; there are few cowboy hats. Friendliness abounds. People talk about where they are staying as "their park"—they build an identity with the facility. They become family. Undoubtedly this comes about as a result of the camaraderie of trailer people.

The parks vary in size. They all have recreation rooms. The big ones have a 10,000-square-foot dance floor, stage, large kitchen, adjacent rooms for pool tables and crafts; outside there's a pool, shuffleboard, and maybe tennis courts.

At Fiesta Village one corner near the kitchen has hundreds of pegs on the wall, each holding a personalized coffee mug. Near the tables and chairs is a sign that says, "Squat and Gobble Café." A wonderful corner to sit and "chew the fat."

At one of the tables we met a couple who had just been to the Winnebago factory at Forest, Iowa, and picked out a new motor home. They felt this was the way to purchase a motor home. There were hundreds to choose from. They will caravan during the year and keep traveling until they have health problems. Then they will hit the rocking chair. They have a great outlook.

Most large facilities have a variety of options to choose from:

1. You can rent a site by the week, month, season, or year. Depending on the size, location, and amenities of the facility, the rentals range from $150 plus electricity for one month down to $120 a month on a six-month basis. The yearly rate is not double the six month rate since "off season" time is included, and is negotiable.
2. It is also possible to buy a site. Costs will vary greatly—depending on the size of the lot, location, golf course availability, recreation facilities available, etc. The price can go from $9,000 to $30,000. This would give you normal water-sewage, electrical hookups, and in most cases a phone hookup as well as a cement pad for the trailer, cement patio, and in some cases a cement pad for a car.
3. Many parks have "park models" already set up and available for sale, with the price including the lot.
4. Lots can also be purchased and small homes built; usually a model home is available for inspection. Costs are in the $40,000 to $70,000 range.

We have seen some fabulous setups. One corner site had a circular drive to the front of the trailer. A large wood frame shingle roof had been built over the trailer, car pad, and even extended over a portion of the circular drive. To the rear of the car pad (big enough for two cars) was a small barn-type storage shed. There were plenty of plants growing, showing a lot of personal pride in the property.

These parks vary in appearance. Some are quite hodgepodge. Others are set up by sections and are well organized. Some have well-kept roads and sites while others have rutty blacktop streets and overgrown sites. One park looked pretty seedy—the activity room was called, "The Wreck Hall." That pretty well described the entire location.

These four options will not be found at all parks. Some are strictly rental operations. In the Lower Rio Grande Valley there are a tremendous number of parks to choose from so you can probably find what you want.

One couple we met from Nebraska has found their ideal solution. He had retired from farming but couldn't sit around all the time. So he went to work for the local John Deere distributor. After a few years of that he retired again. They bought a motor home and during the winter months spent time in Florida and the valley. Then he had a light stroke one and a half years ago. After his recovery, they left the motor home back in Nebraska, drove to the valley, and bought a trailer and lot at a park that they liked. They will now have two permanent homes with a support system of friends at each place. This progression seems quite logical. They used their healthy time to see new things and determined a place to settle in when health restrictions required a slowdown. Their process provided a gradual change and had the advantage of developing a good base of friends.

We found an interesting development in Port Isabel, Texas, which is perfect if you are interested in fishing. This is the town on the "land" side of the 12,510-foot bridge across the Laguna Madre to South Padre Island. In Port Isabel, Outdoor Resorts of America* has built a recreational vehicle resort and yacht club. This complex is clustered around an 18-hole par 3 golf course, Spanish-style clubhouse with a 100 × 100-foot hall and kitchen, heated pool, spa, lighted tennis and shuffleboard courts, game room, meeting room, arts and crafts area, laundry, and convenience store.

It is laid out with a series of canals so that the majority of the lots front on water, giving you the opportunity to moor a small boat at your front door. A typical site consists of: a 40 × 70-foot landscaped lot; a 19 × 55-foot concrete pad and patio; a picnic table; water, sewer, and electrical hook-ups; and a telephone hook-up is available. A waterfront lot, without dock, will cost around $20,000. The lot is purchased on a leasehold basis so there are monthly charges.

By checking the real estate listings in the local paper, we found that some lots were selling for less on the resale market than they were from the developer. A little restraint at the time of the sales pitch and some checking around could save dollars.

CANADIAN PINES TO TEXAS PALMS
▪   ▪   ▪

A park in Weslaco, Texas, called Pine to Palm* attracted our attention because of the uniqueness of the name. Pines are not common in the valley—why the use of pine? We paid a visit, heard a fascinating story, and met some terrific Canadians.

In 1970 the valley was primarily a "short stay" travel-trailer stopover. The four- to six-month snowbird had not emerged to any degree. That year a couple of travel-trailer Canadians from Swan River in the provence of Manitoba stopped off in Weslaco. They saw possibilities for building a trailer park and took an option on thirty-five acres. Back home they were able to interest many Swan River Canadians in becoming investors.

Swan River is far up in Manitoba, Canada, at the very beginning of Route 83. This route goes south through the States and 2,000 miles later becomes the main street of the valley—we referred to this as the longest main street in America.

In January 1990, of the park's 448 lots, 23 were vacant. The manager, Alan Rowe, who was hired to do the original site development in 1970, was proud of the occupancy rate. Mobile home sites cost $960 to $1,092 a year, and travel-trailer or park model sites are $804 a year. There are two organizations. 1) Mantex (derived from Manitoba and Texas) is the company that developed the site and presently manages the park. A concentrated effort has been made to have those who use the park become shareholders. Most people own seven shares of stock. Stewart McLean, a former lawyer and judge in Manitoba and president of Mantex, said, "The return on investment has been good for shareholders."

The other organization is 2) the Tourist Club. All resident activities are planned and implemented by the residents—in essence they control their own social life. Ken Wickett, a retired pharmacist, told us that this involvement has done a great deal to mold the entire community into a cohesive group. He said, "At home the doorbell might not ring but once a month, here it happens three or four times a day."

We were given a Tourist Club Directory. It has pictures of all residents, and a seventy-three-page booklet entitled "Go South Dear Heart Go South," written by Fred Sadler, one of the original park participants.

He captured the essence of what makes this park click. Back home everyone is busy, not yet free of the responsibility of earning a living. When they do have free time they seek out kindred souls with whom they have something in common. Time isn't really available to find out about others. Winter Texans have the time to get acquainted, hence they are open to others and new friendships emerge easily to everyone's satisfaction.

Our stop at Pine to Palm Resort Park was very rewarding. We felt we made some new friends, in this case from a different country.

"I DON'T LIKE THE CLOSE QUARTERS OF A PARK"
■   ■   ■

Through an introduction by Marge Johnson of the Rio Grande Valley Chamber of Commerce* we spent an afternoon with a Canadian couple, Leo and Laura Vincent of Sudbury, Ontario. We were interested in learning more about the experiences of Canadian snowbirds.

The first point that was covered was their desire for more room than a park would offer. This couple rents a small home for the winter season. Neighborliness is difficult because they are "new kids" on the block. This doesn't bother them because their privacy is very important. They have made the winter trip to Texas for seven years, usually staying about three months. Day trips, shopping, and Leo's puttering around the house, even though it's a rental, fill their days.

We discussed Canadian pension plans. They participate in three: Canada Pension Plan, similar to our Social Security; Old Age Security—everyone gets this; and their company pension plan. The Canadian medical plan is excellent, which presents a problem since it doesn't cover them when they are out of Canada. They have to buy private insurance while in the States. Temporary insurance only lasts for six months, then a trip back across the border to Canada is required.

We were told that very few Canadians retire full time in the States. This coincided with the options of the folks we talked to at Pine to Palm. Leo and Laura both agreed that the medical coverage is so good they can't afford to leave Canada permanently. Another problem is the buying of American dollars. This is dependent on the exchange rate. Full-

time retirement in the States could cause a major financial loss if the rate
went the wrong way for an extended time.

The Vincents are accomplishing their objective—getting away from
the harsh Canadian winters and maintaining their privacy. It was a very
informative afternoon with some nice people.

Leo mentioned that his brother Camille winters in Summerfield, Florida, and suggested we might want to contact him. Two months later in
Summerfield a north-central Florida town—fifty miles northeast of Orlando—Camille and Annetta Vincent welcomed us to their home.

After thirteen years of wintering in the Clearwater and Largo area in
their motor home the crowds became too much. They sold the motor
home and bought a small manufactured housing home in a rural area of
Summerfield. This has been much better living during the past four
years. They spend six months here and make sure they get back to the
Canadian border before their temporary medical insurance runs out.

There are nine other Canadian couples in the area and they do some
socializing with them but, like his brother, Cam said, "We prefer more
space and like our independence."

LITTLE QUEBEC—HOLLYWOOD, FLORIDA
■   ■   ■

In far south Florida along Route A1A in Dania, Hollywood, and Hal-
landale, we thought we were in Paris or the province of Quebec in
Canada. Everyone was speaking French! In Hollywood at the corner of
Johnson Street and the Boardwalk we had an international breakfast at
Frenchie's Café. The waitresses were bilingual so we were able to order
our food without any problem. All around us we heard excitable French
conversations.

The small bulletin board had messages written in French and the back
of the bar had wine bottles rather than hard liquor.

Fortunately, the couple next to us knew a bit of English. We were able
to piece together that these were all Canadians. They said there are a
million who come here to soak up the sun. (A million sounded high—we
later found out it is more like 350,000, according to the February 1990
issue of *National Geographic* magazine.) Along the fifteen-foot-wide cement path bordering the beach were shops with French names and a

Left Bank motel was advertised. A French language newspaper was evident and it was fun "listening in" as we walked along.

An interesting morning in a snowbird environment—vastly different from the rest of Florida!

The panhandle of Florida has four distinct seasons—not drastic changes but enough to note the passing of a season. In "winter," cool-weather dress is needed. The mean annual temperature is 67.2° F. and rainfall averages between fifty to sixty days a year.

Of interest to many people is the low pollen count. The beaches face in a southerly direction on the Gulf of Mexico. The white sand beaches are magnificent and disappear in a gently sloping manner into crystal-clear blue water.

This area has had overbuilding in the mid- to late eighties. There were condominium auctions the same as in South Padre Island, Texas. It is on the rebound now. For those who don't mind a jacket in January and February, this location is a paradise.

The Sandestin Beach Hilton* in Destin, Florida, has a snowbird package that they market to Canadians. This resort-type facility has 400 suites, each owned individually. When not in use by the owner they are rented as a regular hotel room. It is located on what is known as the Emerald Coast, halfway between Pensacola and Panama City.

We wanted to determine if Canadians might have views of retirement and adjustment different from those in the States. With the fine cooperation of Ms. Brenda Lloyd, director of the Condominium Owners Association, we invited some of the Canadians staying at the hotel to a 9 A.M. coffee and get-acquainted hour. Fourteen people attended. We explained what we were doing and then opened it up for general discussion. Here are some of their most pertinent comments:

The first thing I did was reorganize the kitchen (his wife smiled and shook her head *no!*) . . . Retirees need something to make themselves useful, a balance of pleasure and service . . . Three to four months of snowbirding is a change of residence, one month is an extended vacation . . . We make new friends down here, new networking, a fresh new life . . . Your book is desperately needed—I was given a golden handshake and before I knew it I was floundering in retirement . . . A person needs to plan to *want* to retire, have a plan to live—it takes a lot of imagination to retire successfully.

Is Canadian retirement different? Not at all!

LOVE CAN BE FOUND AT ANY AGE
■ ■ ■

About two thirds up the Gulf of Mexico side of Florida is the town of Homosassa Springs on U.S. Highway 19, approximately sixty miles north of the Tampa area. Four miles south is Sugarmill Woods.* The name is derived from the pre-Civil War Yulee Sugar Mill in Old Homosassa.

This development covers twenty-five square miles, about half of it usable. There are no beaches, since the mangrove grows out into the water. There are about 1,700 homes, and twenty-seven holes of golf. Many of the homes are rented to snowbirds.

Mr. and Mrs. N.S. of Rochester, New York, have been coming to this community for a three-month stay for several years. There are about eight other people from Rochester who also make the same journey. They rent a two-bedroom town house facing the golf course. It is beautifully decorated and gives them a sense of being at home. They play golf twice a week with their friends, go on picnics, explore northern Florida, and in their words, "We just play for three months and then go back to our more organized activities for nine months."

Not too long ago they both lost their spouses to extremely difficult medical problems. After going through their grieving period they found each other, and the chance at a second life. Mrs. S. asked that we include in our book that, "Love can be found at any age." They went through their time of being single again, and today their happiness is contagious. Even in later life, after a personal disaster, they exemplify that life can still be loving and fulfilling!

NATIONWIDE SNOWBIRDING
■ ■ ■

Our nation has the cold North and the warm South. For those who want primarily to remain in their Northern environment but get away from the extreme cold temperatures, snow, and ice, snowbirding is an ideal answer.

Warm winter costs vary from modest—renting a travel-trailer space at $320 a month or $1,550 for six months—to $1,300 and more a month for a town house. Another option is to purchase a small manufactured housing unit for $25,000 or a condo at $150,000.

One couple told us that it takes them about thirty days to return home in their RV. They stop off at many different places to renew friendships with folks they have met down South. One nice thing about this type of dropping in is that there is no imposition on the people being visited. You bring your own bed and bath!

One question always comes up. What are you going to do with your time? Snowbirds all around the country tell us they have no problem with time. They find that there is always something going on. If they're at a facility where there is a clubhouse so much the better. They freely admit that they probably waste a lot of time over coffee and move at a much slower pace. The relaxed pace is not because of medical reasons, it's just that there's no reason to rush. They know from the onset that their stay is temporary. Their main objective is to get away from the bad weather. Therefore, why worry about what to do. As one lady told us, "We are just lazy down here."

Some people do volunteer work. Those with a strong religious persuasion will become active in a local church. Club affiliations or fraternal organizations will provide many with a base of friendly people and many worthwhile projects to work on. Golfing, fishing, dancing, hobbies, arts and crafts, and side trips occupy the time for others.

EXTENDED VACATION
■　■　■

Our overall impression is that most snowbirds look at their winter months in the Sunbelt as an extended vacation. They appear happy and carefree.

Is this lifestyle for you? Only you know the answer.

6

NOMADING—FULL
OR PART TIME

• • •

LIFESTYLE OPTION #3, RV'ING

We started writing this chapter inside a 26-foot, 9-inch Class A motor home. Our East Texas tall pines campsite is in Mount Vernon, Texas. Recognize the name of the town? It's the hometown of "Dandy" Don Meredith of Monday night football fame. You can't miss it. Along the highway a billboard proclaims: "A Dandy Town, Mount Vernon, Texas."

MOTOR HOME LIVING

• • •

What is it really like living in a motor home? A rental for a few days gave us a taste of RV life.

The appointments of this "House Car," as the Pennsylvania license plates describe a motor home, are attractive. This one sleeps six adults very comfortably. It has a dinette area for four, a couch, and large comfortable chairs for the driver and navigator. There is a microwave oven, four-burner stove and oven, double sink, and refrigerator with a separate freezer. The tub/shower, marine-type toilet, and sink are mini-size. Folding doors give privacy to the rear bedroom and bath. This RV has air-conditioning, LP furnace, and water heater; overhead lighting is plentiful. Inside there are thirty-three drawers and doors for storage; outside, five locked compartments.

KING OF THE ROAD
■   ■   ■

Driving is an experience. This vehicle is built on a truck chassis and you're high above the road on level with the eighteen-wheelers. We traveled interstate, FM (farm to market) roads, and dirt trails inside campgrounds—giving us a variety of driving experiences.

Tornado warnings, high winds, and torrential downpours required a constant two-handed grip on the steering wheel. Large trucks passing us slowpokes caused a significant strong push to the right. Initially we were apprehensive, but eventually driving became routine. We averaged 7.6 miles per gallon.

TOGETHERNESS IS TOTAL
■   ■   ■

Togetherness. When you're on the road there is no escape. A person could close off the folding door to the bed. This would give a 2 × 4-foot section to stand in. Other options are: take a walk, use the camp swimming pool or recreation room, take a nap, or read a book. If it's not too cold, hot, rainy, or buggy, a folding chair under a tree, with a six-pack, is an escape. We're being a little facetious. But the reality is—you are together! There are a few hobbies possible. Those that don't require much equipment. Whittling, painting, writing, photography, handwork such as crocheting, needlepoint, and embroidery are possibilities. These activities would provide a little individuality.

Chitchat with fellow campers is nice. There are a lot of mighty fine people on the road. These casual conversations are helpful. They pass the time and some of the travel stories are fascinating. The only show of status is the size and opulence of the rig a person drives. Other than the rig, a campground is a great leveler of humanity.

In the campground there are some people you could do without. The rambunctious kids, the party-party couples, or the barking dog. There are few secrets. A kid is crying. A father's loud "shut up" echoes throughout the campground. The kid quiets down immediately.

A cross section of Middle America can be found in campgrounds across the U.S.A. We accomplished our purpose. We had a mini-peek into the very large window of nomading.

DEFINITIONS
■ ■ ■

Just what is an RV? It's really not any particular size, style, or brand. It's a nickname. The accepted usage of the term is—a recreational vehicle that is designed for highway movement and provides living space. That leaves a lot of latitude.

We were in contact with the Recreational Vehicle Industry Association (RVIA)* and learned a great deal about this lifestyle. The RVIA is the industry voice to the government and the chief source of shipment statistics, market research, and technical data. It also establishes and monitors compliance of construction standards established by its members. Ninety-five percent of all RV's produced in the United States are made by RVIA members. Their seal on a vehicle indicates the standards have been met.

There are many RV choices—RVIA lists two major groups with five subclassifications in each group. The retail price listed is an average for the U.S. market in 1988.

1. Travel Trailer
   CONVENTIONAL TRAILER—$11,806. Ranges from twelve to thirty-five feet in length.
   PARK TRAILER—$17,441. For seasonal or temporary living, can be connected to utilities.
   FIFTH-WHEEL TRAILER—$18,068. Constructed with a raised forward section that allows for a bi-level floor plan. (A pickup truck with a fifth-wheel hitch is required.)
   FOLDING CAMPING TRAILER—$4,135. Has collapsible sidewalls that fold for towing.
   TRUCK CAMPER—$8,025. A camping unit that is affixed to the bed of a truck.

2. Motor Home
   MOTOR HOME (TYPE A)—$55,248. The living unit has been entirely constructed on a bare, specially designed motor vehicle chassis.
   VAN CAMPER (TYPE B)—$27,639. A panel-type truck to which any two of the following have been added, sleeping, kitchen, or toilet

facilities. Also 110-volt hook-up, fresh water hook-up and storage, and a top extension.

MOTOR HOME (MINI) TYPE C—$34,599. A living unit that is built on an automotive manufactured van frame with an attached cab.

MOTOR HOME (LOW PROFILE) TYPE C—$32,011. Same as Type C above but with an overall height of less than eight feet.

MOTOR HOME (COMPACT) TYPE C—$23,521. Same as above but weighs less than 6,500 pounds.

We have been to many RV shows. The cost of an RV can skyrocket when you look at all the desirable options available. There are some super rigs. Financial restraint will need to be practiced.

What kind of rig should you buy? Your pocketbook will dictate to a large degree the answer to size and style. You can spend over $300,000 for a forty-foot Bluebird Wanderlodge pusher model! Luxury is the only description applicable. Your driving and living are made as easy as possible. It has a self-leveling jack system, a monitor that talks to you when your fuel is low or you're exceeding the speed limit, and a TV screen in the cockpit to survey outside conditions. In addition it comes with heated windshield wipers, a remote control retractable TV antenna, air-powered entry step, intercom, water purifier, a safe, and many more niceties.

You can go higher if you wish. A Mercedes Benz bus can be set up as a motor home for about $500,000. Motor homes in this price range are for a selected few. For the vast majority there is undoubtedly a motor home that will fit more normal needs and not cause bankruptcy.

Want to rent an RV for a tryout? Write the following: Recreation Vehicle Rental Association,* Cruise America,* Go Vacations, Inc.,* Rental Management Systems,* U-Haul International RV Rental Division.* In Canada write: Cruise Canada,* Go Vacations, Inc.,* or Path-finder Vacations, Inc.*

According to RVIA statistics dated November 16, 1989, a University of Michigan study shows there are 8.47 million RV's in the United States. There are an estimated 25 million enthusiasts.

What's the future? RVIA says ". . . in the 1990s as the baby boomers enter the prime RV buying years of age forty-five to fifty-four and achieve their peak earning power, higher market growth rates are likely to occur."

Write the association. They will send you a catalogue of publications about the RV lifestyle and an all-inclusive reference list for RV owners. A wealth of good information.

Any of the above type of RV will get you around the country. The first decision is whether this lifestyle of considerable travel is for you. This doesn't mean constant travel, although some people are on the road 365 days a year. Their RV is their home. These full-time nomads are in the minority. The vast majority of retirees who partake of the open road do so on a part-time basis. They keep a residence as a base of operations.

A point of clarification. Snowbirds are away from home for months at a time. But they tend to settle in at a park for a few months rather than be on the move most of the time. The nomad is much more on the move than the snowbird.

How much on the move? That depends on where you want to go, what you want to see, and in many cases what you want to learn. Seeing the country, visiting off-the-beaten-path places at a leisurely pace could be very attractive. But it could get lonesome. It's true there are other RV'ers at a campground and the conversation is fun, but it's surface talk. It doesn't fill the need for security and belonging. Also, that very close togetherness in an RV could cause stressful situations with little opportunity for relief. Virtually constant sight-seeing, although interesting, doesn't really provide a great deal of meaningful accomplishment.

Our very human need for friendship, belonging, accomplishment, and relief from constant close togetherness could dull the pleasures of being on the road. A solution must be found for this need so satisfaction can emerge.

TRAVEL GROUPS
■   ■   ■

Those people with like interests and needs have banded together through travel clubs and associations. This happens all the time when we are at home. We participate in our church groups, civic groups, and small social groups of good friends. Those on the road do this by traveling together—they form caravans.

Company-Sponsored

Many of the larger manufacturers of RV's sponsor clubs for owners of their RV's. The granddaddy of these clubs seems to be the Wally Byam Caravan Club International, Inc. (WBCCI).* It bills itself as the world's largest, oldest, and most active club.

Wally Byam was a pioneer in the development and manufacture of travel trailers—he was the founder of Airstream, Inc. He produced many trailers but his 1936 Clipper became the prototype of the silver-sided Airstream that we see on the highways today. In 1951 Wally Byam led his first caravan through Central America. From this beginning, the club has emerged today with over 10,000 members. Owners of Airstream trailers can become members of the WBCCI.

WBCCI publishes a newspaper, the *Caravaner.* Comparing a reprint of the first issue (June 1954) with the June 1984 (thirtieth anniversary) issue, highlights the growth of this club, and the changes in Airstream.

The club is composed of 12 regions encompassing 170 separate units. These vary in size from 25 to over 300 members. They run their own program of rallies, caravans, and other activities. Membership in 1 unit entitles a member to attend rallies of all units—over 1,000 rallies a year. There are regional rallies and 10 yearly national rallies. The main event is a yearly international rally, attended by thousands of members. At this rally, a caravan training program is conducted by the International Caravan Committee.

There are also clubs within clubs—amateur radio club, gem and mineral clubs, and a free-wheelers club for members who are single, widowed, or divorced.

Owners of Itasca and Winnebago motor homes can belong to the Winnebago International Travelers Club (WIT).* In addition to rallies and tours WIT offers: special motor home insurance; discounts at selected campsites; weekly mail forwarding; information on travel routes; lost credit card notification; an annual WIT directory; a monthly newspaper; a vehicle ID program; check forwarding; spare keys; and special clubs, including CB, Ham Radio, and 365 Club.

Owners of Coachman RV's can become members of Coachman Caravan Travel Club.* Their list of benefits include: decals and unit numbers; caravan roster; map service; magazine discounts; canoe trips; bi-monthly *Caravan Caper* (magazine); Pete's Market—mail order store; discount film processing; a car rental program; discounted travel accessories; campground manual discount; local state and district activities; trip routing; and an annual rally.

There are many more company-sponsored groups—Sportscoach Owners International,* Avion Travelcade Club,* Carriage/Royals International Travel Club,* and Champion Fleet Owners Association.* The Recreational Vehicle Industry Association lists twenty-eight brand-name company clubs.

Private Clubs

If you have an RV not covered by a company club, there are many clubs to choose from.

Good Sam R.V. Owens Club* (Sam is short for Samaritan), headquartered in Agoura, California. This club has more than 400,000 member families and 2,000 local chapters in the United States and Canada. It offers: a variety of group insurance plans; a 50-percent discount on *Trailer Life* and *Motor Home* magazines; *Hi-Way Herald* monthly paper; discount on *Trailer Life's RV Campground and Service Directory;* a 10-percent discount on overnight camping; a 10-percent discount on RV parts and accessories; a 15-percent discount on car rentals; a trip routing service; credit card loss protection; a mail-forwarding service; Good Sam travelers checks; a discount on photo processing; lost pet service; lost key service; and a full-service travel agency. Good Sam is also active in fighting anti-RV legislation at the national level and through assistance to members on the local level.

The Family Motor Coach Association (FMCA),* founded in 1966 and 65,000 strong, has some unique benefits in addition to many of the usual benefits. The unique ones are:

PINCH-HIT DRIVER PROGRAM. FMCA members who encounter any emergency that prohibits them from driving their coach while away from home will be assisted by a member volunteer who will transport the motor home to the desired destination of the owner.

STOPPIN' SPOT FELLOWSHIP. The annual directory lists members who have volunteered their home facilities to fellow members for a twenty-four-hour emergency stop.

To qualify for membership you need to have at least a one-third interest in a qualifying coach. A qualifying coach is defined as a self-propelled completely self-contained vehicle which contains all the conveniences of a home, including cooking, sleeping, and sanitary facilities; and in which the driver's seat is accessible in a walking position from the living quarters.

The Recreational Vehicle Industry Association lists ten national camping clubs. If you write them for information, enclose a large self-addressed stamped envelope.

Small travel clubs can be found in many places. Our local senior citizens' center has one, one of the fraternal organizations has a club, and in most retirement communities we have visited there is usually a travel club. None of these clubs are very expensive. Yearly membership fees are in the $15 to $20 range. If you want to travel with others it's there for the asking, but you have to take the initiative.

WHAT'S A RALLY?
■   ■   ■

One of the club publications had an article entitled "Speaking of Rallies." They tried to define a rally. It's a gathering of hundreds of RV's —so they are parked in a parking lot. It's a gigantic camp out—so you can camp out any time. The conclusion was that a rally can't be described, it has to be experienced. It's the closeness of being part of an extended family with kin from other cities and states, and in some cases from other countries.

There are planned games and contests, some go golfing or fishing, and many times there is entertainment. There may be tours of local places of interest. Good food, happy hours, and friendly chatter. But the real joy is the opportunity to strengthen old friendships and make new friends.

For many, a rally gives a great deal of personal satisfaction. They are able to plan, organize, and carry out a successful event. Whether they are the elected leader or the doer who barbecues the chicken, there is satisfaction in accomplishing a worthwhile endeavor. From this the "well done" accolades by the participants add to one's heightened self-esteem.

We conclude that a rally is similar to the old-time trip to Grandma's farm. There the relatives congregated on Sunday afternoon to enjoy each other's company. It is a means to a satisfaction of the need for belonging —being a part of.

WHAT'S A CARAVAN?
■   ■   ■

It can be five families traveling down the highway in their motor homes or pulling a trailer on their way to a rally. Or it can be thirty families on a three-month caravan through the United States, Canada, Mexico, or the Orient.

A small group on an overnight trip doesn't require a great deal of planning and coordination. However, long excursions need to have every minute detail fine-tuned. There is a great deal of work in connection with a caravan and it's done by those in the caravan. That provides an excellent opportunity for "meaningful purpose assignments."

Someone needs to be a scout—to go ahead and make sure the scheduled evening campsite is ready. Someone with mechanical ability is needed as the "caboose"—the last RV in the caravan—to be available to help with mechanical problems. The caboose never comes into the campsite until everyone else has arrived.

There has to be a wagonmaster and some first lieutenants in charge of group activities, pot-luck dinners, campfire entertainment, and a host of other things.

Many of the caravans that are advertised in *R. V.* and *Senior* magazines sound exciting. For example, a thirty-one-day twin piggyback caravan. The trip was to start in El Paso, Texas, and end in San Ysidro, California. It included highway travel, piggyback on rail cars, and on board ship.

Creative World Rallies & Caravans* organizes rallies and caravans. For example, you drive to Calgary, Canada, where your RV site is ready and there are reserved seats at the stampede grounds for a rodeo. Many other activities are included at a cost of $695 for two people in a rig. Also scheduled in 1990—Orange Bowl parade and game, Mardi Gras rally, and caravans through Alaska, the Canadian Rockies, and Australia.

If you want to travel with others, a little research will probably find you a caravan to anywhere you want to go.

PURPOSEFUL CARAVANS
■   ■   ■

All caravans aren't just sight-seeing or recreational in nature. There is a group called the RVICS (pronounced Riviks). This stands for Roving Volunteers in Christ's Service.

A United Methodist couple, Mr. and Mrs. Henry Schaeffer, founded RVICS in Sibley, Illinois. He had retired from the grocery business and felt the need to minister unto others—not in the sense of evangelism but rather to use his talents to help others. To do things for others, not for money. United Methodists constitute about one third of the total membership. Other denominations make up the remainder.

The RVICS move in and build or renovate mostly church-related facilities. In three and one-half years they have completed thirty-seven projects in seventeen states. Most involve church camp, schools, and children's homes. More than seventy couples participate in two caravans. One that Mr. Schaeffer leads goes up and down the East Coast and another works the West and Southwest.

On a project the men work three and one-half days a week, the women four mornings. Sponsors supply material and parking space and utility hook-ups near the project. Ideally each project takes about three and one-half weeks. The group disbands during December and two summer months.

One minister, a recipient of help from the RVICS, said, "It is excellent work by highly skilled people. They have a standing invitation to come back any time."

Christian fellowship, worthwhile personal contribution, and part-time nomadic living can be a great combination!

THE 365 GROUP
■   ■   ■

These are the full-time nomads. On the road all of the time. They sell their house and away they go. Their motto is, "Home is where you park it." Complete freedom seems to be the main purpose in the life of the full-timer. In fact, a club has been formed for those on the road all year.

Escapees Inc. (SKP)*

This club was founded by Joe and Kay Peterson in 1978. They first went on the road full time in 1970. Their membership in 1990 was 13,000. Services include mail forwarding, emergency contact, and special services requested by a member. Cost varies based on services provided.

We stopped by the club's headquarters in Livingstone, Texas. Joe and Kay were away at a rally but we had a fine talk with their daughter Cathy. Our feeling is that SKP is a small, close-knit club with much camaraderie. It has a very unique membership—those who are on the road full time. That's *not exactly* correct. Many are people who have trades and who move from job to job. These people settle down for short periods, finish a job, and move on.

One thing common to most of the members is the lack of a home base. What they own is in their trailer. Some nomads are retirees. Unfortunately, figures were not available concerning how many members were retirees and how many were tradespeople.

Naturally there comes a time when it makes sense to come in off the road. But where? This is where SKP really offers a valuable service. It has established co-ops.

These are nonprofit RV parks owned and operated by SKP members. Usually there are at least 120 members. They pool their money to purchase land and pool their talents and labor to build the park. Upon completion, each member has a full hook-up site where he/she can live rent free. Operating costs are shared by co-op members. This provides insurance against the time when illness, loss of a partner, or aging requires permanency. Resale, when required, is made to someone on the waiting list. There are co-ops at Benson, Arizona; Casa Grande, Arizona; Tucson, Arizona; Yuma, Arizona; Zolfo Springs, Florida; Pahrump, Nevada; Lakewood, New Mexico; Roseburg, Oregon; San Antonio, Texas; and Olympic Peninsula, Washington. Additional co-ops are being organized in Madera City, California; Hemet, California; and Rio Grande Valley, Texas. The SKP Maple Leaf Chapter in Crown Cresent, Bradford, Ontario, Canada, is also searching for people interested in starting a co-op.

Rainbow's End

The club headquarters in Livingston, Texas is located at an RV park called Rainbow's End, (same address as the club's) where SKP's can purchase lots. Some unique structures, called sheds, have been built by nomads approaching the time when they have to come off the road. Visualize a large barn-type roof or flattened A-frame roof open at the ends. It is high enough to park a trailer or motor home under the roof and wide enough to park a pickup next to it on one side and build a couple of rooms on the other side. These rooms abut the trailer so they become a part of the total living facility. One shed had a screened-in porch. These sites are landscaped and look nice. When a getaway is needed, it's easy to hook up the trailer and hit the road.

We purchased a couple of Kay Peterson's books. For anyone considering this lifestyle we would recommend *Home Is Where You Park It* and *Survival of the Snowbirds.* These can be ordered from the SKP Club.

In one of her books, Kay Peterson describes one of her techniques to meet fellow trailerites. Under their awning she and her husband set up chairs and a small table with a coffeepot and cups. A sign reads:

> *The coffee is ready*
> *No bother or fuss*
> *If you have the time*
> *Come visit with us*

Someday we will go back to Rainbow's End and have a cup of coffee with Kay and Joe Peterson!

Undoubtedly there could be a long list of pros and cons about full-time RV travel. Freedom would be at the top of the "pro" list, along with seeing the country. At the top of the "con" list would have to be the loss of family and close friends and especially the grandchildren.

Quite appropriate at this time is a bumper sticker that Paul Harvey included in one of his broadcasts—Geritol Gypsies!

A tremendous amount of independence would be a prerequisite for nomadic life. Anyone, either the husband or wife, who has a strong need for close association and acceptance by others would probably have a difficult time.

MEMBERSHIP CAMPGROUNDS
■   ■   ■

Dear Mrs. Lee:

This letter constitutes positive official notification that you have been selected to receive at least one gift from Category A.

A part of the packet of information included a flier with a picture of Roy Rogers, in cowboy garb, urging Mrs. Lee to come visit a Thousand Trails* campsite near Dallas. We did, and sat through a Roy Rogers pitch movie, and toured a campsite which was under construction that members could use. In addition, members had the opportunity of staying at other Thousand Trails camps around the country. All this for $6,500, but you needed to sign up immediately to have the price discounted.

Thousand Trails has been in business since 1969. They have been growing. By some yardsticks they have been successful. "Heard on the Street," a column in *The Wall Street Journal* of November 14, 1984, had some reservations concerning Thousand Trails, Inc. A director and the chief financial officer of Thousand Trails, Inc., stated that if memberships were to fall far short of projection, it would create a lot of difficulties. The obvious question is: what would happen to the commitments made to the members if hard times did overtake the company?

We received a similar "You have already won a prize" letter from a camp affiliated with Camp Coast to Coast.* There we sat through a film narrated by the late Lorne Greene of "Bonanza" fame. The similarity to the Roy Rogers film was fantastic. We toured a campsite under construction and were told of the opportunity to stay at other Coast to Coast affiliates around the country. All this for a cost of $5,500, "but if you sign up right now" other things would be added. (In late 1989 Mr. and Mrs. W.M. paid $7,000 for a membership.) We said, "No, thank you." We received no brochures or "I'll check back with you" suggestion, picked up our prize (we didn't win the Cadillac), and left.

The concept is good and when the facilities are completed according to the drawings, the campsites will be very nice. However, we had a great deal of trouble accepting the no-performance bond or lack of any form of guarantee that the campsite would be completed. Likewise, there was no ownership interest in the parent company. A lot of faith is required.

In early 1990 we ascertained that Camp Coast to Coast and Thousand Trails were still in business.

These two companies are certainly not fly-by-night organizations. A lot of people have bought into the membership camping concept. The column "Your Money Matters," in *The Wall Street Journal* of September 25, 1985, reported that this concept is offered in forty-three states. Promoters of membership camping expected sales between $700 million and $800 million in 1984. The main theme of the column centered around the complaints that people have concerning the sales tactics used by these promoters. An Illinois assistant attorney general said that the questionable sales tactics are a nationwide problem.

According to the column, eleven states now have some type of camp-sales law. The old adage—let the buyer beware—seems highly applicable.

If you're tending toward an RV lifestyle, it may be worthwhile to investigate the membership campground concept. There are additional benefits that we haven't mentioned. Be prepared for a hard sell. Analyze thoroughly and then evaluate against your own criteria—the concept may be right for you.

LONERS ON WHEELS, INC.*
■ ■ ■

As the name implies, this group is strictly for singles. If you tie the knot again, you cannot remain a member. The national organization has over twenty-five chapters in thirty-five states and Canada. A national newsletter, as well as chapter letters, keeps members informed of national, regional, and local rallies.

Yearly dues are modest; in 1990 dues were $24 in the United States and $29 in Canada. Permanent campsites are available for members. The club is described as filling a need for singles who have a sense of independence, a love of the open road, and a desire to belong. A "swinging singles club" it is not.

Mr. L.A. of Snyder, Texas, feels that membership in the club has helped fill a void in his mother's life that "is fantastic." After his mother made the initial adjustment to her husband's death, the LOW's became an integral part of her life. She belongs to an Oklahoma chapter called the SOONER-LOW's.

Age is no barrier. Some members in their eighties still drive their own motor home to the rallies. Why not? As long as one still has the physical ability to drive the companionship of other singles around the campfire has to be very fulfilling. An added bonus is the possibility of meeting that certain someone with similar interests and values.

A letter from the president, Dick March, who lives in California, and a copy of the January 1990 *LOW Newsletter* indicates a very active national group. Dick has been an RV'er for twenty years and active in LOW for nearly eleven years. He loves the freedom of RV'ing, which provides a change of scene or area of interest at will and a continual accumulation of new friends. He said, "LOW is not a matchmaking or dating service." "However they constantly go off with one of our 'good and true'—in round numbers we get three new members and lose two."

The newsletter has a slogan—"Never let 'em past the gate without a greeting and a hug." There is a listing of rallies, chapter meetings, caravans, and camp outs. It has an interesting section called "Mail Call." Members send in brief notes of their activities. The following excerpts portray the real meaning of being a member:

P.L. (NY) . . . Loner family has certainly hung in with me . . . thank you all for being friends and family to me. Life is good.

D.P. (VA) LOW is a wonderful organization and my only inspiration since losing my husband of thirty-seven years.

B.B. (CA) . . . How great that Loners can be with those who care rather than longing for unavailable persons who have gone. Have spent too much of my life in that dismal pursuit, longing to go to a party to which I was not invited. No more!! I have LOW, thank God . . .

Edith Lane founded LOW twenty years ago. The organization raised over $2400 to pay for her trip to the twentieth-anniversary rally at Death Valley Sunshine Campground. From her wheelchair she wrote, "Never in all my life have I felt so loved and so appreciated."

From these comments it's obvious that the organization is the conduit that fills an important need—a bonding among members; it offers good times and assists in the adjustment to being single.

RV'ING CONCLUSION
∎   ∎   ∎

A lot of time and effort can and should go into a study of the different types of RV's available. A realistic evaluation will pay off in the long run.

Nomading, full or part time, can be an extremely satisfying lifestyle. If you haven't been an RV enthusiast before retirement, a lifestyle change of this magnitude can be very traumatic. A tremendous amount of time should be spent researching before a decision is made.

Renting an RV for an extended trip is a must. Visiting travel clubs and getting acquainted with members should be high on the list of important things to do. Search out some folks who have come off the road and find out why! Ask current nomads what kind of adjustments they went through. How did they cope?

Bookstores are full of paperback books on the subject. Pour through these. Use two different color highlighters. Underscore the good things with one color and the concern items with the other color. Both husband and wife should do this. Then analyze the results. Most important of all is to surface differences and come to a resolution.

The close quarters of RV living require a nearly complete acceptance of the lifestyle by both parties. Giving this lifestyle a try without close to 100 percent agreement will lead to a high level of dissatisfaction—only trouble will result.

Assuming it's for you, the study and decisions necessary in deciding which kind of RV best suits your needs can be a fun time. It will be the beginning of a new adventure. A time of freedom and happiness.

Pulling a rig or driving a motor home is a clear-cut lifestyle. It would be entirely possible to become completely engrossed, providing both physical and mental stimulation. A critical need is to prepare for the time when a person must come off the road. Until that time, those who choose this lifestyle and become involved will undoubtedly have a very fulfilled retirement.

7

RETIREMENT AREAS

. . .

LIFESTYLE OPTION #4, RETIREMENT AREA LIVING

"We didn't know where to retire . . . we just loaded up the car . . . locked up our house in Rye, New York . . . started driving south to Florida . . . then west through the Sunbelt states. Our frustration got to be unbearable . . . we were really confused . . . ready to head back east . . . happened to stay in a motel in Hemet, California . . . liked the town and bought a mobile home."

That's exactly what Mr. and Mrs. G.R. told us. They also said that Hemet is a nice town and they like their home. We don't doubt their decision but it seems to us that if they had done some investigation of different retirement areas they could have saved themselves a great deal of confusion and frustration.

The "urge to move" seems to prevail among a lot of people when retirement comes along. This urge probably stems from the concept of a new beginning. Starting with new surroundings, new home, and new friends. This provides excitement and can be very invigorating.

During our travels we have found pockets of retirement areas around the country. Chapter 12 deals with retirement in Hawaii so we will stay on the mainland in this chapter. Our purpose is not to recommend any area. We will give you our findings and our impressions, refer to various resource materials, and then it's your decision.

We have already covered some pros and cons of moving. This chapter is based on an assumption—you want to move or are open to considering a move to a retirement area, to starting a new lifestyle in a new environment.

Wherever you live there will probably be a retirement facility or complex nearby. This may be a planned neighborhood, apartment complex with age restrictions, or perhaps a life care community. When we refer to retirement areas we mean areas of the country that have drawn retirees in fairly large numbers.

Most of these areas will be in the moderate weather part of the country. Some people like the challenge of zero-degree wind-chill factors with icy roads and snowdrifts. We have found many retirement pockets where these conditions exist. Most people don't want the hassle. Especially in the latter stages of retirement when physical conditions make life more difficult.

MOST POPULAR SUNBELT STATES (CENSUS BUREAU FIGURES)
■ ■ ■

The populations of Arizona, Florida, Texas, New Mexico, and California grew by more than 15 percent from 1980–87. Only three other states had that kind of growth—Nevada, Utah, and Alaska.

The most popular retirement states are expected to show continued growth. According to the Census Bureau

Projected Population Growth from 1980 to 2010 will be:

STATE	1980/1990	1990/2000	2000/2010
Arizona	+38.0%	+23.1%	+15.2%
Florida	+31.5%	+20.3%	+13.7%
Texas	+24.5%	+14.1%	+10.2%
California	+23.1%	+15.0%	+11.5%
North Carolina	+13.7%	+11.8%	+ 9.0%
South Carolina	+13.7%	+10.1%	+ 7.6%

Apparently the popularity of following the sun will continue.

It's evident from the above that the milder climates are a drawing card for retirees with the "itch to switch."

MANUFACTURED HOUSING
■   ■   ■

Before explaining various retirement areas the subject of manufactured housing needs to be discussed. In all probability this type of construction will be new to most people. In fact, to many readers the words "mobile home" or "manufactured housing" will be thought of as substandard or second class.

There are a great many communities, especially in the warmer climates, that are exclusively manufactured housing.

NEW MOBILE HOMES PLACED FOR RESIDENTIAL USES
(IN 1000's)*

1987	TOTAL	NORTHEAST	MIDWEST	SOUTH	WEST
Number of Homes	239.2	26.6	40.0	145.5	30.1
Average Sales Price	27.7	25.6	23.7	21.9	31.0

* SOURCE—U.S. BUREAU OF CENSUS, CONSTRUCTION REPORTS—SERIES CZO

In the past there probably was a great deal of mobility since many were used as temporary or transportable homes. Today most mobile homes are moved once—from the manufacturing facility to the home's permanent location. We have seen thousands of these homes on permanent foundations. They were beautifully landscaped with porches, patios, window boxes, carports, and all the trappings of a "stick-built" (normal construction) home. In some cases perhaps better construction. Some had roofovers with insulation to deaden roof rumble. Two roofs would seem to make good sense.

Although these mobile homes can be moved there is little likelihood this would take place. They are bought and sold just like any other home and are eligible for FHA and VA long-term mortgage financing.

All manufactured homes built since June 15, 1976, are constructed to a uniform set of construction and safety standards, which are administered by the Department of Housing and Urban Development (HUD).

This national building code regulates design, construction, strength and durability, fire resistance and energy efficiency, insulation, and performance of heating, plumbing, air-conditioning, thermal, and electrical systems. Included in the above are standards dealing with ceiling heights, light, ventilation, exit facilities, smoke detectors, pop-out egress windows, flame-spread limitations, body/frame and transportation movement.

Each home built to these specifications is required to have:

1. A seal affixed to the house specifying HUD compliance.
2. A diagram provided by the manufacturer showing the required number and position of placement piers and positioning for anchoring devices.
3. A certificate explaining the performance that can be expected from the heating system within a specified range of outside temperature and wind velocity.
4. Maps indicating the zone for which the home has been built insofar as resistance to wind and snow loads.
5. A consumer manual informing the purchaser of proper home maintenance, avoidance of potential safety hazards, and remedies available under the National Manufactured Housing and Safety Standards Act of 1974.

The state of Florida requires that homes be anchored. Apparently this safety requirement is worthwhile. According to the Florida Manufactured Housing Association, the 1979, 110-mph hurricane David didn't dislodge a single manufactured home in the Cape Canaveral area.

Some homes are very large—fourteen feet wide by as much as eighty feet long. Put two of these together and you will not hurt for room.

As in any housing purchase, the more information you have the better will be your decision. Your library or bookstores have many publications on this subject.

As we rambled around the States we used Peter A. Dickinson's *Sunbelt Retirements* (AARP) as a statistical reference. If your retirement plans are incomplete and you're considering a jaunt around the country, we strongly recommend having a copy of this book with you. The book is updated every few years so be sure to get the latest version.

Woodalls Retirement Directory also has good information about Sunbelt housing; however, this is heavily oriented to mobile home housing (Woodall Publishing Co., 500 Hyacinth Place, Highland Park, IL 60035).

NORTHEAST
■   ■   ■

Far up the East Coast has to be for the more hardy individualistic type. The rock-bound coast of Maine is rugged; beautiful but rugged. Winters follow the same pattern. Northern Vermont, New Hampshire, and New York are likewise havens for those who relish huddling up by the wood stove. Nothing wrong with this but these areas don't draw large numbers of retirees.

Going south a bit brings you to Cape Cod.* A major vacation spot and a rapidly growing retirement haven. Mr. and Mrs. W.M., formerly of Stamford, Connecticut, have chosen a two-home approach to retirement. They have a modest waterfront home in Wellfleet on the Cape and a small home in Williamsburg, Virginia. The Cape has been their vacation ground for years so a retirement haven here was a natural. Why not full time? They feel that from October on it's bleak and lonesome, hence the Williamsburg home.

A projection by the Massachusetts Institute of Social and Economic Research indicates that from 1985 to 1995 there will be a 94-percent increase in the number of people older than eighty on the Cape, and an increase of 18 percent of people aged sixty to seventy-nine. Everyone doesn't like this growth. The "townies"—lifelong residents—find it difficult to accept these outsiders. Most prominent town government positions are held by the "townies." Already crowded roads will be impassable in the future—there's no land available to build superhighways. Perhaps that fits into many retirees' philosophy of taking the slow lane.

Lower New York and Connecticut have drawn many retirees to two planned communities, both developed by the Heritage Development Group. These are not totally retirement-oriented. In fact they are listed as adult communities. You have to be in your early fifties to qualify.

The first, Heritage Hills of Westchester,* is located in the hilly area of

Somers, New York, very close to the boundary line of Putnam and West-chester counties. Some residents commute to midtown Manhattan by chartered bus or take a mini-bus to the railroad station. Either way it's a long commute.

Somers is referred to as the cradle of the American circus. The Barnum and Bailey Circus was spawned in Somers—Hachaliah Bailey had a menagerie business which evolved into the famous circus.

There are all kinds of activities here—golf, tennis, swimming, and the normal range of interest clubs. In addition, there is winter. Not the severe winters of upstate New York but enough to feature cross country skiing as an activity.

Further east among the hills and valleys on 1,000 acres of Connecticut countryside is Heritage Village,* an adult planned community of 2,500 condominium homes. It's located fifteen miles from Hartford and eighty miles from New York City. Mrs. E.F. has retired to this community. Her condo is part of a four-plex unit nestled in a well-landscaped setting. Maid service is available so when she travels someone stops by once a week to care for her plants. Her condo has eight thermostats—one in each room! All doors will accommodate a wheelchair.

When her husband died she moved to Heritage Village. This enabled her to be somewhat close to her friends but in a community that fits her needs. She told us "this lifestyle is great and the somewhat mild winters are easily handled. I feel very secure here among my newfound friends."

Both communities are very nice but carry with them the higher cost of any area on the environs of New York City.

Throughout the Northeast there are many towns that have that legendary New England charm: narrow macadam roads, stone fences lining each side, large trees forming a canopy over the roads, and rambling old houses. A moonlight night casting shadows on a new-fallen snow is long to be remembered. Towns such as Sturbridge, Amherst, Williamstown in Massachusetts, and Litchfield in Connecticut are models of the classic New England mold.

NEW JERSEY
■   ■   ■

The 127-mile shoreline has been highly influential in the emergence of a large retirement area in southern New Jersey. All along the coast are many picturesque seaside communities. Of course the closer to the ocean, the higher the price.

Inland is where a host of planned communities have sprung up. Since this area is within commuting distance of New York City these communities are not exclusively for retirement. The Garden State Parkway and New Jersey Turnpike offer good access to many large cities: Philadelphia, Trenton, Newark, and New York City. Going south not too many miles is "Vegas by the Sea"—Atlantic City—with its casinos along the Boardwalk.

The area is flat, sandy, and is called the Pinelands of South Jersey. The winter climate is moderated by the offshore Gulf Stream. But there is still winter—January has many days in the 20° F. range.

Some of the planned communities in this area are: Clearbrook*; Crestwood*; Holiday City*; Leisure Knoll*; Leisure Towne*; Leisure Village West*; and Rossmoor.* For those with close ties to any of the big cities along the mid-Northern coast this area offers a lot of advantages. However, any place in comparative proximity to these big metropolitan areas carries a higher price tag.

EASTERN PENNSYLVANIA
■ ■ ■

Among the historic small towns of eastern Pennsylvania there are a surprisingly large number of life care facilities. (See Chapter 18 for details of this type of lifestyle.) The rolling countryside is beautiful and when an Amish horse-drawn carriage comes down the lane it's like a return to the turn of the century.

Four of the life care communities are sponsored by the Religious Society of Friends (Quakers): Foulkeways at Gwynedd*; Crosslands*; Pennswood Village*; and Kendal at Longwood.* Other facilities are: Pine Run Community*; Dunwoody Village*; Fort Washington Estates*; Gwynedd Estates*; Southampton Estates*; Rydal Park on the Fairway*; Cross Keys Village*; Luther Crest*; Martins Run*; and Peter Becker Community.*

SOUTHWARD THROUGH VIRGINIA
AND MARYLAND
■ ■ ■

These two states are on the fringe of the major retirement areas. There's still winter, not very harsh, but winter clothes are required. Most likely the major reason there is not a rush to these areas is cost. The proximity to Washington, D.C., and the Chesapeake Bay area carries with it higher land costs.

The southern part of Virginia, closer to the border of North Carolina, offers a much more reasonable cost opportunity for the retiree. It's still not what can be considered a major retirement area. Perhaps this will happen but the Carolinas have a big head start.

Even in southern Virginia a small lot in a developing golf course community in Williamsburg is $50,000. Bordering the golf course would be much more.

ELEGANCE
■ ■ ■

The Georgetown* has to be one of the most elegant retirement facilities we have come across. It is located on Q Street in Washington, D.C. The brochure states that all suites look out on the courtyard. There is daily maid service; mail and your newspaper are delivered each morning; and a private chauffeured limousine is available.

Meals can be served in your suite or you can go to the dining room. The Green Room hosts weekly cocktail parties and the lounge has complete bar service. There is a Sunday champagne hour in the lounge or served in your suite. Religious services for all denominations are held in the chapel. A professional nurse is on duty around the clock and a corps of aides is available to run errands, serve tea at 3 P.M., or bring you a bedtime snack. Oh yes, formal tea is served on Fridays at 3 P.M. in the Green Room. A three-room suite is over $100 a day for one person. Meals are included.

NORTH AND SOUTH CAROLINA
■   ■   ■

Here's where you can get frustrated! North Carolina is the northern-most state considered in the Sunbelt. This state is making a real push to outdistance Florida as *the* major retirement state. Accordingly, there are many, many choices of places to consider. This can cause frustration.

In the past these two states have been primarily quiet and peaceful. The Pinelands have been a golfer's paradise. Seashore areas such as the Outer Banks, Myrtle Beach, or Hilton Head Island have always been attractive as vacation spots. In the interior, college towns such as the Research Triangle of Raleigh-Durham and Chapel Hill have always at-tracted those with intellectual yearnings.

The retiree with the urge to create a new beginning has added a new dimension to the Carolinas. The retirement-age population in North Carolina grew 32 percent from 1970 to 1980. The Carolinas are a half-way haven—halfway between the harsh winters of the North and the long-drawn-out steamy summers of the far South—a day's drive back home to families in the North and a day's drive to vacation resorts and sunny beaches in the far South.

Climate and geography provide a pleasant blend, and more choices. There are three distinctly different areas of the Carolinas.

1. *Coastal Plains*—North Carolina has 338 miles of beaches. South Carolina has a 281-mile Atlantic seaboard, which features the Grand Strand, 50 miles of beaches that are warmed by the Gulf Stream. The temperature of the Strand averages only 2° colder than St. Augustine, Florida.

2. *Piedmont*—Mid-state in North Carolina, this is about 150 miles wide. An area of gently rolling hills that separates the coastal plains from the Appalachian Highlands. Included in this area are the sandhills where golf is played twelve months of the year. The Pied-mont narrows in South Carolina as the southern part of the state becomes a much flatter terrain.

3. *Appalachian Highlands*—The western part of North Carolina has good-sized mountains. Mount Mitchell in Yancey County tops out at 6,684 feet. Towns in the Highlands area such as Hendersonville, Asheville, Brevard, and Tryon are at 2,000 feet and above. It gets

cool, averaging eighty freezing days a year. There are four definite changes of seasons. On into South Carolina there is a much greater moderation of elevation and much higher temperatures. Myrtle Beach, in the center of the Grand Strand, averages fifty-four freezing days and twenty-eight 90° days.

Both states have to be rated as major retirement areas. Well worth an in-depth examination if you want a four-season mild climate. You will have your choice of coastal plains, rolling hills, or mountainous country.

We saw many fine small communities. New Bern, where the Neuse River empties into Pamlico Sound, is Southern charm personified. Tryon Palace, where the royal colonial governors lived, adds a great deal to the overall Southern living atmosphere.

Greenville, South Carolina, was exceptionally nice and Clemson, South Carolina, home of the Clemson University Tigers, had that college town feeling of enthusiasm. As we left the interstate to enter Clemson we followed large yellow tiger claws painted on the exit ramp.

North Carolina Trivia

Two books about retirement areas are: *Places Rated Retirement Guide* (Rand McNally, 1983) and *Retirement Places Rated* (Prentice-Hall, 1987). Both books evaluate selected retirement areas, usually counties, and come up with a ranking.

The authors, Richard Boyer and David Savageau, talked to several demographers, government officials, and academicians in order to come up with the 107 counties in the 1983 volume. The 1987 book has a little different slant. Its list of 131 counties was determined from demographic evidence, advice of experts, and recommendations of many older adults. Factors evaluated are:

■ Money matters—local prices, part-time job market, economic forecast.

■ Climate—where the temperature stays closest to 65° F.

■ Personal safety—crime and violence.

- Services—including health care.

- Housing—cost comparisons, taxes, and utility bills.

- Leisure living—recreational and cultural opportunities.

North Carolina ratings were:

1983 (Total of 107 in 25 states)   *1987 (Total of 131 in 38 states)*
Brevard #1   Asheville #21
Asheville #2   Henderson/Brevard #32
Hendersonville #35   Chapel Hill #92

Not included in the ranking system are personal visits. There is a tremendous amount of good information in these books—a good data base to use when starting your own evaluation.

MARCHING THROUGH GEORGIA
■ ■ ■

Tall pines. Tall pines. Tall pines. Southern Georgia seems to have a supply that is inexhaustible! At least that's what we thought as we traveled some of the back roads. Between the southernmost point of South Carolina and the far northern extreme of Florida there is about 100 miles of Georgia seacoast. Actually, the extreme irregularity of the coastline probably gives Georgia several hundred miles of actual coastline.

The town of Brunswick serves as the entryway to what is labeled the Golden Isles. St. Simons Island is Southern charm. Stately trees, Spanish moss, the hunt club and equestrian center, the golf club, the shopping center that blends into the natural beauty and is hardly noticeable, the Heritage*—a life care facility with plantation-style housing, all reinforce the aura of comfortable Southern leisure living. Small road signs that are rugged-looking with their wood-burned letters add confusion as you try to find your way around.

Sea Island is the site of the Cloister—a world-class resort. The third island, Jekyll, is state-owned and land is leased. It is a tourist mecca with many motels, a convention center, and other tourist attractions.

Sea Island is out of reach for those below the wealthy classification.

Jekyll Island seems to be primarily a cottage-rental, motel area. St. Simons offers some possibilities for those who consider themselves in the average to above average income classification. However, this area cannot be considered a major retirement mecca. There is plenty of vacant land and perhaps some day developers will converge—much to the consternation of those on the island.

Farther north in Georgia, up close to the South Carolina/North Carolina and Tennessee border, there is an entirely different topography. There are rolling hills and in the distance you can see the mountain peaks of the Appalachian region. The mild four-season climate can be very attractive to those who tend to a more rugged environment.

FLORIDA—LAND OF SUN, SAND, AND SENIORS
■ ■ ■

According to the 1989 Statistical Abstract of the United States put out by the Census Bureau, a lot of seniors call this land of silver hair and Social Security home. In 1987 the state's population was 12,023,000. Of this 2,139,000 were over sixty-five. Following right on their heels were 1,353,000 aged fifty-five to sixty-four.

Florida is a big state. It extends 400 miles from north to south and in the northern panhandle area it extends 400 miles east to west. That's a large area in which to make a choice of where to live.

Searching out a community in Florida can be extremely confusing. In some places there are communities one right after the other. We were overwhelmed with the number of entryways along Route 19 going north out of Clearwater.

After stopping at many of them and seeing signs as far as we could look down the road, we said, "That's enough." If we had been pressured to come to some decision we would both have had an anxiety attack.

Doing research before on-site visits will cut down on the aggravation. A postcard to any Chamber of Commerce will bring you a wealth of information. Retirement magazines such as *Modern Maturity* and *New Choices* have many ads extolling the benefits of particular retirement communities. A call to their toll-free numbers or a postcard will help you create a large research file.

Because of the large availability of communities in Florida, we have found some basic choices that are clear cut and require answers. You can narrow the selection problem by choosing:

1. A waterside community or an interior community?
2. If a waterside community—on the Gulf Coast or on the Atlantic Ocean?
3. If an interior area—do you want to be near a freshwater lake or not?
4. Living below the frost line (about Stuart) or above it?
5. A distinct four-season climate in the panhandle?
6. Town living or planned community/park living?
7. If you chose a planned community—do you want planned activities/clubhouse or not?
8. A golf course as part of the facility?
9. Is manufactured housing acceptable?
10. If you chose manufactured housing, do you want to buy or rent a lot?
11. A high-rise condo or single family?
12. On a canal with boat dockage?
13. Easy access to major city cultural advantages?
14. Easy access to major airport?
15. Easy access to major or specialized medical facilities?

Assuming you like subtropical to tropical climates with high humidity and rainfall averaging around fifty-five inches a year, you can find any kind of living that you want in Florida. That includes price. A $40,000 place isn't a mansion but if that's all you can afford, a decent place can be found. At the other end of the price spectrum, Palm Beach can cost you in the millions. In between, there's something for everybody.

The panhandle area is the least developed part of Florida. Climate has undoubtedly held this area in reserve. In November, December, January, and February average temperature is in the fifties. That's not extremely cold but since that's an average there can also be some freezing days.

In the panhandle area we had written contact with a Chamber of Commerce that informed us of a retirement community right on the waterfront. We were also given the name of a realtor to contact on site. Here is the exact wording sent to us:

Lanark Village, five miles east of Carrabelle, is a complete planned retirement community. Located directly on the Gulf of Mexico, Lanark Village features a par-3 golf course, a marina and club house and a restaurant and lounge for the enjoyment of its members.

We visited. What a disappointment! It was a former World War II base. It consisted of long one-story barracks made up in small units. These places were the exact duplicate of the veterans' housing we lived in back in 1947.

The golf course looked as if it had just three holes and a sign said you could play all day for $2.00. The marina was boarded up. It had about ten boat slips but no boats. The old officers' club was boarded up and overgrown. There were many kids running around. The former PX had a small restaurant and an office occupying its space. We inquired about a brochure. They didn't have one but ran off a copy of a plot plan. A small unit could be purchased for about $10,000. A bystander told us that this wan't a retirement village, they let anyone in. He warned us against buying.

The location was great—a beautiful view of the gulf—but we were disappointed and relate this experience to urge you to call ahead and question recommendations before making a trip. Fortunately we had not made a special trip to see this place. We were in the vicinity checking out the panhandle area and made sure this place was on our route.

Florida Trivia—Reverse Migrants

All who move to Florida don't stay. The reason they don't stay may be different from what you may think. A six-state Elderly Retirement Migration Study covering the years 1960 to 1980 uncovered an interesting trend. From 1970 to 1980 more than 9,000 residents moved from Florida to New York. Of those who moved, 56 percent were born in New York. This is more than *double* the number that returned to New York during the preceding decade, 1960 to 1970. New Jersey, Pennsylvania, and Ohio showed a similar trend. The average age of those moving to New York was seventy-three; 42 percent were seventy-five or older. Of those going to Florida, 76 percent were married; 49 percent of those returning to New York were widowed.

The obvious conclusion is that when old old age takes its toll on one's energy there is a need to be nearer family, especially one's children. Deep down there is probably the acceptance that one isn't as independent as one used to be. Also, coping with widowhood is easier when a family support system is nearby.

Other problems may emerge, such as a disruption of the living pattern of the children, but the returnee feels more secure.

ALABAMA, MISSISSIPPI, AND LOUISIANA
■ ■ ■

The Deep South. Charming, quiet, slow, conservative, protective, Bible Belt, low tolerance level, humid, and hot. Any big city will have pockets of newcomers. They are there for business reasons. The Gulf Coast shoreline will have resorts, some exceptionally nice such as the Grand Hotel at Point Clear, Alabama, and the normal motels and cottages for rent.

Retirees? They will be found throughout, as in any state. Outsider retirees? We weren't able to unearth any sizable retirement communities. Everyone doesn't necessarily want to live in a retirement community. We're not trying to say they are for everyone. But if they are not around it means outsider retirees will be plowing new ground. Being the "new kid on the block" carries with it some tough hurdles to overcome. Especially if the "new kid" doesn't have a Southern drawl.

There will be many fine towns in these states that certain individual retirees would find highly acceptable. However, we don't consider these states as major retirement areas.

ARKANSAS
■ ■ ■

In 1970 the population of Arkansas was 1,923,322 and in 1980 it was 2,286,435—that's almost a 20-percent increase!

By 1987 the estimated population was 2,388,000. Why? Because of what the demographers call in-migration. There's a major area of resort/ retirement facilities primarily in the northwest sector of the state. In the area known as the Ozark Highlands. These highlands have drawn many retirees to hill country towns such as Eureka Springs* (the Little Switzerland of America), Mountain Home,* Bentonville,* Berryville,* Yellville,* Fayetteville,* Harrison,* and Flippen.*

Two large planned retirement communities are in the hills. Bella Vista Village* is five miles from the Missouri border, covering 36,000 acres with seven golf courses, eight lakes, and 7,000 residents. It is common to see a car towing a golf cart from home to the course. Not too far away is Cherokee Village,* with two golf courses, two recreational and community centers, and seven lakes spread out over 13,000 acres. There are 4,000 residents and 24,000 property owners.

If you like the ponies, there is Hot Springs Village,* covering 26,000 acres with 6,300 residents and about twenty miles from the Oaklawn track in Hot Springs.

Arkansas can definitely be considered a major retirement area. For additional information about Bella Vista Village and Hot Springs Village, please see Chapter 10.

Arkansas Trivia

While checking out the Eureka Springs area we saw the Great Passion Play. A cast of hundreds, outdoors in a natural setting—inspiring. One evening a walk around town brought us to the lobby of a very small hotel. There we joined others as the local Ukulele Club of fifteen members held their weekly meeting. We stayed on for a couple of hours listening to the old tunes played by some folks who made us feel as if we belonged in Eureka Springs.

Several months after writing about our experience in Eureka Springs our local paper carried a major story about this town of 2,000 people. Over the past seven years a developer has been slowly acquiring property nine miles west of town. Land—2,650 acres—has been bought for the purpose of building a $400 million theme park called White Wind. Surrounding the 650-acre park—more than 200 acres larger than Epcot Center—will be hotels, condominiums, golf courses, tennis courts, and stores.

The land is outside the town limits so there is no zoning control over what can be built. The first year of operation is expected to bring 5 million visitors and employ 4,000 people—that's twice the town's population.

When this takes place the quaintness of Eureka Springs will disappear.

The Ozark lifestyle will be gone. Those retirees who had bought into the slow pace would face a dilemma—stay put amid the fast growth or move. The best-laid plans would have gone astray, but that's progress and progress brings change. We can't help but wonder if there will still be a Ukulele Club. *Update:* at this writing construction had not begun on the theme park.

TEXAS
■   ■   ■

Big! It's 801 miles in a north-south direction and 773 miles in an east-west direction. The total area of Texas is 262,840 square miles of land and 4,499 square miles of inland water. The coastline is 367 miles.

The physiography of Texas is varied. The far north panhandle and for some distance south is part of the Great Plains and so is very flat. In an easterly direction it changes into rolling prairie land culminating in the hill country in about the center of the state. Farther east and south it becomes a pine belt. Due south of the hill country it becomes the Rio Grande Plains and at the southern tip it's subtropical. The far west (the area south of New Mexico) is a continuation of the Guadalupe Mountains leading into the Davis Mountains and the Big Bend area. The northern panhandle experiences 0° F. and blizzards; the lower Rio Grande Valley has palm trees and orange groves. Altitude varies from 8,751 feet above sea level at Guadalupe Peak to sea level along the coast.

Texas is big, it has variety, and its population is growing. The 1980 census showed 14,228,400 people and the Census Bureau estimated 16,841,000 in 1988. Government demographers estimate that by the year 2000 Texas population will be 20,739,400.

Large Retirement Communities

Except for sprawling mobile home parks in the Rio Grande Valley, there are no large retirement communities in Texas. At least we haven't been able to find anything that compares with developments such as the Sun Cities, Leisure Villages, or Leisure World—very large communities that have been designed for retirees and cater to their needs.

There are a multitude of retirement facilities throughout the state— condo/townhouse complexes of 300 to 400 people, life care units, and retirement residences—but no big self-contained communities such as those we found in New Jersey, Florida, Arizona, and California.

Where Are the Retirees?

San Antonio—Population Metro Area (Estimated) 1987—1,298,117. A delightful, not too big and not too small city with a Latin flavor. It's hot, but not too humid. Located 140 miles from the Gulf of Mexico there are 111 days a year above 90° F. Annual rainfall there is 28 inches and there are 81 precipitation days. There is a short winter—December through March. There are no 0° F. days and about 22 freezing days. The snowfall is negligible.

Going northwest the terrain goes up to the Edwards Plateau—Bexar County goes from 500 feet to 1,900 feet. To the southeast the terrain slopes downward to the Gulf of Mexico, 140 miles away.

The Alamo city is a haven for military personnel. There are six major military installations—Kelly Air Force Base, Lackland Air Force Base, Brooks Air Force Base, Randolph Air Force Base, Fort Sam Houston Army Post, and Brooke Army Medical Center. Logically many of the military will want to remain in the area when retirement muster is called. In 1980 there were 42,330 military retirees in San Antonio.

In 1983 it was estimated that the number of retirees in the greater San Antonio area was between 150,000 and 200,000—about 15 to 20 percent of the population. Since there are no large retirement complexes, this large group of retirees has disappeared into the community. As a result there is no big awareness that San Antonio is a retirement city. In fact, this same conclusion can be drawn about other cities in Texas. The retirees have come to Texas but have been absorbed into the community rather than segregated into certain parts of the community.

Lower Rio Grande Valley. The retirement mecca of the Lower Rio Grande Valley encompasses about the last seventy-five miles of the Rio Grande River before it spills into the Gulf of Mexico, and goes inland about thirty-five miles. McAllen, Pharr, and Edinburg are only three of the towns along Route 83 that draw Winter Texans (snowbirds) in very large numbers. The other towns are Mission, San Juan, Alamo, Donna, Weslaco, Mercedes, Harlingen, and Brownsville. To the east right on the Gulf of Mexico are Port Isabel and South Padre Island. Refer to chapter 5 for additional information.

This is subtropical country. August is the hottest month with a normal maximum temperature of 93° F. May is 87° F., June 90° F. The coldest month is January with a normal maximum of 69° F. and a minimum of 51° F. for an average of 60° F.

Needless to say, many people go north for the summer. During the winter it's great.

Austin—*Population Metro Area 1987—749,612.* The capital city. On the fringe area of the hill country and on the Colorado River. Summers are hot, occasionally hitting 100° F. with relative humidity around 67 percent. Winters are not severe but there will be about twenty-five freezing days.

The University of Texas is located in the center of town, and there are five other colleges. Needless to say, the Longhorns of Texas dominate the town—burnt orange is a featured color around Austin. Medical and cultural advantages are in Austin but good living can be found outside of town in resort/adult communities. Along the Colorado River many lakes have been formed. There are clusters of developments all around these lakes.

Lakeway* with its famed World of Tennis Complex draws many retirees. Mr. and Mrs. W.G. of New York City moved to Lakeway, have a nice home overlooking the water, not too far from the golf course, and find the hilly terrain invigorating. As far as they're concerned life is great. Farther out of town Meadow Lakes* to the west offers similar living.

We found a very unique retirement facility in this same area, right on Lake Travis. In fact, it's completely surrounded by Lake Travis. The Island on Lake Travis* is plush, unique, expensive, in the country, and new in 1989.

Visualize an approach to an island that is completely covered by a very large three-story castle-type structure. A manned security gate bars your way to the 500-foot two-lane road across the water to the complex. On each side of the gate and above the gate are offices. To the left is a visitor parking area and marina. There is clear water to the right.

With our escort we drove across. Parking is on the ground level in a completely enclosed concrete parking area with reserved spots for each resident.

By elevator we went to the first floor where the exercise room, mail room, convenience store, beauty shop, large lap pool, craft room, and other meeting rooms are located. All apartments are around the perimeter of the building, each with a fabulous view. The interior of the complex has gardens, patios, a gazebo, grassy areas, extensive walkways, and a heliport. The second floor has lounges, library, and small meeting rooms with a spectacular curved mahogany stairway to the third-floor dining room.

There are some drawbacks. The closest convenience store off the premises is eight miles away. The complex is secluded, although a van with scheduled service is available. We asked about the nearest medical services—it's thirty miles away, that's why they have a heliport. We were told that a person could be at a hospital in thirty minutes.

A number of ladies were using Lark-type three-wheel electric carts. The size of the complex is too large for some folks and they need help. However, our marketing representative told us she felt these carts had become a status symbol. The "in" thing to have among the elderly set.

This complex has 212 apartments, monthly rentals range from $795 for a one-bedroom to $2,900 for an 1,830-square-foot three-bedroom apartment. This includes one meal—breakfast, along with weekly housekeeping, utilities, parking, etc. It is 60 percent occupied as of February 1990.

It's a beautiful place, but expensive and out of the mainstream.

Athens*—Population 1988 (Estimate)—11,000. Athens is seventy-two miles southeast of Dallas. There are about ninety-five days with temperatures 90° F. and above. Freezing days average about thirty-five. The average yearly rainfall is thirty-eight inches.

We stopped at the Chamber of Commerce and inquired about retirement areas. There aren't any. People move to Henderson County and its many small towns and are absorbed into the community.

We also stopped at the Henderson County Senior Citizens Center. A nice new facility. We talked to many of the seniors—they were very enthusiastic about the center. A lot of activities take place and they have a party at least once a month. This center is part of the Area Agency on Aging. These agencies (AAA) are found throughout all states and came about as a result of the Older Americans Act of 1965. The director of this facility was extremely cooperative. She told us that the group has developed into a support system for one another—a form of extended family. When one of the regulars doesn't show up someone calls to make certain he or she is all right.

We liked the town very much. It is clean, neat, and not too far from the advantages of a large city. Along the roads there are signs indicating that this section of the road is being kept clean by a particular church or city organization. It's part of the adopt-a-road program. Certainly indicative of a great deal of community spirit.

Three lakes are comparatively close to Athens. Lake Athens—about ten minutes away and Lake Palestine and Cedar Creek Lake about half an hour away. We surveyed Cedar Creek Lake and since it's seventy-five miles from Dallas it's pretty well built up. The 328-mile shoreline seemed to be full of houses. We found one attempt at a big development. Many roads were built but have now badly deteriorated. Some lots had pickup truck campers on them, others had beat-up trailers. Not a very nice place.

Kerrville*—Population (Estimate) 1987—20,500. This town is in the heart of the hill country and right on Interstate 10, which spans the Southern United States from Florida to California. The closest large city is San Antonio, about sixty-five miles south and east. Kerrville climate is near ideal—the summer average is 79° F. and the winter average 47° F. The elevation of 1,616 feet allows for cooling off at night. The annual rainfall is 32 inches and snow is possible, perhaps an inch a year.

Back before the major breakthroughs in medical science, tuberculosis was treated by building hospitals in areas that had exceptionally clean air. The patients would then sit outside and take in the good, clean air. A hospital for this kind of treatment was built in Kerrville. There is also a veterans' hospital.

Many fine housing developments are located in the hills. Some are first class. A retired company president has a beautiful valley view but the stream down in the valley was quite some distance away. Along the front of his home he built a stream! It's probably the length of a football field. The water gushes down the rock-lined cement trough loud enough to be heard. It's very calming. At the low end of the stream the water is recirculated back to the high end of the stream.

The hills abound with all kinds of game. A ride through the back roads always produces a wildlife show, including wild turkey.

It's sixty-five miles to San Antonio but that doesn't take too long using Interstate 10. All in all a very nice small town.

KERRVILLE TRIVIA. In 1954 James Avery came to Kerrville and set up shop in a garage to design beautiful jewelry. Today his works are sold nationwide and are no longer made in a garage. Visiting his studio is fascinating.

Fredericksburg*—Population (Estimate) 1987—7,670. Fredericksburg is only twenty-four miles north of Kerrville so the climate is about the same. This town has charm. Main Street has many old buildings that have been renovated and designated as historic buildings. It is clean and orderly with no litter. The senior citizens building is one of the nicest we have seen.

There is a heavy German influence, stemming from the early German settlers who arrived in 1847. Main Street has an abundance of German restaurants.

Texas Choices

Take your choice of living style: an expanding big city, a small town, a prairie mini-ranch, an inland lake, the seashore, or hill country. There are four seasons, including blizzards as well as subtropical temperatures. Y'all have fun making up your mind!

NEW MEXICO
▪ ▪ ▪

Also called "The Land of Enchantment," New Mexico is big with relatively few people. It is the fifth-largest state with a total area of 122,000 square miles, and a population of 1,500,000 (1987 estimate).

A love for nature and scenic wonder, an appreciation of open spaces and outdoor life, and a desire for a simple life at a slow pace are the necessary attributes for those thinking of retirement in New Mexico.

Sprawling Albuquerque, adobe Santa Fe, the capital city, and commercialized Carlsbad are different from one another, but nonetheless are similar to other communities in the Southwest.

You have your choice of desert areas and the warmer climate or the high altitude towns with their spectacular mountain views.

There are no large retirement communities that are designed for retirees. However, many towns have very active senior citizens programs and committees promoting the town as a good place for retirees.

For example, the retirement committee in Silver City* will put you in direct contact with a retiree who will act as your sponsor, answer your questions, and give you some personal opinions and insights into the area and why he or she chose Silver City.

This town of 10,000 people is in southwestern New Mexico and is referred to as "the Gateway to the Gila Wilderness." It is in the foothills of the Pinos Altos Mountains at an elevation of 5,900 feet. The Continental Divide runs close to the city limits. January has an average low of 22° F. and a high of 46° F. June is the hottest month with an average low of 52° F. and a high of 86° F.

In Silver City there is an interesting small retirement community being developed. The Gardens* will feature atrium buildings, each with eight condominiums constructed around a 22-foot-high covered 28- × 64-foot courtyard. There are plantings, furniture groupings, and a heated brick floor. A nice gathering place for the residents of the condominium.

The city of Deming, 30 miles from the Mexican border, has a special brochure about retirement. The population is about 10,000 and the altitude is 4,355 feet. There is an attractive senior citizens center and a retirement community, Kingdom of the Sun,* downtown. The old section of this community is regular housing but the new part is subsidized housing.

New Mexico Trivia

Fourteen miles away is the 250-acre Rockhound State Park, the only state park in the United States that encourages visitors to take home whatever rocks they want!

Santa Fe* is the oldest capital in the United States. At an altitude of 7,000 feet this city is located at the base of the Sangre de Cristo Mountains. Stringent zoning and building requirements have kept this city of 58,000 as an adobe oasis. It is unique, artistic, colorful, and a tourist mecca. At the height of the season it gets crowded. Having checked out the city during Indian Market in August, we could see there is no question about its luring the tourist. The preservation of many of the original buildings and roads adds its charm and congestion. Also in the downtown area is El Castillo*—a small retirement facility.

The Santa Fe Opera, orchestra of Santa Fe, the symphony, the New Mexico Repertory Theater, and many more presentations in music, dance, and theater make Santa Fe a center for the performing arts.

The hub of New Mexico is Albuquerque. At 5,314 feet this city has about one third of the total population of New Mexico. This would be retirement in a big city.

In keeping with the desert Southwest is the architecture of La Vida Llena* (the Full Life). This life care facility in Albuquerque with its tile roofs and stucco exterior melds into the countryside. The panoramic vistas of the Sandia Mountains and the twinkling lights of Albuquerque add to the ambiance of this 350-person complex.

If you yearn for the wide-open spaces and beautiful mountain views, New Mexico may be the place for you.

ARIZONA—
THE GRAND CANYON STATE
■ ■ ■

The sixth-largest state in the United States and one of the big five retirement states, along with California, Texas, Arkansas, and Florida. Arizona has 113,900 square miles of widely diverse topography and climate.

The southwest section of the state is desert country. Yuma,* Phoenix,* and the area known as "the Valley of the Sun" are in the low desert region. Summer temperatures are high—very high. Average summer high is 105° F and 48° F in the winter. Average annual rainfall in this area is 7.11 inches. When we lived at Sun City West* for a week the 1917 and 1949 record of eighty-eight consecutive days without rain was exceeded.

The high desert area starts north of Phoenix and goes toward the southeast. In Tucson* there's a little more rain—10 to 15 inches annually. Tucson, at an altitude of 2,390 feet, is in a desert valley and is surrounded by mountains. However, an hour away is Mount Lemmon, which is over 9,000 feet.

North of Phoenix are the highlands with altitudes ranging from 4,500 to 12,000 feet. Prescott* is at an altitude of 5,389 feet with an average snowfall of 20 inches a year, while Sedona,* in the Oak Creek Canyon

area, is at 4,300 feet and has an average yearly high temperature of 74.7°
F. and a low of 45° F.

Higher in the mountains is Flagstaff* at 7,000 feet; it sits at the base
of the San Francisco Peaks (elevation 12,600 feet). Winter sports are big
in this area. On average it receives 90 inches of snow per year. Yet about
130 miles due south is Phoenix and the desert heat.

More than half of the state's population resides in the Phoenix metropolitan area, which includes Chandler,* Glendale,* Mesa,* Scottsdale,*
Sun City,* Sun City West, Tempe,* and several smaller communities.
Tucson is the second-largest city with a population of 399,300, according
to a 1987 estimate.

The run to the sun continues. A U.S. Census Bureau report shows
that from 1980 to 1984 the sixty-five-plus population of Arizona increased 22 percent from 307,000 to 374,000. It is estimated that the
sixty-five-plus population in 1987 was 444,000.

Retirement communities are popular in Arizona, especially in the
greater Phoenix area. The biggest, Sun City, with close to 50,000 residents and the new Sun City West, with 17,568 people and growing to
25,000, are adjacent to Phoenix. We will cover these in great detail in
Chapter 9.

Leisure World,* Fountain of the Sun,* and Westbrook Village* are
other communities in the Phoenix area. Farther south is Green Valley,* a
planned adult community of 16,500 people located about twenty-five
miles south of Tucson. Continuing care and life care facilities can also be
found in the greater Phoenix area.

Mobile home parks are plentiful and are heavily used by the snowbirds. These are found throughout the Valley of the Sun and south
toward Yuma and the Mexican border.

During our corporate years we had business reasons to make frequent
trips to Phoenix. For over twenty years we watched the original Sun City
grow from a small community to its present size as a mature community.
It is somewhat crowded, but a nice retirement haven for a large number
of senior citizens.

Phoenix grew very rapidly during those years, as did Scottsdale. A little
crossroads called Carefree* grew into a large definitely upper-class retirement community. Our last trip to Sedona caused us great pain. A delightful small town nestled at the southern entrance to Oak Creek Can-

yon has mushroomed into a crowded tourist stopover. Complete with masses of souvenir and Indian jewelry shops.

The spectacular natural beauty remains and once we got away from downtown we felt better about Sedona. From the mesa, where the small airport is located, you overlook a valley that defies description. Adjacent to the Masonic Temple on the mesa is a stone platform where Easter sunrise services are held. We have never been there for this sunrise experience but it must leave an unforgettable impression. Maybe some Easter we will go back.

Many of our Phoenix trips were in July and August. The very low humidity helps but it's hot. Very hot! A small getaway place in the mountains would be a lifesaver.

Peter A. Dickinson, author of *Sunbelt Retirement* and other books, publishes a *Retirement Newsletter.** He highlights Kingman,* Arizona, in the northwest corner of the state. The town is located on a high plateau and surrounded by wide-open land. It is adjacent to Hualapai Mountain Park. The Lake Mead recreation area is about 100 miles away and Las Vegas is only an additional 25 miles. Sounds like a great setting for a summer place away from the heat of the Valley of the Sun.

Greater Phoenix and Tucson are big and getting bigger. But there are also many small cities that should be considered and probably represent an opportunity for getting in on the ground floor.

Arizona Trivia

Dickinson's newsletter offers this rule of thumb. Every 1,000 feet of altitude causes the average temperature to drop five degrees. Every 75 miles south you go the average temperature increases 1°. You might want to keep this in mind as you evaluate areas of the country.

CALIFORNIA
■   ■   ■

California runs along 1,200 miles of Pacific coastline, with each mile offering a spectacular view. The farther north you go, the more spectacular the view. But for years retirees have flocked to Southern California, especially the area from Santa Barbara south. Their reason for this choice: the mild climate. Basically there are two seasons: a mild summer and a spring that is a little cooler. The summertime is dry with temperatures reaching into the nineties. The sea breezes keep the temperature comfortable and dry.

In San Diego the average July and August maximum is just over 75° F. and the average low for January and February is 46° F. Rainfall is about nine inches a year. Most of the rain comes in the spring. On average there are 150 clear days, 117 partly cloudy days, and 98 cloudy days during the year. Fog and low clouds can be bothersome.

From San Diego* north to Los Angeles* and perhaps 60 to 70 miles inland there is town after town with a heavy concentration of seniors. To go much farther inland leads into the desert country where one should heed the map warnings. Their basic advice is to stay on the main highways and avoid turning off desert roads. California has its share of extremes. Within 100 miles (as the crow flies) is the highest point in the lower forty-eight states, Mount Whitney, and the lowest point, Badwater in Death Valley National Monument. Throughout California there are mountain ranges that separate the seacoast from the desert plains.

It goes without saying that the closer you live to the shoreline, the higher the cost will be. We didn't spend a lot of time surveying San Diego because of these high costs. There is a very high concentration of retired naval personnel in the San Diego area. Housing is the same as in any large town, from the small to the luxurious. Retirees are absorbed into the city of San Diego and are served by an aggressive senior citizens program. The city itself administers the Senior Citizens Services.*

An interesting retirement hotel is the Balboan* in downtown San Diego, adjacent to Balboan City Park. This former commercial hotel with 150 units offers downtown city living. It provides daily maid service, three meals a day, an emergency call service, indoor parking, and an activity program. A two-room suite for two people costs about $2,000 a month. Their ballroom is used by outside groups and residents are given free admission to any of these dances.

A few miles north of San Diego is Escondido.* From a retirement standpoint it is probably best known for the Lawrence Welk Resort.* (More about this facility in the next chapter.) Twenty-five minutes from San Diego International Airport is Rancho Bernardo—a total planned community. (Chapter 10 contains more about this development.)

Going north on Route 78 about thirty-five miles north of San Diego is Leisure Village Ocean Hills.* A long winding road to the top of a knoll brought us to a very nice entryway. Farther up the hill they have just completed a beautiful clubhouse and a golf course. The first of their two-story condos were under construction. They have a very nice layout, but of course the price of a two-bedroom villa reflected the surroundings, about $165,000.

One of the many small retirement towns is Hemet.* About midway between San Diego and Los Angeles and about fifty miles inland in the San Jacinto Valley. The climate in Hemet is different than that of the coastal areas. May through October the average high is 93° F and the average low is 54° F. November through April the average high is 72° F and the average low is 40° F. This is primarily a mobile home town. Along Route 74 there are mobile park signs one after the other. A retiree told us that 67 percent of the population are retirees. The Chamber of Commerce lists thirty-eight churches and there seemed to be a lot of scheduled community activities. In the Hemet area there are six golf courses; and fun in the snow and mountains is only a half an hour away.

Thirty miles east are the desert resort towns of Palm Springs* and Desert Hot Springs.* We felt a little let down as we drove around this area. Our expectations were clearly much too high. We expected everything to be luxurious, after all this was the desert hideaway country for the wealthy. There were nice places that were tucked away but the main roads with their fast food places and so-so stores didn't seem to fit this image.

We were also searching for a retirement village that didn't exist. We had received a very nice brochure and some handwritten notes on a form letter about the village. We were informed that "the project will be 100% subscribed within a few months" with a handwritten note adding that subscription was already past 50 percent.

We found the address, but there were just some desert flowers. We thought we had the wrong address so we called the phone number listed in the brochure and were told construction would not begin for a year. This was even a church-related development, which proves you have to be extremely careful.

We followed up on this and construction did start. By the time this book is published it will undoubtedly be in full operation.

Another development that was in its planning stages when we were in Palm Springs and is now operational is the Outdoor Resorts Palm Springs RV Resort and Country Club.* Outdoor Resorts of America has eight resorts throughout the United States. We have followed the development of one of their resorts in the Lower Rio Grande Valley in Port Isabel, Texas very closely. It is now complete and has sold out. South Padre Island is just across the causeway from Port Isabel. The concept is unique and would seem to be a natural for Palm Springs. The basic idea is that a person purchases an RV pad for $30,000 to $40,000. When not in use by the purchaser, the pad is rented out and the management and purchaser share the income.

The complex in Palm Springs will eventually have spaces for 1,320 RV's, which will be built around an eighteen-hole golf course. Construction is taking place in phases and when completed there will be a total of ten swimming pools, fourteen tennis courts, eight bathhouses, a restaurant and clubhouse, a pro shop, and a health spa.

Palm Springs with its average temperature of over 100° F. from June thru September is a good place to leave during the summer. The Outdoor Resorts concept removes the need for two homes or a home and a vacation condo. Start up the RV and take off for cooler places during the summer, and then return to a well-appointed RV resort during the winter months. If you like RV living this could be the way to go.

West of Palm Springs is Sun City,* a sister city to Sun City, Arizona, and Sun City, Florida. This complex was founded in 1962 and has about 9,000 residents. Its elevation is 1,470 feet, mean average temperature is 63° F., and rainfall averages 13 inches per year.

As in any mature community the people are bound to be much older. Those who moved to Sun City in the 1960s are now in their late seventies or eighties. The activity level throughout the complex is slow. Although the buildings have also aged, they have been well cared for and the surroundings are neat and attractive.

Continuing west, all the way to the coast and the Seal Beach area is Leisure World-Seal Beach.* It is located seven miles from Long Beach and twenty-eight miles from Los Angeles International Airport with the San Diego Freeway running along the northern edge of the facility. The surrounding area is crowded, there are oil wells nearby, and it's easy to tell you are in the greater Los Angeles area.

This facility encompasses 6,482 apartments on 543 acres housing 9,000 to 10,000 people. Most apartments are ground level with a few three-story buildings throughout the campus. There are golf courses, medical facilities, clubhouses, churches, and outside the very closely monitored entryway is a post office, a bank, a savings and loan, and a supermarket. The apartments are owned by fifteen mutual corporations which provide housing to stock owners on a cooperative basis. Residents from each of the mutual areas elect their governing boards, whose members determine community policies. The general policies of the area are administered by a professional management organization.

The community has been sold out for quite a while. All units are now sold as resales.

Farther south is Leisure World-Laguna Hills.* Located fifty-nine miles south of Los Angeles and seventy miles from San Diego, this facility is seven miles from the Pacific Ocean and Laguna Beach. It is big, with over 21,000 residents. There are six clubhouses with hobby shops, game rooms, billiard rooms, and meeting rooms, five swimming pools, lawn bowling greens, shuffleboard and tennis courts, individual garden areas, a library, a twenty-seven-hole golf course and a driving range, a nine-hole executive course, and a riding stable where you can board your horse or rent one.

A closed-circuit television station provides residents with entertainment and community information.

Resales are all that are available. The ownership and management are similar to the Seal Beach Leisure World. Prices range from $65,000 to $400,000. Freeways are adjacent to the over 700-acre development so it's easy to get from one place to another, during nonrush hours that is. Inside the complex it's a retreat. Outside it's big-city congestion and activity, Los Angeles style.

In lower California one has many choices. There are planned retirement communities of all sizes and towns with mobile home parks restricted to adults with a heavy concentration of retirees. Little enclaves of manufactured housing are also found throughout this area. There are clusters of about 100 to 150 homes with restricted entry, a small clubhouse and pool, and an association that fosters pancake suppers, a monthly party, and a feeling of camaraderie.

Then there's the regular classic neighborhood—each residence a separate entity and everyone doing his/her own thing.

There are two things in common among all of these California choices —nice climate and very high prices.

It is common knowledge that housing in California has skyrocketed. Mr. and Mrs. W.C. of Dallas returned from a survey trip to the Los

Angeles area and announced that their "$200,000 Dallas home would cost $500,000 in the L.A. area."

A duplex or home in a mobile park would be affordable but the emotional adjustment of this lifestyle could cause a difficult situation.

California Trivia

For a while we traversed Highway 1 en route to San Francisco. About forty-five minutes south of Carmel by the Sea in Big Sur country is Ventana Inn. Our travel agent recommended the inn and we made reservations months in advance. A quiet place tucked away among redwood, oak, and bay laurel trees. A retreat for notables, although there weren't any when we were there.

Checking in was an experience. We sat at a desk and an attractive young lady explained the various amenities. Our mouths dropped open when she told us of the sun deck and heated pool where swimsuits were optional. We recovered quickly and murmured an acknowledgment.

No swimming for us, we were too chicken!

OREGON
■   ■   ■

Rugged, beautiful, damp, scenic, and cloudy—an adventurer's paradise. Oregon is inexpensive when compared with California. Denims and plaids are always acceptable in this informal environment. There are many small towns with a great deal of community spirit. Retirees yes, but from the above description they are "special." Not the average run-of-the-mill retirees.

When thinking of retiring in Oregon, weather conditions should be taken into consideration. Anyone with nasal problems might think twice.

Ashland and Medford are towns along Interstate 5, near the California border and about 80 miles inland, at an altitude of 1,298 feet. Annual rainfall in this area is about 21 inches per year with roughly 100 days of precipitation. This area is a sportsman's paradise while also offering many cultural advantages. In Ashland there is a nationally recognized Shakespearean Festival; a few miles away in Jacksonville, the Britt Festivals are held. There are five festivals annually in the area each of which features first-class artists.

In Medford (population 46,000) is the Rogue Valley Manor,* a retirement community comprised of 230 apartments in a 10-story high-rise and 113 contemporary cottages spread out over the campus. The high rise is highly visible. It is situated on a hill overlooking the town. This is a continuing care community with a 60-bed skilled nursing care facility.

Also in Medford is one of the many Madison House facilities in the United States, Madison House/Medford,* a rental community composed of 85 apartments.

Farther north, about 40 miles from the coast and halfway to the Washington border, is the city of Eugene (population 106,000). Precipitation averages 43 inches of rain a year. It generally rains 137 days each year.

WASHINGTON
■   ■   ■

Natural beauty and climate in the state of Washington parallel that of Oregon. For example, Olympia, the capital city, located at the southern tip of Puget Sound, has an annual rainfall of fifty-one inches and nineteen inches of snow.

We were in Seattle when we heard people saying, "the mountain is out," meaning that Mount Rainier was visible. Many people talked about this, it seemed like a holiday celebration. We have to admit that it was a beautiful sight.

We found many retirement facilities in Washington. Madison House has three facilities: one called Madison House/Totem Lake* in Kirkland, one in Yakima,* and one in Edmunds.* Panorama City* in Lacey and Pacific Regent* in Bellevue are both life care communities. Covenant Shores* on Mercer Island, a modified life care residence, has a 700-foot frontage on Lake Washington and is a beautiful setting. In Centralia is Stillwaters Estates,* where you can purchase a home and should you choose to sell there is a guaranteed buy-back by the Stillwaters Estates Retirement Community. In Issaquah, Providence Point* offers home purchase with adjacent health care.

The beauty of the Pacific Northwest is a prime attraction. But there is a downside. One retired resident told us, "We have to get out of here in the winter, it gets very depressing. There are too many dark, damp, drizzly days."

No state, city, area, or retirement community will be perfect. You should make a thorough study of all aspects of a location. Making an informed decision on the basis of a factual study increases the chances of making the right decision. Not everyone does this.

While attending an Elderhostel program, one of the student couples told us how they made their decision. When they were on vacation in Florida they liked a town, bought a small house, and then went back to their hometown, retired from their jobs, sold their house in a week, and moved to Florida!

It sounds exciting to make a decision on the basis of an impulse! Was it the right decision? They said they were happy but there was no real enthusiasm about their lifestyle choice.

With many productive years ahead of you, time and energy spent on a thorough analysis, including a tryout or practice time, will pay big dividends.

Throughout our lives the important decisions were never easy to make. Your decision about retirement is important—give it your best shot.

8

CLUB/RESORT/ VACATION COMMUNITY

. . .

LIFESTYLE OPTION #5, LEISURE/SOCIAL- CENTERED LIVING

CLUB COMMUNITIES
. . .

We hit the brakes and pulled over on to the shoulder of the road. That's a nuclear power plant! Right on the shore of the lake. But we had just passed a sign that said Keowee Key was three miles ahead. Could that be? A large country club/marina development right next to a nuclear plant? We drove on and very shortly checked in at the information center of Keowee Key.* Our condominium was nice. Our neighbor was a nuclear plant!

The nuclear plant really didn't bother us. More than anything it was the surprise of seeing it so close to a country club/marina community. The brochure that we had received didn't mention its proximity.

Duke Power owns the plant and most of the lake that isn't a wildlife refuge. Its official name is the Keowee-Toxaway Complex. We toured their visitor center and were very impressed with their displays, the enthusiasm of their staff, and their well-kept grounds.

Keowee Key

What would the lifestyle be like living in a large planned recreation retirement community? One that was somewhat isolated and in the foothills of the beautiful Blue Ridge Mountains? To answer this we took advantage of a four-day, three-night package. The brochure highlighted "one small string attached": we had to take an escorted tour of the facility. That was fine with us.

Keowee Key is located fourteen miles north of Clemson* and fifty miles west of Greenville,* in the far northeastern corner of South Carolina. There are a total of 1,500 acres available for development, which is being accomplished in two phases. When we were there phase one, 1,200 homesites, was nearly sold out. Work was starting on phase two, which would be very similar to the original development.

The property is on a peninsula on Lake Keowee—18,000 acres of water with about 300 miles of shoreline. The countryside is beautiful. We were there in the fall when the trees were at their height of color. The lake has no commercial establishments around it—no neon signs— no fast food litter—no hordes of weekenders. The terrain is very hilly. In the distance can be seen the Blue Ridge Mountains, which are snow-capped in the wintertime. The median year-round temperature is about 61° F., while relative humidity ranges from 51 to 79 percent and the yearly snowfall averages 2.7 inches.

At Keowee Key there are two pools, a 6,625-yard golf course, a pro shop, a clubhouse with a restaurant, a marina, an exercise room, and tennis courts. Everything is in excellent shape.

Villas, town houses, and most individual homes are rustic in appearance and blend in well with the countryside. Some new homes were being constructed. The echo of hammers rattling back and forth among the hills was disconcerting. The distraction would continue for many months to come.

Although the lots have been sold there are not many homes. Those that were built were spread throughout the grounds. In fact, there weren't many people around. It was very quiet in the clubhouse all day, even during happy hour.

There are little hill country crossroads towns nearby. Clemson with a population around 8,500 is the closest town of any consequence.

A golfer or a freshwater sailor would most easily become an active part of this community. For those not so inclined, over a period of time acquaintances would be made and activities would emerge as a result of common interests, as in many places.

The *Keowee Key Courier,* a seasonal publication which is primarily a promotion piece, doesn't mention many activities. One newcomer was quoted as saying, "There is plenty of entertainment here but the community takes things in moderation." We had that very same feeling, things seemed to be very low key. Perhaps it goes with being in the hill country. That could be good or bad, depending on how you see it.

Lots go from $35,000 up. A small home built by FORDCO, which does all the building, would cost $120,000 and up. Fees for taxes, community maintenance, insurance, water and sewer, garbage collection, energy costs, and golf membership were estimated at about $250 a month.

A home with no steps could be built to take care of the time when there might be physical difficulties. But the rest of the place would be off limits. The hills make for a pretty environment; however getting to the clubhouse, pool, marina, etc., would be difficult for a person with a physical problem.

The availability of the golf clubhouse, marina, and pools offers an opportunity to meet people and become involved. Memorial Day, the Fourth of July, and other special day celebrations offer additional means of becoming a part of the community. These kinds of activities provide a little more social opportunity than moving into an established neighborhood in "any town, U.S.A." We felt there was no particular lifestyle associated with Keowee Key other than retirement in a beautiful setting.

Sand Hills of North Carolina

The sandhills, about 1500 square miles, are located in Monroe County, right in the middle of North Carolina. The area is 500 feet above sea level with the Appalachin Mountains on one side and the Atlantic Ocean on the other. The mean temperature for the year is 61.6° F., normal rainfall is fifty inches a year with about four inches of snow. Fayetteville* is the nearest large town, about an hour's drive east on Interstate 95.

The 1980 census showed the population of the main golfing areas in North Carolina as, Pinehurst, 3,420; Southern Pines, 8,620; Whispering

Pines Village, 1,160; and Foxfire Village, 153. The total for Moore County is 50,505—projected 1992, 59,324.

Throughout the area there are small developments very carefully designed to blend into the environment. Naturally a place on a golf course gets to be expensive, but away from the very center of activities the price becomes affordable to the average golfer.

We had another "deceptive experience" when we visited this area. The brochure we sent for described many amenities that were nonexistent when we visited the site. We should have expected this when we received two copies of a deed agreement already typed in with the cost of a lot at $12,900 and detailing 84 payments of $192.75.

Another interesting section of the agreement gave us this privilege: "within 6 months of your purchase you may inspect your property on a company guided tour and if not completely satisfied, receive a refund of all months paid."

It's hard for us to believe that someone would buy property sight unseen.

The World Golf Hall of Fame, established in 1974, is located on the famed Pinehurst Number 2 Course overlooking the fourth green and the fifth tee. Although we aren't golfers, a shrine of this nature, memorializing the golfing greats, is truly inspiring.

Within a fifteen-mile radius of the heart of the pinelands there are: 27 golf courses, i.e., 91.03 miles of golf; 131 tennis courts; 6½ miles of racetrack; and 3,460 acres of lake and pond waters.

There are nineteen country clubs in the area. Big names in course design abound—Donald Ross, Pete and P. D. Dye, Jack Nicklaus, and Arnold Palmer. (Write Sand Hills Area Chamber of Commerce* for more information.)

A definitive lifestyle would certainly emerge in this locality: playing golf. Hopefully both spouses would be a participant. If not, possible problems are on the horizon. Anyone contemplating this lifestyle would do well to review Chapter 1, "Five Key Questions," in depth. This resolution of both persons' views is critical to a happy retirement.

Golf talk morning noon and night, 7 days a week, 365 days a year, could easily cause someone not interested in golf to tune out. In some cases a click of the hearing-aid switch would accomplish the same thing. Noncommunication results and then real trouble emerges.

At social functions we move away from golfing enthusiasts. As long as someone will listen they go through every shot on every hole which can be extremely boring for the nongolfer.

Another club lifestyle experience can be found at Lake Fairways* in Florida. This is a manufactured housing development built around an executive-type golf course. We have visited many club facilities around the country. This one seemed to be unique.

Lake Fairways is located on Florida's southwest coast near Fort Myers.* This is 120 miles south of St. Petersburg.* It is built on 300 acres and there are 935 sites.

One of the unique characteristics of this community is its layout. All homes are built in a cul-de-sac or cluster design instead of rows. A golf course and 27 acres of small lakes meander throughout the development. A series of roads tie each cul-de-sac neighborhood together. Most neighborhoods have 15 homes in a circle, each on a pie-shaped lot, approximately 85 feet in back, 38 feet along the street, and 92 feet deep. You might call each cul-de-sac a "circle of friends."

One thing different from most Florida developments is you can buy a lot or lease it. In each case you buy the home. Most places it's an "either/or" decision.

The golf course would turn off the avid golfer. It's only 3,006 yards, or less than half of a regulation course, with 6 par 4's and 12 par 3's. This means that most everyone can handle the course, but it's not a pushover. Par is 60. Most greens are built up and that causes trouble for a lot of people. The fifteenth hole has an elevation of 52 feet. Again, it's not an easy course. No one, even the pro, has shot less than a 55.

We were intrigued with the layout of this course. A husband and wife could easily negotiate this length of course on a close to even basis. It looked so inviting that we agreed if we had a course like this in our backyard we might once again try golf.

An excellent clubhouse, a pool, tennis courts, shuffleboard, and activity rooms round out the development. Cost of a home ranges from $42,000 to $85,000; golf and general maintenance fees are extra.

Their quarterly publication, called *Lake Fairways Lifestyle*, contains a very full activities calendar.

Lake Fairways is completed and in March 1990 the model homes went on sale. Immediately adjacent is Pine Lakes,* a carbon copy of Lake Fairways, with a more grandiose community clubhouse and golf facilities.

It has the same cul-de-sac neighborhood arrangement around the golf course and the meandering lakes.

There are two sections, the estate section where you purchase the land and the lease section where you have a lifetime lease on the land. Basic house prices, exclusive of land costs, range from $50,000 to $85,000; golf and maintenance fees are extra.

Each development has a guarded entryway but one identification pass serves both Pine Lakes and Lake Fairways. The guard said, "It's all the same place."

WHAT ABOUT MENTAL STIMULATION?
■   ■   ■

A casual club community lifestyle emerges from this type of environment. This lifestyle is different from a normal country club membership. It would be less formal, less competitive, and more conducive to husband and wife joint participation than to single living.

There is a danger. A life of fun and games all the time may cause mental stagnation. Some degree of balance is generally needed. A club community requires leadership positions, innovative projects, and creative thinking. Mental stimulation could be found by becoming involved at the planning level not just at a participation level.

Another danger may emerge: tunnel vision: i.e., becoming completely engrossed in a club community could cause a person to have a limited perspective on the outside world. There should be a degree of balance. You should make a determined effort to become involved in at least one nonclub related activity.

RESORT COMMUNITIES
■   ■   ■

Another possible lifestyle, very similar to the club community, is a resort community. By this we mean living on the resort grounds. This involves owning a condominium or cottage and utilizing the resort facilities.

Innisbrook*

This resort is located on the Gulf of Mexico, on 1,000 acres, at Tarpon Springs, Florida. It is twenty-five minutes from the Tampa International Airport.

At Innisbrook there are 24 lodges containing 900 guest units. These condos are part of a rental pool. You don't have to rent out your condo. There are special lodges for those who wish to live at the resort full time.

The facility has three golf courses, a tennis and racketball center, five climate-conditioned swimming pools, a health club and spa, and a shuttle to the beach. A surprising part of the facility were the peacocks that roamed around the grounds.

It's a busy place with over 100,000 guests a year and a conference center capable of handling meetings of up to 2,000 participants.

There are some retirees but not very many. When we were there it was a hustle and bustle with people of all ages looking for a good time. Most resort areas that we have been to have secluded homesites away from the commercialism of the resort. According to the management, most of the condos are bought for investment purposes. The rental pool distribution has been very good.

Tamarron*

Golf Hosts, Inc., which operates Innisbrook, also operates Tamarron in Durango, Colorado. If snow skiing is your thing the Purgatory ski area is nearby. Ownership at Innisbrook includes a club membership at Tamarron.

On the subject of snow skiing another resort community, in this case a town, is Vail,* Colorado.

Vail

In 1962 construction was started on a resort on Vail Mountain. The twentieth birthday of the now-incorporated town of Vail counted 5,000 permanent residents and accommodations for 20,000 visitors. It's a one-industry town, a resort town.

We couldn't get a handle on retirees. When we were there a political argument was taking place concerning a site for a HUD Senior Housing

Project. The facility would provide forty units of low-cost housing and a senior center.

The meeting calendar didn't list any senior associations or activities. There are plenty of condos and homes. If you're ready for 325 inches of snow (on the mountain) along with a lot of other avid skiers, Vail might be for you.

Hilton Head*

Located thirty miles north of Savannah, Georgia, and ninety miles south of Charleston, South Carolina, Hilton Head is a boot-shaped barrier reef that juts out into the Atlantic along the South Carolina coast. It is about twelve miles long and up to five miles wide, covering approximately forty-two square miles.

Year round the climate is mild; the warm ocean water which envelops the island moderates the changes in seasons. Normal daytime temperatures range from the mid-forties to fifties in the winter to the mid-eighties and nineties in the summer. Hilton Head Island is referred to as a completely planned resort community. All of the accoutrements are there—golf courses, tennis courts, marinas, fine shops, and a McDonald's.

It is low country. The highest elevation is twenty-five feet above mean sea level. The approach on the mainland is through marshes and tidal channels followed by a high bridge to the island. Here the road becomes a wide boulevard among palmettos, live oaks, pines, and magnolias. The threat of coastal storms playing havoc is always present; i.e., the devastation of the Carolina coast by Hurricane Hugo in 1989.

We talked with retirees Mr. and Mrs. R.T., who have a villa at Hilton Head. Resort areas are called plantations, such as Hilton Head Plantation, Port Royal Plantation, and Sea Pines Plantation. Each plantation is self-contained. Sea Pines Plantation where the R.T.'s have their villa is 5,000 acres, containing an inn, restaurants, shops, golf, tennis, rental homes and villas, plus over four miles of beach.

They are extremely pleased with their retreat. They spend a lot of time there but consider Roanoke, Virginia, home. Although the island gets crowded they said a well-planned master design keeps things flowing pretty well. They have a lot of friends there and have become active in various organizations. According to them, "It's a great life."

Most people, not all, would agree that retirement time should allow a person to ease up on the strain of fast-paced living. A resort community lifestyle seems to be centered in the fast lane. This would provide a challenge for some and a pain in the neck for others.

VACATION COMMUNITIES
■   ■   ■

Logically, the attributes that draw people to a vacation community will also be attractive to retirees. From the standpoint of a retiree, vacationers could cause a lot of disruption. Maybe there's a happy medium, but that depends on your likes and dislikes.

Cape Cod*

We mentioned Cape Cod in Chapter 7; however it needs to be mentioned here as a vacation community possibility.

Millions of vacationers make the trek to the Cape and old roads were not designed for that volume among other problems.

Cape Cod Trivia

An article in the *Cape Codder*, a newspaper serving the entire Cape, is entitled—"An Offal Situation in Harwich That Can't Be Ducked Anymore." A flock of 500 to 600 varying types of ducks and geese have taken over the dock at Saquatucket Harbor. As they loll around on the dock waiting for the next carload of vacationers to bring bread and corn you can imagine what happens on the dock. It's hosed down every day but that has just caused the water to become polluted.

These park birds don't leave. Why should they? They have found a good food supply with virtually no predators. The flock continues to get larger and larger. They have interbred with each other and created their own little variety of bird.

The vacationers find it fun to "take care" of these cute creatures of the wild. The harbormaster doesn't see the birds in the same light. Even though the daily hosings clean off the dock surface, what is left allows algae and lichens to grow. It's very slippery and causes rot.

Saugatuck, Michigan*

Another vacation haven is located about fifty miles south and west of Grand Rapids, Michigan. Near where the Kalamazoo River empties into Lake Michigan, a large harbor has been formed. About a mile downstream is the actual mouth of the river.

Saugatuck was incorporated as a village in 1868 and achieved city status on July 1, 1984. For years vacationers have come to this harbor city. First by large side paddle wheel boats, which made it an overnight trip from Chicago. Later by interurban coaches from Holland, Michigan, twenty miles to the north.

Today many of the original buildings are still preserved, although one of its major attractions is no longer there, the Big Pavilion.

Saugatuck remains a popular vacation spot. The boats still come from Chicago but now they are luxurious yachts. The beaches are good, as is the fishing. Occasional power boat races add excitement. It's a clean and pleasant town.

Mr. H.M., the town supervisor of Ganges, an adjacent township, related to us the story of a couple who were captivated by Saugatuck. They vacationed there a couple of summers, liked the activity, met some nice people, and decided Saugatuck would be their place for retirement. They sold their home in Cleveland and bought a place at the beginning of the next summer. It was a fun-time summer. After Labor Day it started to get quiet as some of the shops closed. By November the boats were gone and the weekenders no longer made the trek to the small town. Winter was getting close. The only people in town were farmers going to the pharmacy, the bank, or the American Legion Hall.

When the snow came and the wind off the lake howled they found everything to be quiet and confining. They sold out and went back to Cleveland.

A little different from a lot of locals who look forward to the departure of the short-termers. Small-town living isn't for everyone. The Cleveland retirees checked out the town during their vacations. That's good. But they failed to remember there are four seasons in the North. They checked only the fun days of summer. When checking a retirement possibility remember it's a twelve-month living arrangement.

Many places are not necessarily vacation communities, but do attract a lot of touring vacationers. The overnight or tour bus vacationers also bring along a lot of continuous activity.

We found that there was never a dull moment at the Lawrence Welk Resort. First of all, if you don't like Lawrence Welk and his champagne music you might just as well forget this section. At this facility you can't get away from the fact that this is Lawrence Welk country.

A part of this resort is a manufactured housing retirement village, which was started in 1964. We first became acquainted with the facility in 1979 when there were 204 mobile home spaces and the motel had 54 units. An expansion took place in 1984, increasing rental spaces to 456 and adding 90 units to the motel. The village has been "sold out" for a long time, but resales are available.

All homes have to be a minimum of 24 feet wide. Some on the resale list are 34 × 62 feet. They must be owner-occupied and no one under eighteen can be considered a resident. The golf courses and resident activity area are at the lower elevations. The roads meander up the hills and lots are at various levels. Some sites have excellent views, hence a wide variance in site rental fees. The entire complex is well groomed, neat, and, in the residential area, free of litter.

The village is located midway between Los Angeles and the Mexican border. It is 8 miles north of Escondido on Interstate 15. Escondido is at an elevation of 660 feet above sea level, has a yearly average temperature of 62.5° F., and 16.11 inches of rainfall a year.

Expansion has continued. In early 1990, the entire resort complex covered 1,000 acres. There are now 134 rooms in 6 separate lodge-style buildings. Three golf courses are included: a par 3, an executive course of 4,100 yards, and a 6,500-yard course with another 18-hole course nearby. In addition the following is also available: a vacation time share operation; a conference center; Broadway musicals at the Lawrence Welk Resort Theater; a restaurant; gift, craft, and clothing shops; a market and a deli; a beauty shop; and medical offices. There is a very large parking lot servicing these attractions. When we were there it was busy all the time. Many tour buses were parked waiting for their riders to return. We toured the shops and it was a trip down memory lane. However, we didn't go into raptures as some folks did as they tried to figure out what to buy.

To some people the availability of a dinner theater, accessible by hourly tram service, would be a tremendous draw. Those same folks would probably also like to "people watch" the tour bus riders. Nothing wrong with that, but some residents would have trouble with the constant turmoil created by tourists and the constant movement in and out of vacationers at the resort. Some homes in locations up in the hills could be pretty well isolated from the rumble and exhaust of tour buses. Location would be extremely important if you wanted a great deal of solitude.

Lawrence Welk Resort Trivia

Each residence must have a seventy-five-foot section of hose permanently attached to the water outlet on the site. From the standpoint of fire safety this makes a great deal of sense.

In this chapter we have tried to point out some of the difficulties that may be encountered in a club resort or vacation community. The excitement of these environments and the glamour of this lifestyle could be contagious and a decision made without a complete analysis.

Whenever there is a great deal of general public interaction there is a high probability of some negative happenings. This must be factored into the analysis of what's right for you.

9

LARGE RETIREMENT VILLAGE/CITY

▪ ▪ ▪

LIFESTYLE OPTION #6, TOTAL RETIREE-DOMINATED LIVING

DEFINITION: A large community for adults only, requiring one person to be at least fifty years of age. Within the community there are usually houses of worship and many types of recreational facilities, including golf, shopping, restaurants, banks, professional services, hospital or medical services, and police and fire protection. A self-sufficient community.

Reactions are varied, ranging from "Great, best move we ever made," "Always something to do," "Clean, neat, no litter," "Feel safe and secure," and "Quiet, no noisy kids running around" to "Never should have left the old neighborhood," "Boring," "Regimentation, too many rules and regulations," "Feel cooped up behind guard stations," and "All you ever see are a bunch of old people."

To experience firsthand what this lifestyle is like, we took advantage of a "Vacation Plan" and lived for a week in Sun City West, northwest of Phoenix, Arizona. We chose this community because it's large, set apart from other communities, and the Sun City retirement concept is one of the oldest in the United States. We have visited retirement communities throughout the United States, mostly in the frostbelt and Sunbelt.

SUN CITY WEST
■   ■   ■

Del E. Webb, now deceased, a businessman and owner of the New York Yankees, opened the original Sun City on January 1, 1960, not to be confused with Sun City West, its sister community.

Sun City was started in the middle of a cotton field that was surrounded by open desert. Eighteen years later all of the residential property in the 8,900 acres had been purchased by close to 50,000 adult residents.

Two other Sun Cities were started, one in California and one in Florida. Then in 1978, a few miles northwest of Sun City, a new community was started—Sun City West. Sometime after the turn of the century, it will be filled up with over 25,000 people. When we were there the population was 17,568. That was six years after the opening.

A unique approach was taken by Del Webb. At the original Sun City he built the main recreation center, golf course, shopping complex, and other amenities before offering any houses for sale. Home buyers didn't buy in on the basis of promises, the buildings were there. The same concept has been followed at Sun City West.

Going northwest on the road from Phoenix to Las Vegas you turn into Sun City West. There is no guard house, although there is a concrete wall around the perimeter of the property. A divided extra-large four-lane boulevard, nicely landscaped with saguaro cacti and other desert vegetation, leads you into the core of phase one of Sun City West.

The core is a very large oval with a commercial area at one end and an eighteen-hole par 72 golf course at the other end. In between is the R. H. Johnson Recreation Center, the Sundome, vocation center, and restaurant. Around the perimeter of the oval are the Camino Del Sol shopping center, vacation special apartments, fire station, gas station, model homes, houses of worship, library, and medical center.

Fanning out from the oval are homes. Interspersed among the homes are more golf courses, another recreation center, and a shopping center. Additional neighborhood recreation centers and golf courses will be built as the growth continues.

The home area is divided up by units. As one unit is built another is started around the perimeter. There is a constantly creeping armada of bulldozers, trucks, and construction workers. They leave in their wake miles of roads and acres of homes.

You pick out the lot that you want, the house plan that fits your needs, and the Del E. Webb Construction Company does the building. You have no choice concerning who will build your home. A large model home area of twenty homes shows you exactly what you get. Single families, duplexes, and villas range in square footage from 1,038 to 2,790 and are priced from $70,000 to $180,000.

There are many amenities attached to Sun City West. There are seven eighteen-hole golf courses including a private country club. The R. H. Johnson Recreation Center is a forty-acre complex including fifteen regulation tennis courts; eight paddleball courts, plus handball and racketball courts; swimming pool with a separate diving area and a Jacuzzi; two oversized hydrotherapy pools; an exercise room; twenty-four bowling lanes; lawn bowling; table tennis; a twenty-five-table billiard room; an eighteen-hole miniature golf course; indoor shuffleboard courts; a quarter-mile running track with pacing lights and an adjacent eighteen-station parcourse fitness circuit; a 1,000-seat social hall; and individual crafts rooms for ceramics, lapidary, woodworking, weaving, painting, silvercraft, sewing, copper enameling, woodworking, etc.

The Beardsley Park Recreation Center includes an indoor-outdoor pool, facilities for stained glass, pottery, and china painting, a photography studio, and meeting rooms.

Their 7,169-seat Sundome is the largest single-level theater in the United States. Dinah Shore was performing when we were there. There is a 203-bed hospital. The library has a stack capacity of 40,000 volumes, a reading room, and a periodical section. More than eighty stores and services are available.

We sampled many of these amenities and they were all first class. Whether or not you use any of these facilities, there is a nominal yearly fee for each resident excluding golf, which is extra.

Activities

There are 150 chartered clubs and organizations—with 237 activities scheduled each week. If there isn't one that excites you and there is sufficient interest from others, you can start your own. Some unusual clubs listed in the monthly activity calendar are mah-jongg, copper cookers creation, gold panning, tap dancing, yoga exercise, water ballet, leather carvers, rosemaling, and jazzercise. Three clubs should be highlighted.

PRIDES (PROUD RESIDENTS INDEPENDENTLY DONATING ESSENTIAL SERVICES). This group of 300 volunteers help keep the litter off the streets and maintain public landscaping. Every Saturday morning, armed with brooms, clippers, rakes and trash bags, they hit the roads. They have two vans to transport equipment, a safety wagon (golf cart), and they all wear reflector vests. They are successful. In all our visits to different communities around the United States we have never seen a place as clean as Sun City West. We made a game of trying to locate litter when we traversed the roads and walkways. We couldn't find any!

SUN CITY WEST POSSE. These volunteers—250 of them—serve as the eyes and ears of the Maricopa County sheriff. Twenty-four hours a day they police the grounds in official vehicles. They receive training from the sheriff's department and are supported by contributions from the residents. Members who take advanced training can be qualified to carry sidearms. They are also successful. A resident told us there is "never any crime; occasionally an outdoor chair is taken."

LENDING HANDS. Supported solely by donations, this group lends thousands of items yearly to residents. From baby beds for visiting grandchildren to specialized hospital equipment.

Many clubs sponsor countywide functions. Couple these with Sundome scheduled activities and there is always something going on.

Our Impressions

Is this utopia? To some, yes; those that like it stay. Others who don't like the lifestyle leave. Hence, those that we talked to were really enthusiastic about the community. This also spills over into the pride that everyone seems to have in his/her own home and the community in general.

We had an in-depth conversation with Mr. and Mrs. D. S. formerly of Milwaukee. They left the North and retired to Palm Springs, California. Neither of them cared for this location because of the class consciousness of the residents. People paid a great deal of attention to what year and style of Cadillac you drove and what your work title had been.

They then moved to Leisure World Laguna Hills in California but didn't care for the high-rise concept. Now they have a very large home, 3,500 square feet, on the golf course, a pool, and most importantly—a place for their golf cart.

He plays golf twice a week with the boys and twice a week with his wife. They do not participate in any interest groups. A few small trips during the year and one major foreign trip satisfy their wanderlust.

We asked how they handled the heat in the summer (average high temperature in June is 101.5° F., July 104.8° F., August 102.2° F., September 98.4° F., and an average rainfall of 7.05 inches). Their reply was to do outside things early in the morning and hibernate in the air-conditioned spaces during the afternoon. Many people go North or to the nearby mountains for the summer. We stopped by the area where motor homes and trailers were stored. It seemed as if there were miles and miles of RV's.

Rules and regulations didn't appear to bother them. They agreed with the fifty-year-old age restriction, the rules that no business could be run out of your house, that a guest could stay only one month, and that an RV could not be parked in front of a house longer than twenty-four hours.

Most people belong to the residents' association, which does a lot of good. Mr. and Mrs. D. S. did find the remoteness of the facility irritating. It's forty miles to Sky Harbor Airport in Phoenix, and twenty-two miles to the nearest regional shopping center. They were also irritated by the occasional noise of a fighter plane from Luke Air Force Base. But all in all they said, "We're really happy here."

Within the complex it seemed as if everyone used his/her golf cart for shopping, going to and from the recreation center, and visiting. It takes a bit of getting used to. Unfortunately, we had to leave just before a golf cart rally was to take place. The scheduled activities included cheerleaders, bands, food, drink, and a five-mile parade through the community. Also, a race and a "most beautiful golf cart in the world" pageant. On the roads we saw some really dolled-up carts. It was hard to believe they were *just* golf carts.

The roads are wide—very, very wide—so there is plenty of room to maneuver. It seemed as if the speed limit were ten miles an hour. People drive slowly! We were told that even if you couldn't pass a regular driving test, it was possible to get a special driver's license permit which is valid within the complex.

We likened this lifestyle to 365 days a year on the *Love Boat*. Any responsibilities or time constraints are self-imposed. This could be a lifestyle completely centered around leisure activities of your own choice. A complete 180-degree shift from the workaday world prior to retirement.

THE OTHER SUN CITIES
■ ■ ■

The Original Sun City in Phoenix

Some of the original small homes built in 1960 that sold then for about $8,900 need some attention and are now selling in the $60,000s. The streets aren't very wide and traffic backs up a bit. Naturally, everything shows some sign of wear and tear. This is now a mature community. Those moving here in the early days of the community are now in their late seventies and eighties. Canes, walkers, and wheelchairs are very visible. With these limitations, it follows that everything that needs attention doesn't always receive the TLC that it requires.

Both Sun City and Sun City West are unincorporated. The Del E. Webb organization has acted as a substitute for a normal city government. It encourages a great deal of input from the residents. It appears this has been a very good arrangement. However, the Webb organization moved from Sun City to Sun City West, leaving the governance up to Maricopa County. Some people feel this is less than desirable. They have many concerns about rezoning, adherence to the age restriction, and common grounds maintenance.

Another thorn in the side of some residents at Sun City is the ban on smoking in the seven recreation buildings. A recreation center member's vote was being contested in Superior Court by the Equal Rights for all Sun Citians Group. The Non-Smokers Association of Sun City was defending the legitimacy of the election. This caught the attention of national television. The "Today" show reported that 1,000 smokers demonstrated against the ban.

Living in Sun City West, but exploring all parts of Sun City, gave us the opportunity to see how the Webb company has learned from its experiences. The wide streets, the use of boulevards, rockscaping and desert plantings, large parking lots, more use of color, large lots and deeper set-backs, and a greater number of house styles add much to the newer Sun City West.

The comparison of these two Sun Cities leads us to the following recommendation. A recent retiree in his/her early sixties who chooses this lifestyle would be much better off moving to a new developing community rather than a mature facility. Being in the company of young/old rather than old/old would offer more interest compatibility. Friendships would be easier to establish. Being a part of a "near the same age" group allows the group members to grow old together. There would be a reciprocal support group that is a vital necessity as the aging process takes its toll.

Sun City, California

This unincorporated community in Riverside, California, was founded in 1962 in the same manner as the Arizona Sun City. Located seventy-five miles south of Los Angeles, seventy-five miles north of San Diego, and twenty-five miles from the Riverside/San Bernardino area, its population is 9,000. It is another clean and neat facility which is showing a bit of age. The older population is quite evident as you compare the activity level at the various recreational buildings here and at Sun City West.

There are two golf courses; one is an executive-type course. The recreation building has the usual craft rooms, two pools, and two auditoriums that accommodate 1,000 residents.

A widow who is a homeowner told us her feelings about Sun City. When she decided to sell her large home in Palos Verdes Peninsula she looked at Sun City West in Arizona, but felt it was "so huge." She settled on Sun City, California, because she wanted to be close, but not too close, to one of her daughters who lives one and one-half hours away.

One of her concerns is the occasional sound of the ambulance siren. This is very depressing. There is also a problem with robberies. However, she feels secure in her home on the golf course, which has wrought-iron grillwork across the back lanai; the front is latticed over with a wall and locked gate. There is a movement to annex the community to a larger city nearby. She favors this because it would offer better police protection.

When she moved in four years ago there was no welcoming process and no community singles group. However, all in all, she feels it was a good move and is satisfied with her lifestyle.

The business section of Sun City, California, includes supermarkets and other stores. There is a mobile home section and an apartment complex that includes maid service and meals. The Sun City Chamber of Commerce gave us an economic profile that seemed to encourage business and industry to locate in Sun City.

Sun City Center, Florida*

Started in 1962, the community is located 25 miles south of Tampa. There are over 11,000 residents in this 5,500-acre complex; 200 social clubs and organizations provide plenty of activities along with 108 holes of golf. Homes are priced from $60,000 to over $200,000.

Mr. and Mrs. C.M. make a yearly commute to Sun City Center from their house on the ocean at Cape Cod. Health problems caused them to leave their retirement home on St. Croix and they decided on the Cape Cod/Sun City combination. Their life is full and they enjoy this lifestyle.

SUN LAKES*
■ ■ ■

South out of Phoenix, Arizona, toward Tucson we stopped at Sun Lakes. We arrived as church was letting out and small groups were forming to walk to the country club for Sunday brunch. One thing was different; they seemed younger. You only have to be forty or above and not have anyone younger than nineteen living with you to be able to live at Sun Lakes.

Mr. & Mrs. W.D., who left South Haven, Michigan, and the cold winds sweeping off Lake Michigan, told us this was one of the reasons they chose Sun Lakes. Although they are in their late sixties they like the younger look.

This community of 3,500 acres and 8,000-plus residents is one of the newer large communities. It is growing rapidly. Nineteen lakes interspersed around three country clubs and three eighteen-hole golf courses provide the key to the name. The developer was formerly associated with the Del E. Webb Company so there are similarities with the Sun City communities: two shopping areas, churches, sheriff's posse, a 10,000-square-foot civic center, and an arts and crafts building.

A small villa plus lot costs about $100,000. Larger homes on choice golf course or lake lots exceed $200,000. There is a monthly fee for each homesite, which includes use of all club facilities, security, fire protection, and emergency response. Golf fees are extra.

It's a lively place with a tennis club, a camera club, a Republican club, a Scandinavian club, a super singles and solo club, a 40/50 (age) club, a VFW and American Legion, an Italian/American club, a hiking club, the dancin' grannies—and the list could go on.

GREEN VALLEY, ARIZONA*
■   ■   ■

Twenty-five miles south of Tucson and forty miles north of Nogales, the city divided by a fence along the Mexican border is Green Valley. Located in the Santa Cruz River Valley with the Santa Rita Mountains to the east and the Sierritas to the west, the desert setting at 2,500 feet is inspiring. It's easy to visualize the Apaches prowling the ridges of the foothills.

Sprawling along both sides of Interstate 19 are the homes of 16,000-plus residents. A master plan approved by the Board of Representatives would accommodate up to 85,000 people in the 210-square-mile valley. The unincorporated town of Green Valley would take up 48.4 square miles.

Fairfield Communities is the prime developer. They expand the community by subdivision. When 60 percent of the homes have been sold the subdivision is turned over to the residents for self-administration. As a result, there is much more consistent road and neighborhood planning, along with common area beautification, than there was during the early development in the mid-sixties. It's obvious that administration by the residents is more effective.

On average, there are 300 days of sunshine each year.

Month	Average Temp. (° F.) Daily Max.	Min.	Average Precip. Inches	Average Humidity 5:00 P.M.
Jan.	67.1	31.0	0.66	33%
Mar.	75.2	37.8	0.50	27%
Apr.	84.3	43.5	0.25	16%
June	101.1	60.6	0.29	13%

| | Average Temp. (° F.) | | Average Precip. | Average Humidity |
Month	Daily Max.	Min.	Inches	5:00 P.M.
Aug.	98.6	66.3	2.03	33%
Nov.	74.5	40.4	0.58	28%
Year	84.9	48.0	10.86	25%

Mr. and Mrs. M.H. moved to Green Valley from Colorado. They had previously lived in Scottsdale, Arizona, for seventeen years and were partial to desert living. Before their permanent move to Green Valley they spent winters there for seven years. They knew the territory before their move. They enthusiastically said, "The climate and people" were their prime reason for their choice of the valley. Mr. H. said, "Even if it hits over 100° F. during the day, in the evening we can sit on our patio and be very comfortable—it's the low humidity." When asked their overall opinion about the community they said, "Fantastic!"

Another resident said, "It's like family here." There are 150 clubs and organizations, 9 social centers, each with a swimming pool and Jacuzzi, 2 private and 2 public golf courses. There are 2 shopping centers with 130 businesses and 8 financial institutions, and 5 medical centers. The closest hospital is in Tucson, and it's a two-hour drive to Mount Lemmon (9,000 feet) for snow skiing.

In the Canoa Hills Development a freestanding home, 1,450 square feet, costs $120,000; a town house, 1,350 square feet, $100,000; a larger town house, 2,050 square feet, $150,000. These costs do not include landscaping, patio construction, or extras that many people want. This includes the lot but no view. Add $20,000 to $40,000 for a premium lot. Homeowners yearly subdivision costs are $350.

There is one distraction: the dirt wall of the open-pit copper mine that borders on the southwest. It will be years before natural growth appears on the wall. Operation of the mine is further north so there are no trucks or traffic problems. However, theft is another problem. Interstate 19 is a direct route to Mexico and some travelers take side trips through the community.

In 1989 we took advantage of a three-day vacation package and stayed in one of the casitas. It was a delightful experience.

SOUTHERN CALIFORNIA
■   ■   ■

There are two large communities in the vicinity of Los Angeles. Leisure World-Seal Beach has 6,482 apartments. This has been sold out for years. Resales are handled by local real estate companies. Leisure World-Laguna Hills has over 21,000 residents. This was started in 1964 and has also been sold out for a long time. Resales are listed with local real estate companies.

Each of these communities has a complicated cooperative or condominium arrangement involving the Golden Rains Foundation. Everyone must join the foundation, which holds in trust common area facilities such as clubhouse, stables, golf course, streets, etc.

We have been unable to locate new large retirement developments on the West Coast. There are multitudes of small communities of under 1,000 residents that have been built in recent years. Undoubtedly the high cost and limited availability of large tracts of land inhibits the development of new large retirement communities in California.

SOUTH JERSEY COAST
■   ■   ■

As previously mentioned in Chapter 7, the Pinelands of South Jersey have become a major geographical center for retirees. This area is about fifteen miles inland from the Atlantic Ocean and is in the vicinity of Lakehurst, New Jersey, the site of the German zeppelin *Hindenburg* disaster, May 6, 1937. This area is approximately sixty-five miles from New York City, fifty miles from Newark, New Jersey, fifty miles from Philadelphia, Pennsylvania, and fifty miles from Atlantic City. The average temperature during the summer is 72° F., the fall, 56° F., the winter, 33° F., and the spring, about 60° F. The terrain is low, flat, and sandy.

In this general area we made on-site surveys of five facilities: Crestwood, Holiday City, Leisure Knoll, Leisuretowne, and Leisure Village West. In addition to these large communities, there were many smaller retirement complexes.

Holiday City

This community of approximately 20,000 residents is located five minutes away from Toms River, New Jersey. Express buses go from Toms River to New York, Newark, and Philadelphia.

Private community buses provide service around the community and to local shopping centers on a regularly scheduled basis. There is a neighborhood shopping mall with a variety of shops and medical services.

A clubhouse with meeting rooms is the center of activities. Nearby are a pool, tennis courts, shuffleboard courts, and an area for playing boccie.

The December 1989 newsletter the *Southwind* indicated an active environment. There were volunteer chairpersons listed for fourteen activities including bingo, ceramics, exercise, and tap dancing. Eight sports chairpersons were listed and seven club presidents, including a singles club. This club had just finished their fourth annual flea market. A Christmas luncheon was planned on a BYOB basis, along with a long list of trips and other events.

Holiday City is located in Berkeley Township. A civic committee monitors local government and school board meetings. Increased taxes and water company rate hikes are the current interest. There is a volunteer fire department and a first aid squad.

Homes and lots are purchased. It is not a co-op or condominium community. A "club" membership is required. Common areas, trash pickup, snow removal, and lawn cutting are handled by the club. There is an age restriction. Residents must be at least fifty-five.

Holiday City has been developed by areas. The latest is called the New Holiday City. One-story-home prices vary from $111,900 to $149,900. October 1989 monthly estimates for a $122,900 home are:

Club Membership	$ 24.00
Minimum Water Rate	2.85
Sewage Rate	13.67
Estimated Taxes	131.40
Monthly Total	$171.92

This home has two bedrooms, two baths, kitchen, combined dining and living area, fireplace, sun room with atrium, a one-car garage, and a porch. Front lawns are sodded and have a sprinkler system. All utilities are underground and there is a ten-year homeowners warranty.

A sales brochure from a nearby community, Crestwood, highlights some reasons for making a move. Is the old neighborhood deteriorating? Is the old home appropriate for future years? Is the bathroom where needed? Are there stairs to climb? Are there unused rooms to heat and clean? Is it time to replace the major appliances? Is it time to redecorate? Also included is the release of frozen capital assets in an existing home: i.e., sell, take advantage of the $125,000 capital gains tax exemption, buy a lower-cost retirement-sized home, invest the balance in income-producing liquid assets, and live better from this increased income.

As we surveyed these various communities and talked to residents it was very evident that most of the residents had not made a cross country move. The New Jersey/New York accent was very pronounced.

New Jersey Trivia

We went further south down the Atlantic Seaboard to Atlantic City. For retirees with the urge and wherewithal to gamble, we found the modest Fox Manor Retirement Hotel. They advertise themselves as a hotel for senior citizens, not an old-age home or a nursing home. The hotel is located on Pacific Avenue between Illinois and Indiana avenues, one block from the Boardwalk. Recognize the names from the last time you played Monopoly?

IS THIS LIFESTYLE FOR YOU?
■   ■   ■

There are many more of these large self-contained retirement communities that we have visited around the country. They have the advantage of easy living. You don't have to go too far for your essentials. Activities are readily at hand. The means to meet people with similar interests are readily available. The surroundings are quiet, proper, and in keeping with the values of the twenties and thirties generations. Other than some occasional flaps—such as the smoking ban at Sun City West, or the intense discussions at Leisure Village concerning the expansion of Willow Hall—rooms for TV and cards should be separate rather than one big room with distractions from conversation—there isn't going to be a lot of "rocking the boat." There will be some personality conflicts within activity groups but these can be handled—just move to another group.

If you're a harried business person—an entrepreneur being run ragged because you can't find good employees—a volunteer getting burned out helping in a hospital—a machinist who is sick and tired of clocking in at the same gate for the past thirty-five years, then this lifestyle might sound really great. It would be a departure from your present lifestyle. From stressful living to easy living.

But there is another side to the evaluation of this *ease of living* life-style. We talked to Mr. and Mrs. R.V., who moved from Ohio to the original Sun City in Phoenix. They stayed for many years and then moved back to Chardon, Ohio—a place known for its heavy snowfalls. They liked the sun, the craft work, the tours to Las Vegas and other places of interest. But as their area matured they turned off to being with old people and listening to their complaints about aches and pains. They felt depressed when the ambulance was seen more frequently. They wanted a more rounded life. They moved back to their native state.

It's possible that the self-contained retirement community could pro-duce self-contained residents. Retirees who *because of the ease of living become encased in a cocoon.* It would be very easy to slip away from other aspects of life—children, young adults, young marrieds—and the changes taking place in a contemporary society.

Is this good? Bad? Right? Wrong? No one can answer this except you and your spouse. What's best for you is a personal decision. We can only relay what we have found and heard and present conclusions that seem logical—then the ball is in your court.

SINGLES APPLICABILITY
■   ■   ■

The opportunity to meet people is built in. A little aggressiveness in searching out the right interest groups will provide ample opportunity to become acquainted. Smaller housing can be found so there will not be a lot of unused space. All in all, this lifestyle should be tailor-made for the single.

10

TOTAL PLANNED
COMMUNITY

. . .

LIFESTYLE OPTION #7, PLANNED
INTERGENERATIONAL LIVING

One of the objections to a facility such as a Sun City is that it is designed completely for retirees. There is no involvement and participation by varying age groups. This doesn't mean that all retirees want a lot of children running around. Most people want their peace and quiet but some people don't want to be in a cloistered environment of older people, a geriatric ghetto!

To satisfy this need for a more well-rounded life experience two approaches to total planned communities have emerged.

1. Large master-planned communities with separated sections for singles, married-no family, families, and retirees.
2. Large master-planned recreational communities open to anyone. Natural divisions occur as prospective buyers survey the community. Those with children look for areas where there will be companions for their children. Seniors look for other seniors and a more secluded quiet environment.

In both approaches, shopping, total community activities, church, and an evening's walk will involve a cross section of the community. If the community is large enough to have a weekly newspaper, activities and goings on at all age levels will be covered. This provides a well-rounded update on the "big picture."

LARGE MASTER-PLANNED COMMUNITIES
■ ■ ■

Rancho Bernardo

One of the first total planned communities was Rancho Bernardo, in California, started in 1962. Located twenty-three miles north of downtown San Diego, this community is located on 5,800 acres of gently rolling countryside. It is part of the city of San Diego and is served by a centrally located fire station, U.S. Post Office, library, police station, and ambulance service.

The community is completely developed. Resales are handled by local real estate firms. It is clean, neat, and well manicured. We found no rundown areas. There is obviously a great deal of community pride. There are no clear-cut delineations between the six neighborhoods.

Westwood. This is an area of single-family homes and town houses for active families, with schools nearby. The Westwood Club, open to Westwood homeowners on an annual-fee basis, has a fully equipped gymnasium, swimming pool, lighted tennis courts, little league baseball diamonds, and a full-time director and staff.

Oaks North. This neighborhood, developed around a twenty-seven-hole executive golf course, is an all-adult community for the over-forty-five group, with no children under twenty-one living at home. The Oaks North Recreation Center has a swimming pool, therapeutic pool, arts and crafts rooms, auditorium, lounges, lawn bowling, and tennis courts. We talked to an avid lawn bowler who travels around the country competing in lawn bowling tournaments; he told us that 99 percent of the people in Oaks North were retired.

Green Homes and Villas. Here single-family homes and villas are built around a private golf course. Nearby is the swimming and tennis club, which includes a large pool, a wading pool, tennis courts, little league ball fields, and meeting rooms.

Seven Oaks. This is an area of homes and villas for those over fifty with no children under twenty-one living at home.

The Trails. For those interested in horseback riding, this neighborhood would be most attractive. Homesites are one to three acres, adjacent to the large Rancho Bernardo Saddle Club. A ten-foot-wide bridle path winds among the estates.

High Country West. This is the newest area of single-family homes and duplexes for growing families.

COMMUNITY FEATURES. There are a total of eighty-one holes of golf available for residents and guests. A tennis college is located at Rancho Bernardo Inn, a 150-room resort. Numerous recreation centers are available along with the swimming and tennis club and the saddle club.

Five shopping centers are within the community, one featuring major department stores. In addition, there are twenty-four-hour medical and dental facilities. The industrial park encompasses 635 acres and is occupied by many high-tech companies.

Also in the community is Rancho Bernardo Inn, a nationally recognized resort and meeting complex. The Remington Club* is a full-service rental retirement community with on-site skilled health care. They have just opened Phase II, which provides an additional 100 one- and two-bedroom apartments.

Rancho Bernardo Trivia

Rancho Bernardo Realty, Inc., has a poem which seems to express the spirit of Rancho Bernardo.

CHRISTMAS EVE IN BEAUTIFUL
RANCHO BERNARDO

" 'Twas the night before Christmas and all through our town,
No noses were frozen, no snow fluttered down.
No children in flannels were tucked into bed,
They all wore their shorty pajamas instead.
To find wreaths of holly was not very hard,
For holly trees sprouted right in the back yard.
In front of the houses were daddys and moms,
Admiring the bushes and beautiful palms.

The slumbering kiddies were dreaming in glee,
And hoped they'd find water skis under the tree.
They all knew that Santa was well on his way,
In a Mercedes-Benz instead of a sleigh.
And soon he arrived and started to work;
He hadn't a second to linger or shirk.
He whizzed o'er the highways and zoomed up the road
In a shiny new sports car delivering his load.
The tropical moon gave the city a glow
And lighted the way for Santa below.
As he jumped from the auto he gave a wee chuckle;
He was dressed in Bermudas with an Ivy League buckle.
There weren't many chimneys but that caused no gloom,
For Santa came in through the patio room.
He stopped at each house, staying only a minute,
And lightened his sack of the gifts that were in it.
Before he departed he treated himself
To a glass of orange juice left on the shelf.
Then he turned with a jerk and bounded back to the car,
Remembering he still had to go very far.
He stepped on the gas and put it in gear
And drove throughout town singing with cheer.
And I heard him exclaim as he went on his way,
'Merry Christmas, Rancho Bernardo, I wish I could stay!'"

—AUTHOR UNKNOWN

Ahwatukee

This is another master-planned intergenerational community. Pronounced AH-WAH-TOO-KEY, the name is derived from an Old Crow Indian word meaning "house of your dreams."

It is a total planned community located in the Valley of the Sun, twelve miles southeast of Phoenix, Arizona, near the juncture of the Sonoran Desert and the Salt River Mountains. It is adjacent to Tempe, home of Arizona State University.

"Ahwa" (as the residents call it) was started in 1974 by the Presley Development Company, a publicly held company listed on the New

York Stock Exchange. This 2,500-acre community has areas for separate family, adult, and retirement living. These three lifestyles are blended into the community. Although segregated, they don't appear that way.

The retirement living area is adjacent to one of the two golf courses and has its own recreation center with an Olympic-sized pool, Jacuzzi, sauna, exercise room, billiards club, craft rooms, lawn bowling, etc. When we toured the center and talked with the activities director and retirees, we were impressed with the informality. The smallness of this retirement area seemed to add warmth to the conversation. We felt comfortable.

There is a separate large family community center that has recreational facilities for all ages. The adult area has its own swimming pool.

Toward the rear of the development, near the equestrian center and in the shadows of the Phoenix Mountain Preserve, are the executive series homes. Here are large lots which are perfect for building the "house of your dreams."

A shopping and medical plaza offer essentials. The country club and a separate tennis club round out the development.

It has a well-rounded atmosphere—senior citizens, adults, kids, school house, athletic fields, and day care center. Yet the somewhat secluded retirement area was like a haven—a quiet retreat.

On the negative side was the merchants association appeal in the newspaper. They were asking parents to police their kids. There had been a rash of shoplifting in Ahwatukee Plaza.

When we first surveyed Ahwa there was a lot of room for new homes. An aerial picture of the area with the community superimposed showed nothing but desert for miles around. When we resurveyed in 1989 we were in for a surprise. Not only was Ahwa completely full but there were homes for miles around. Resales are handled by local real estate firms. It still looked like a nice community but there were no open spaces.

The Del E. Webb Company announced that it was not going to build any more "city-size" communities such as their Sun Cities. The lack of large tracts of land at an attractive price makes this kind of development impossible. It is expanding by buying a large tract in a master-planned community. There are two of these, one in Tucson, Arizona and one in Las Vegas, Nevada.

Eleven miles northwest of Tucson is a 7,700-acre master-planned community called Rancho Vistoso. It is described as a community which will allow its residents to work, play, and live in a self-sufficient environment. It is located in the desert foothills of the 9,000-foot Catalina and Tortolia Mountains, surrounded by the 256,000-acre Coronado National Forest; 3,700 acres have been dedicated to natural open spaces.

We talked with the developers and viewed a topographical mock-up of the entire project. Areas have been designated for housing with very low, low, medium and high density residential. Space has been set aside for a hospital and medical facility, primary and secondary schools, religious facilities, town center, and a resort hotel. Work areas are designated commercial and campus park industrial.

Sun City Vistoso*

Sun City Vistoso's 1,000 acres within the Rancho Vistoso complex will eventually be occupied by 5,000 residents. In early 1990 there were 1,000 residents. We surveyed in early 1989 and were impressed by the entire development. There is a beautiful sixteen-acre $5 million recreational center, which includes lighted tennis courts, shuffleboard, boccie courts, swimming pools, raquetball courts, jogging track, large auditorium, several multipurpose rooms, an arts and crafts village, an eighteen-hole golf course, and the Double Eagle Restaurant and Lounge. In 1990 housing costs on a standard lot were:

Single family home—1,035 square feet	$96,300
Single family home—1,524 square feet	$122,300
Single family home—2,328 square feet	$183,800
Patio homes—1,214 to 1,753 square feet	$98,000 to $136,800

Lots with "a view" are much more expensive.

Sun City Vistoso is alluring if you are interested in desert living at 2,400 feet and want to be part of a large intergenerational community in its infancy.

Sun City Summerlin*

Howard Hughes Properties is developing a similar community in Nevada. Sun City Summerlin is a 25,000-acre master-planned community located eight miles northwest of downtown Las Vegas. In the foothills of the Spring Mountain Range, it is being built on 1,050 acres high above the city, offering evening views of the lights of Las Vegas. The Sun City Summerlin complex within the Howard Hughes development parallels the Vistoso development in style, size, amenities, and prices.

Summerlin Trivia. There is a story in the Summer 1989 *Summerlin Profile* (a promotional newsletter) about the start of a family compound— five family members recently purchased four homes and there is a possibility of a fifth joining the group. It started with Shirley Buzzalini and her husband purchasing a home for themselves and her mother, followed by three aunts each buying a home. Mr. Buzzalini's folks live in Las Vegas and may possibly make the move.

Sun 'N Lake*

This complex is in Sebring, Florida, which has world prominence at least once a year as the site of the twelve-hour Sebring Auto Race. The 7,000-acre planned community is home to more than 3,000 residents. Sebring is in the rolling terrain of central Florida along U.S. 27 about seventy-five miles south of Orlando.

One eighteen-hole golf course has been built and another will be ready in late 1990. There is already a grade school and a Presbyterian church, and negotiations are underway to build a large shopping center. A medical and office park is nearing completion.

The master plan calls for a very small airport, a large recreational area, apartments, patio homes, and residential family estates. A $450,000 home is under construction facing on the golf course. However, most homes are in the $60,000 to $70,000 range. A 170-unit retirement community called Sun Lake Towers has been built.

LARGE MASTER-PLANNED RECREATIONAL COMMUNITIES
■   ■   ■

Cooper Industries* is a developer of very large recreational communities. We will detail two of them.

Bella Vista Village

This community is located in the Ozark Mountains in the extreme northwest corner of Arkansas. The first residents arrived in 1965. The complex is very large, covering 36,000 acres. There are 7,000 full-time residents and a total of 35,000 landowners. Recreational facilities include six eighteen-hole golf courses, one nine-hole course, three clubhouses, five recreational/community centers, a yacht club and marina, a shooting range, and shopping centers.

While on vacation in Cancun, Mexico, we became acquainted with a group of "young in spirit" retirees from Bella Vista. Their endorsement and enthusiasm about Bella Vista and the lifestyle it offers knew no bounds. As far as they were concerned it was, "The way to go!"

Residents are not all in one area but in many communities spread throughout the 36,000 acres. Bentonville is 5 miles south, Fayetteville is 38 miles away, and Tulsa, Oklahoma, is 150 miles to the west. The town center has restaurants, a supermarket, clothing stores, and most of the goods and services needed. Cunningham Corners has similar stores.

School-age children are bused to Bentonville, Gravette, or Pea Ridge. There are thirteen churches on the grounds as well as Concordia at Bella Vista,* a modified life care community. It is beautiful country with four distinct seasons without the extremes of the far North or Deep South.

Hot Springs Village

In the heart of the Diamond Lakes country in the southern part of Arkansas is the very old town of Hot Springs. The forty-seven hot springs bubbling out of the mountainside first drew Indian tribes and later others who wanted to take advantage of the healing waters. The area was declared a national park in 1921 and numerous handsome bathhouses were built on what became known as Bathhouse Row. Magnificent hotels were built, which are now surrounded by motels. The spa business and Oaklawn Park Race Track with three months of horse racing make up the town.

Twenty-two miles northeast is Hot Springs Village, another Cooper complex. Opened in 1970, this 26,000-acre self-contained community has grown to 6,300 full time residents and 28,000 property owners. Although not as spread out as Bella Vista, this community contains four eighteen-hole golf courses, two clubhouses, two recreational and community centers, three swimming pools (one indoors), and many other recreational attractions for all ages. There are seventy-five civic and social clubs. Three shopping centers provide ample stores and restaurants.

Good Samaritan Cedar Lodge,* a modified life care facility, is also on the grounds.

Twelve congregations meet in the village. School-age children are bused to either Jessieville or Fountain Lake. The average annual temperature is 62° F. We have been there in the summer when it was sweltering.

Other Cooper communities are Cherokee Village in Arkansas, Tellico Village* in Tennessee, and Savannah Lakes Village* in South Carolina.

Ms. Nancy Goben, marketing director for Cooper Industries, suggests, "Purchase property today and become a member of a growing recreational retirement community. Come back and vacation, and later relocate to an active retirement lifestyle."

Good advice for some but not for all. Mr. and Mrs. F.W. purchased a lot in Bella Vista as they prepared for retirement. When decision time came they decided against this move because of the remoteness of the community. They ended up in lower California, closer to family.

One couple, Mr. and Mrs. J.C. spent time at Hot Springs Village. They were trying to put together a retirement plan. They said, "It was a very sterile environment living in a contained retirement community—a weird feeling."

Mr. and Mrs. D.C. own a lot in Hot Springs Village. They spend considerable time with friends at the village. As they get closer to retirement they are questioning their plan. They live in a large metropolitan area and are concerned about the remoteness and lack of cultural opportunities. In all probability their lot will be up for sale in the near future.

Conversely, Mr. and Mrs. J.M., the first residents of Tellico Village, moved there after six years of retirement in Florida. The heat and humidity of Florida caused them problems. They wanted to move a little farther north but didn't want the winters they experienced while living in Michigan. South Carolina, a halfway climate, met their needs.

There are no right or wrong answers—only personal choices.

11

SMALL RETIREMENT COMMUNITY

■   ■   ■

LIFESTYLE OPTION #8, PARTIAL RETIREE-DOMINATED LIVING

Thus far we have covered retirement lifestyles that are, to some degree, of a specialized nature: motor home or trailering, either full time as a nomad or part time as a snowbird/Winter Texan; living in a retirement area where most everything is geared to retiree needs; club/resort/vacation communities offering a lifestyle that centers around the club, resort, or vacation area. A leisure-oriented lifestyle; the big self-contained retirement communities and total planned communities, which are quite structured and revolve almost entirely around community-planned activities.

There is still another lifestyle that can be found around the United States—neighborhood complexes. More and more of these communities/complexes are being built, tucked away among other subdivisions. Most are restrictive, usually requiring a minimum age of fifty to fifty-five. Some are referred to as a preretirement/retirement complex.

They don't have medical facilities or a golf course but will usually have a modest swimming pool and a recreation center. Volunteers from the residents' association do the planning and running of community affairs; there is no paid staff. Since they are very small, when compared with the Sun City or Leisure World developments, a person's life will of necessity also involve activities outside of the neighborhood.

They are popular because they fill a very well-defined need. When the kids are gone many people feel they don't need the big house and large yard. Although not retired, they want more freedom time. Finding a small house normally leads to first-home neighborhoods. Naturally, younger people in their first home look forward to moving on to bigger and better homes, so there is a lot of turnover. In addition, there are few common interests.

An adult community, eighteen years of age and up, is similar to the first-home community. The turnover is high and finding neighbors with similar interests may be difficult, especially if your neighbor is a nineteen-year-old contemporary music addict with a high-powered sophisticated sound system.

The preretirement/retirement complex fits the bill for those seeking an escape from closed-off rooms in a large house and a weekly half-day ritual devoted to cutting the lawn. Retirement planning should be so fixed that another move isn't necessary when actual retirement takes place.

Lower California and Florida are the two meccas of the small-neighborhood-type retirement complex.

LAKE PARK SANTA ANA NORTH*
▪ ▪ ▪

Santa Ana, located in Orange County, is a suburb south of Los Angeles. It's adjacent to Anaheim and Disneyland. The complex itself is a long-term, land-lease manufactured housing community of 212 homes with conventional lots and low-maintenance sites. The property is completely walled with a controlled gate. Entry is gained through the use of the second button on each homeowner's garage door opener.

The entryway, found in every complex, is nicely landscaped and expansive. Since the first impression is so important, all entryways are on the lavish side. Here, there is a figure-eight rock-walled lake with two fountains. Beyond the lake is the community pavilion, swimming pool, and patio. The clubhouse has an exercise room, Jaccuzi, bridge room, billiard room, fully furnished kitchen, and a great room that can seat 250 people.

What's it like being retired in this type of complex? We asked this question of Mr. and Mrs. F.W., who had moved to the facility from another state. Their first comment was, "We never realized we could be so busy when we retired." Every Wednesday is card night, every Friday there's a cocktail social where everyone brings a snack. There's a potluck supper once a month, and the last Sunday of each month the men put on a pancake breakfast. In addition, there is bingo, general association meetings, committee meetings, and holiday parties.

Mr. W., an avid do-it-yourselfer and former service manager for a major office forms company, fulfilled a lifelong dream of working in a hardware store. He does this two days a week and plays golf once a week. He also is in charge of the pancake breakfast and the purchasing of food supplies, including liquor, for the clubhouse. Mrs. W. writes the monthly newsletter, which puts her in contact with the various committee chairpersons, arts and crafts, golf, bereavement, socials, etc. She also volunteers at a home for battered children. They see their daughter, son-in-law, and two grandchildren occasionally and explore the mountains and seacoast. All in all they are very happy.

An interesting design feature of the complex is the planting of trees. Each street has the same kind of tree but the trees on one street are different from the trees on other streets.

The houses vary in size from 1,250 to 2,100 square feet. Home sites range from 3,700 to 6,000 square feet. Your home arrives in three sections and the garage in the front of the house is built on site. After the cement work is completed the house can be livable in three weeks. Resales are listed with local real estate firms.

Anyone coming from a large house and lot will have to make an adjustment. It's easy to say "We want a smaller house," but initially it's a shock. A thorough evaluation needs to be made because the house is a compact model and the neighborhood is compressed. Land rental costs are in addition to the building cost and include maintenance of the community. Association activities are on a pay-as-you-go basis.

According to Mrs. W., 98 percent of the residents come from within a radius of fifty miles. The F.W.'s are the only people from outside the state. Many are preretirees and have sold large homes in preparation for retirement. "We're all family here," sums up the feeling of Mr. and Mrs. F.W.

What's it like after the newness has worn off? We did a follow-up. The entryway gate has presented a problem. Guests and others can't get in without a coder. It's been left unlocked and there have been a couple of robberies.

The community remains close-knit. Most residents have learned not to meddle unless asked. When needed, the community responds. There is a "We Care Committee," with each committee member responsible for a page in the community telephone book (about fourteen to a page).

Everyone has his/her share of aches and pains. "We make light of them because we're all in the same boat," says Mrs. F.W.

About ten or fifteen people have moved for various reasons: business transfers, money problems, the loss of a spouse, a desire to move closer to their kids, a move back to the old hometown. No one moved because of a dissatisfaction within the community. When asked, "Would you still recommend this lifestyle?" the reply was, "Love it!"

A definite lifestyle emerges from a complex such as this. Members of the community become part of an extended family. It is not for everyone, of course, but for those in need of substitute family warmth and support it's there. Our mobile society has caused partial deterioration of the traditional close family. This lifestyle can help fill the gap.

SWANSGATE
▪ ▪ ▪

We were surveying South Carolina and while passing through Greenville came across a beautiful entryway. The ironwork on the gate was unique—white swans. We investigated and discovered Swansgate.*

The facility was under construction so there wasn't much there except the well-manicured entryway. Our initial guess was that it was a retirement facility since it was right next to Greenville Memorial Hospital. The location was in the historical district of Greenville.

Greenville is in what's called up-country South Carolina in the northwestern corner of the state. It is not too far from the Cherokee Foothills Scenic Highway and a few minutes off Interstate 85, equidistant between New York City and New Orleans and between Chicago and Miami. It is a good mid-trip stopping place.

The climate is moderate. There are four seasons but extremes are rarely reached in the summer or winter. The population is about 65,000.

We asked to be put on the Swansgate mailing list and soon started receiving promotional material. In the next year and a half we received a large brochure, six follow-up letters, a Christmas card, a postcard, and their first newsletter. The developer is U.S. Retirement Corporation, a subsidiary of U.S. Shelter Corporation.

On a later trip we resurveyed Swansgate. A very nice facility, it is a preretirement community. Entry age is fifty-five and up and the average age is sixty-two. Many residents are still gainfully employed.

There are 135 patio homes and 24 condos in a manor house building, reminiscent of the old days in the Deep South. Most of the area has been utilized. There are only 35 sites available. Patio homes, 2 or 3 bedrooms, start at $125,000 and a 2-bedroom condo is $70,000. Residents pay their own utilities and there is a monthly fee of $140 that covers the upkeep of the common grounds, security, taxes, and exterior maintenance of all the buildings.

There is a club building, including an exercise room and a party room with kitchenette. A pool, tennis courts, and walking trails are also available on the grounds.

An arrangement has been made with the hospital for medical care when needed.

BRISTOL VILLAGE*
■   ■   ■

While browsing through the October 1985 issue of *Atlantic* magazine a one-inch classified ad with a "Retirement Living" heading caught our attention. It read: "Retirement living. Enjoy happiness, security, and contentment. Beautiful Southern Ohio small town flavor. Easy driving to major cities. Independent living, individual homes starting at $19,000 (life lease or rental), modest monthly fee. Generous refund policy. Bristol Village, Waverly, Ohio 45690."

The ad was on a page called "Classified Section." It was tucked away with ads for Cape Cod estate living, an English/Spanish translation service, ancestors researched, a brownie recipe, an authentic Christmas Pudding recipe, a wildlife and cultural expedition, and an Argentine nature tour.

We checked; the population of Waverly was about 5,000. What would a retirement lifestyle be like in a small town in southern Ohio? Our inquiry brought some brochures and an on-site survey gave us the "flavor" of small-town retirement living. We discovered Bristol Village.

Bristol Village is one of the very first large senior housing facilities in the country. Waverly is in the rolling hill country of southeastern Ohio, sixty miles due south of Columbus. It is in the Scioto River Valley.

This county-seat town of Pike County had its first boom during the construction of the Ohio-Erie Canal and was a busy trading center during the canal's heyday. The decline of the canal caused the town to become a typical rural trading center.

The second boom came in 1952. In August of that year, the *Waverly Republican Herald* headline—eight columns wide—read, PIKE COUNTY TO GET ATOMIC PLANT. This once quiet rural town erupted. There would be 4,000 workers requiring 1,000 new homes. In-state and out-of-state real estate developers flooded the town. By late 1955 there were 865 new homes. Included in this building boom was a subdivision of 325 three-bedroom frame houses called Bristol Homes.

The boom deflated and by the spring of 1961 the projected employment of 4,000 had diminished to an actual payroll of 1,800. The Federal Housing Administration took title to a large number of unoccupied homes including 323 Bristol Homes. In 1961 proposals were invited by private persons or institutions for the purchase of the Bristol Homes. By this time the homes were in rough shape—broken windows, overgrown yards, peeling paint.

Bristol Village was born on August 15, 1961. John R. Glenn, senior pastor of the 1,800-member Boulevard Presbyterian Church of Columbus, Ohio, spearheaded the purchase of the homes to be used as retirement residences.

From the beginning residents went "beyond the call" in helping make the village a success. This single-mindedness pervades the village today. In all our travels we have never felt the closeness of residents in any other community as we did during our visit to Bristol Village.

Some residents told us of minor differences but they were always shunted aside with a positive deep feeling about the village and the people.

There is no activity director, yet the activity center is well run. A volunteer is responsible for the center each day. While talking with the volunteer on duty, we felt he had the same concern as a high-priced building superintendent. Resident volunteers man the reception desk, library, drive the van, and handle other services in the village. This spirit lends itself into a friendly neighbor helping neighbor atmosphere.

In the early days Waverly residents were concerned about "all those old people." That feeling now is long gone. BV'ers, as they are known, have become active in such activities as receptionists, file clerks, and pink ladies at the local hospital. There is a continuous supply of BV-made layettes for newborns.

We have closely followed the progress of the village. When we were there Jay Early had just been appointed executive director. He was a former Boy Scout executive in Dallas. The village has expanded its facility and updated its administrative procedures. Much of the village's success has to be attributed to his leadership.

In early 1990 there were 460 residents, 193 couples, 160 single women, and 24 single men. There are residents from 38 states and 14 foreign countries. The age range goes from 49 to 103. Jay Early says, "There is a cross section of America—missionaries, doctors, ministers, and milkmen."

A concentrated effort is made to acquaint prospective new residents with the community. Members of the Proud Residents Program are assigned as hosts. They answer questions, take visitors to neighborhood block meetings, committee meetings, and have them meet other residents.

In the quarterly newsletter a prospective resident said, "Coming to visit alone I wondered what I would do when I was staying at a Welcome Inn. . . . My mind was put at ease when I knew someone was coming to pick me up." She later became a resident.

Financial arrangements are unique and somewhat confusing. There are now 395 single-story homes. You can choose between a home that has been renovated or one that you wish to renovate to your specifications. Standard renovations such as painting, new carpeting, new kitchen and bathroom fixtures, and changing closets are extra. For this you get a life lease. There is an entry fee which varies in cost and is dependent on the size of the house chosen and remodeling required. A monthly fee covers services and the cost of operating the village, and includes extra maintenance of roof, siding, lawn fertilizing, building insurance, gas furnace maintenance, and property taxes. Utilities are paid by each resident.

Three entry payment options are available. The Life Use Plan ranges from $20,000 to $68,450. During the first fifty months of residency if a person leaves for any reason including death a refund minus a one-time 10-percent fee and 2 percent for each month of residency is made. The Capital Recovery Plan ranges from $35,000 to $119,750. At departure, 85 percent of the entry fee is refunded regardless of how long a person has been there. The Monthly Payment Plan requires a $1,000 per person entrance contribution. There is a fixed monthly payment ranging from $302 to $941 per month. (This is in addition to the monthly maintenance and service fee.) Every household pays the monthly maintenance and service fee, which ranges from $292 to $339.

There are some other miscellaneous charges. Medical care is extra and is provided on three levels. The Homemaker/Home Health Care Plan provides services such as bathing, administering medication, light housekeeping, grocery shopping, etc. The Assisted-Living Unit consists of sixty-two apartments. The nursing home is fully licensed, Medicare/ Medicaid approved and has fifty beds.

For many years there was a waiting list. Today there are vacancies. The increase in retirement facilities around the country brings with it the element of competition. Beautiful three-story brick buildings with professionally decorated lounges, library, and dining room in a large campus-type setting offer a great deal of competition.

If a modest well-kept area in a small Ohio town, along with a "spirit" that will be hard to beat, is for you, further investigation of the BV community should be on your calendar.

BV Trivia

John R. Glenn, who spearheaded Bristol Village, was president of National Church Residences.* This organization is an outgrowth of the original group that had a dream of what a ghost town of 323 run-down homes could become. Today NCR's ministry includes 7,000 residents in 75 facilities in 20 states. This best describes NCR: "Since 1961, combining compassion with professionalism in its national housing ministry to seniors."

From small-town country living to living in the big city requires a drastic change in perspective. In order to describe a condo-type complex in Dallas we have had to jolt ourselves back into reality—traffic, people, congestion, and security considerations.

MEADOWSTONE PLACE*

■   ■   ■

In July 1983 and February 1984 we attended two newspaper-advertised meetings billed as seminars on preretirement planning. From these meetings eventually emerged Meadowstone Place.*

We found it very interesting to follow the developers through their marketing and construction process. The meetings were well attended by gray-haired couples. Retirement needs were solicited at the first meeting through a questionnaire of twenty questions. The older speaker was very low key with a slow drawl and a homey attitude. He pointed out the negatives of certain types of retirement facilities. High crime in resort areas. Bankruptcy of some life care facilities. Charges for some health care services that you may never need, and charges for a golf course that you might not use. No mention of the word death, rather he talked about the time when one spouse remains. From this presentation it was easy to foresee what kind of facility they would eventually be marketing.

The second meeting unveiled what needs were discovered, along with a review of the disadvantages of life care, residential hotel, and other types of retirement facilities. The plans for Meadowstone Place and how it came about were explained. A five-step price list showing the advantages of a presale sign-up was distributed along with a priority reservation agreement and deposit receipt.

An interesting aspect of the meeting was the secrecy of the exact location of the facility. The developers said they had an option to purchase an existing apartment complex. A large geographical area was described—Meadowstone Place would be someplace in that area. The priority reservation agreement had an escape clause. You could cancel once you found out the exact location of the complex. Quite a few people went forward at the end of the meeting. We didn't stay around to see how many signed up. We had a couple of cookies and left.

We received many progress brochures and we drove by a few times to watch the renovation of the apartment complex. The two-story hollow square 146-unit facility was spruced up. Elevators and covered walkways were added. A central commons building was constructed. This contained the offices, restaurant, exercise room, and large lounge. There were no medical facilities but each condo had an emergency hook-up to a nearby hospital. TV cameras constantly monitored the two automobile entrances.

Located in a densely populated area of Dallas, the facility layout is crowded. All parking is in the interior of the complex along with two swimming pools. It is not a campus-type layout. All in all it seemed like a nice city-type complex. Purchase price for a one-bedroom condo was $95,000 plus a monthly fee.

We constantly received brochures announcing new residents, activity programs, and an upbeat sales approach. In late 1985 we were sent Vol. 1, No. 3 of *Prime Times* (the facility newsletter and promotion piece). The activity calendar was sparse but indicated some things were taking place. The restaurant menu seemed adequate. However, there was one announcement that caused us some concern. It read: *"LEASE PRO-GRAM NOW AVAILABLE:* In response to recent requests Meadow-stone Place now has a limited number of condominium-homes available on a lease basis. This program offers an acceptable alternative to the person who may not wish to purchase. It must be emphasized, however, that very few condominium-homes are available in this program. Meadowstone Place is first and foremost an 'owned-home' community. So act now if you are interested in the lease program."

A red flag! This had to indicate trouble. We didn't receive any more brochures nor did we see ads in the paper. Our on-site meeting with the manager in late 1986 was interesting but sad. Ownership of the complex had changed twice and Chapter 11 bankruptcy proceedings were now in process!

The reason for the demise seemed plausible. Dallas had experienced a severe economic slowdown in the last couple of years. Many seniors had signed up for a condo on a contingency basis. The problem was that they couldn't sell their home.

Activities within the complex were drastically curtailed. The original brochure featured "Smile it's just like home." Needless to say, that bro-chure is no longer valid. We could not help but reflect on the original development meeting. We recalled that the speaker had highlighted problems that many life care places had experienced which eventually caused their bankruptcy.

A resurvey in early 1990 indicates that the facility is still operating. Thirteen units are owned by the original residents. The remaining one hundred and twenty-six units are rentals. There are seven vacancies.

Noon meals are served on Tuesday, Wednesday, and Thursday, at a cost of $5.25 each. A lifeline emergency call system is available at an additional cost. Scheduled transportation for shopping, doctor appointments, and banking is still available. Movies are shown in the lounge each Saturday at 7 P.M.

Quite a change from the activities that were originally planned. Fortunately those who bought years ago continue to have a place to live.

PROVIDENCE POINT*
■ ■ ■

While surveying the Pacific Northwest we were house guests of a couple whom we include among our very dear friends. Like us, their kids are on their own. He is a retired executive and life is good.

After hours of reminiscing they mentioned their interest in selling their big house. They had looked at a couple of retirement communities. One was a high-rise life care community which turned them off—all the canes and walkers.

They had heard of Providence Point and said they were going to check it out. Ironically this community was on our survey list so we decided to go out there the next morning. What developed was a tremendous opportunity for us to participate in the actual process of evaluation and emotional trauma of a possible move to a new way of life in a retirement community.

That evening our host did the cooking and as we sat around the country kitchen we philosophized about their next move. Would it be the last? Was it throwing in the towel? What would it be like in a community of older people? How many common interests would they have with these people? Our conversation led into aging's aches and pains and into a tone of finality. So we moved on to a more practical discussion. What would they do with all their furniture? A long list of knick-knacks they couldn't part with developed. We all strove to take a positive approach as we joked about things but inwardly many of the deep thoughts remained.

Providence Point is located in a country setting near the town of Issaquah, pronounced Is-a-qua, and is about fifteen miles from downtown Seattle. There was a guard at the gate and a long winding road that traversed the sloping terrain of the 180 wooded acres.

Center Village is a large three-story semi-Victorian-type structure with a glass captain's walk at the top. This is referred to as "downtown." It is the activity center with offices, meeting rooms, exercise room, etc. Nearby is a pool, putting green, and tennis courts. The LaPointe restaurant serves breakfast, lunch, and afternoon tea each day.

We heard a very well-presented "pitch" about the Point, a condominium community for people age sixty-two and above. Each condo is in a single-floor building in a cluster of three or four units. There are five villages: Forest, Hilltop, Center, and Meadow are finished, and Garden is still under development.

A two-bedroom, two-bath model—the Versailles—was chosen. It had 1,476-square feet of living space, a 445-square-foot garage, and a 445-square-foot courtyard and patio/deck. An end unit overlooking the forest looked good.

It was exciting to visualize furniture placement, and a small addition to the family room. In fact we became enthusiastic about the possibilities, although we weren't the buyers. It was fun. This unit would run about $200,000 with all the changes and additional amenities. Much smaller units would be close to $90,000. As it was a condominium community there would be a monthly fee.

We left our friends and spent some time with the president of the developing company. He told us an interesting history of the property. The Sisters of Providence had owned the land, intending to build a convent and a residence for the elderly. This changed and the land was sold to the Lutheran Bible Institute. They developed part of the land into their campus and searched for a company that would build a retirement community.

Thirty developers applied and Swanson-Dean was chosen. This company donated part of the land to the Sisters of St. Joseph of Peace, who built a $6 million health care facility. (This is not a part of the community but is accessible.) They are trying to find a long-term care insurance policy that could be offered to the residents on a group basis.

When we rejoined our friends they were still in the throes of trying to determine furniture placement. We could see the problem of losing cherished pieces of furniture. Some of the enthusiasm for moving to a smaller house was waning.

That night we again went over the pros and cons of the move. Our friends decided to go back and meet some of the residents to try and determine if they had common interests and to learn more about the activities offered in the village. They eventually signed up. We wished there was a community of this nature in a semi-rural area of Dallas. We were very impressed. All in all a great experience!

HEARTMEADOW*
■ ■ ■

A small village of sixteen cottages built on church grounds in West Hartford, Connecticut. Mr. R.S., a leader in the church, is enthusiastic about the possibilities of this type of retirement village. He maintains that throughout the country there are multitudes of churches that are situated on large beautiful grounds and contends that these unused spaces could be used as a church community outreach program—a small retirement village.

This seems to make a great deal of sense. Most likely many people in a congregation would find this cottage-type living to their satisfaction. They would also have continual contact with their church friends but not be dependent on them. Church membership would not be required.

Each cottage has two bedrooms, is freestanding, and faces the church green. Residents make a contribution to the church, are charged a monthly maintenance fee, and are guaranteed life occupancy so long as they can care for themselves.

A fellowship among the residents of the sixteen cottages would evolve to include members of the congregation. The end result would be a strong mutual support system. This could be very comforting during times of distress.

Instead of talking outreach, this congregation practices what it preaches.

CHANGE
■ ■ ■

Fred's aunt Doris and his uncle Jay retired and moved to a small town on the eastern coast of Florida in the late 1960s. They purchased a modest two-bedroom, two-bath home with a large Florida room. The small neighborhood community was developing and soon filled with retirees from the North. There was a residents' association that looked after neighborhood affairs and a small meeting facility. There was no activity director, perimeter fencing, automatic gate, pool, or golf courses, just a nice little neighborhood full of Yankee Floridians!

They all enjoyed the sun and the orange tree in their backyard. Getting to know all the neighbors was easy. The meeting house served as a common ground. Potluck dinners, shuffleboard, the ceramic kiln, which Aunt Doris used extensively, drew the neighborhood together. Everyone had much in common. These were truly their golden years.

More roads appeared and new houses were built. These new neighborhoods were on their own. They weren't a part of this nice compact neighborhood. To meet their needs other activity centers were built.

We visited them many times. At first the meeting place was a beehive of activity. At many of the homes three-wheel bikes vied for space with the family car under the small carport. Then the life cycle started taking its toll. Attendance at the meeting center decreased. Small groups of widows banded together. They used the meeting place but it was a lot more quiet. Aunt Doris became a member of the widows' group.

When we visited, Aunt Doris would take us to the meeting house. The center was okay but it was starting to show its age. We met some of the newcomers to the area—folks who had bought homes from those who moved to nursing homes or were forced to the shelter of their kids' homes. But it wasn't the same—it was very quiet.

The newcomers tended to cling together. Naturally so since there was a generation gap. Some of the original neighborhood gang were approaching eighty. They had sold their three-wheel bikes or hung them from the roof of the carport. The numbers at the meeting house became minimal.

Aunt Doris needed involvement. Despite her share of medical problems she was not one to settle cozily into her chair and constantly watch TV. The involvement she lost at the meeting house, she found in her church. Their Super Sixties program has satisfied her. She also goes to a nursing home once a week and leads the group in an old-fashioned sing-a-long. Undoubtedly, many of the people she helps are younger than she is. Over the years she has continued to be active in preserving the natural beauty of the seashore. She has a tremendous outlook on life and is a joy to be with.

Nothing remains stable. There is always change. Sometimes rapid, sometimes a slow progression. The change in Aunt Doris's community evolved slowly. It went from the high activity of a band of recent retirees to a constantly decreasing involvement as a result of the aging process. This is inevitable. All of us would wish it were different. Aging is a change agent and brings with it new requirements. Different needs have to be met. From the slower walk, to the occasional helping hand, to the assisting arm, and then the care and comfort of nearby help.

Chapter 15 explores in greater detail this Phase Two of retirement.

12

PAU HANA
IN HAWAII

Pau means finished. Hana means work.

■   ■   ■

LIFESTYLE OPTION #9, HAWAIIAN LIVING

To an island! The relaxed life. The slow Hawaiian pace and the friendliness of Hawaiian people. No more wool dresses, white shirts, coats and ties, just muumuus, aloha shirts, and cutoffs.

But which island? Full-time retirement living or snowbirding? Big-city living, Honolulu, population 830,600 (1987 estimated)? Small-town living, Kapaa, Kauai (population 5,000+)? Koolau (windward) or Kona (leeward) side of the island? Sea level warmth (and humidity) or the coolness of the mountains? Country-club living on Maui? A ranchette near Parker Ranch in the mountains of the Big Island? Resort-area living along the Kona Coast of the Big Island? On any island a single-family residence or condo with: A makai view (toward the sea)? A mauka view (toward the mountains)? Facing on a swimming pool? Facing on a golf course? Looking onto a bay with a boat dock at your front door? Or a downtown condo near Waikiki Beach in Honolulu? A quiet residential area?

Still another choice throughout the islands is whether to purchase the land and building—i.e., real estate for which the owner has the power over the title, referred to as a fee simple purchase—or choose a leasehold contract in which the real estate is held under a contract for a specified term. A leasehold arrangement is cheaper than a fee. The vast majority of properties are leasehold. The seller makes this decision.

There are choices, choices, choices! Over the years we have made

many trips to the islands. Most of our time has been spent on Oahu—
both in Honolulu and the far northern tip of the island—Kauai, and the
Big Island of Hawaii.

Fred had a consulting client in Honolulu. This company built large
condominiums and other commercial properties. The president of this
construction company advised us to bypass Maui. He did a lot of building on Maui. He referred to it as the jet-setters island and costs skyrocketed accordingly. We have been to Maui a few times but have not
concentrated on that island as much as we have on Oahu, Kauai, and the
Big Island.

What would retirement be like in Hawaii?

Authors John and Bobbye McDermott, in their book *Our Hawaii*
(Orafa Publishing Co. 1985), describe "the aloha spirit" as "one which
expresses love."

We have found that there are two aloha spirits. There is the aloha
spirit as perceived by the tourist, and then the true aloha spirit known by
those who live the spirit.

As seen by the tourist Hawaii is the land of the hula show, leis, luaus,
an all-you-can-drink sunset dinner cruise aboard a catamaran, and
Waikiki, renowned playground of the Pacific. There's a tremendous
amount of promotional material—each with a coupon for a good deal—a
free aloha coffee mug at the Muumuu Fashion House, a free frosty
passion fruit float at a plantation store, or one free dish of sweet and sour
spareribs at a Mandarin restaurant.

Tourism is the largest business in Hawaii. The image makers have
done a superb job fostering "a trip to savor the tropics—with a little
imagination one flirts with the stuff of legends, ocean voyages to the rest
of Polynesia, and veritable escape from the twentieth century."

This is not to say it's bad. The islands would have troubled times
without tourists. But retirement living is full time. Once the touristy
things are done they become old hat. One hotel luau is enough, one
commercial hula show is enough!

What is the true aloha spirit that is known to those who live in Hawaii
and make it such a wonderful place?

Authors John and Bobbye McDermott further describe the spirit as—
aloha—we care—you express aloha when you give because you want to
give.

Although not residents of Hawaii, we have experienced this true aloha spirit. We attended Sunday services at the Kahuku United Methodist Church at the far northern tip of Oahu. Early in the service we were recognized as visitors—we were the only ones—and a little Hawaiian girl put a shell lei around our necks and gave us a hug. When the Hawaiian minister prayed he went to the foot of the large rugged wooden cross, looked up, and "talked with God." Just prior to the close of the services he bid aloha to a Caucasian couple who had been attending for the past few months. The lady replied with glowing terms of endearment about their love for these parishioners, how they had openly accepted them and how much she and her husband would miss their friendship and love. All this while unabashed tears streamed down her face. As the service closed we arose, formed a circle, joined hands, sang the closing hymn, and received the benediction. At the door we shook hands with the minister, and he invited us to his home for lunch!

A large stalk of bananas appeared one morning tied to the railing of the building in which we had our rental condominium. A full-time retired resident told us that the previous week a plant had been left at her doorstep, and this week a bag of fresh fruit greeted her when she opened the door.

We listened to an excited gardener tell a lady that he just heard that Mrs. C. had returned. He said he would for sure bring her some fruit. That's the Hawaiian loving, caring, sharing.

But it's a two-way street. We have been told this emphatically. The full-time resident who received the plant and the fruit told us that she has many Hawaiian friends that she dearly loves; she does her part. She is learning to play the ukulele and will soon start classes to learn the Hawaiian language.

On Kauai we spent a great deal of time with Mrs. Elsa Holtwick, Executive Director, Kauai Senior Centers, Inc. This is a private, non-profit, Kauai United Way Agency. Mrs. Holtwick, the widow of a design engineer for a major sugar company, started this agency over fifteen years ago.

She emphasized that the newcomer from the mainland has to earn acceptance. When you move in next door you are a competitor. She warned that the newcomers should not expect the razzle-dazzle that the tourist gets at the hotels and tourist restaurants. She likened the acceptance of the *haole* (foreigner) moving into a neighborhood to a black moving into a WASP neighborhood twenty-five years ago. The *haole* faces the problem of acceptance just as blacks did. You have to earn acceptance. The old adage—your actions speak so loud I can't hear what you say—certainly applies.

Of course, any move to a new environment requires a great deal of adjustment. Whether it's on the mainland or in Hawaii, you have to do your part. But a move to Hawaii is a move to a different culture and ethnic customs.

Those born in the twenties and thirties, the Depression generation, have undoubtedly accepted racial differences. However, this "older generation" has been generally conservative in its racial views. Few of this generation have been active demonstrators fighting for civil rights for the oppressed. We passively accepted these changes. Most have come to know minorities from a business standpoint, but not from a social standpoint.

We have driven through neighborhoods on every island looking at the names on mailboxes. We saw relatively few stereotyped American names such as Smith or Jones, etc. Most names we saw we couldn't even pronounce. This graphically illustrates who would be the minority—the *haole!*

With a couple of exceptions if you have trouble accepting on equal level the different races, you should probably not consider a move to the islands. You can't look down on people and earn acceptance. It's just not possible.

However, in a big city such as Honolulu you could probably find enough people of your own persuasion and thinking to affiliate with and not have to associate with the locals. This would probably be a rather shallow existence.

On all the islands there are developments that are primarily second homes to people from the mainland and other countries. Even in these complexes we have found many names we couldn't pronounce. There will probably be enough people to form a small select closed group. The turnover within the group would be high since these would be second or vacation homes. This could also be a very shallow existence.

The complete acceptance of racial differences—the Hawaiians—the Japanese—the Chinese—the Filipinos—and others of Asian backgrounds—is a very sensitive subject. Including this subject in this chapter might be unsavory to some. However, we felt it important enough to highlight since it will have a major impact on your having a great retirement in Hawaii.

There's still the "big choice"—what are you going to do with your time? Island living can offer some new opportunities as well as restrict some activities.

AN OVERVIEW OF THE STATE OF HAWAII
∎ ∎ ∎

It was on August 21, 1959, that Hawaii officially became the fiftieth state. We purchased *Ronck's Almanac* (compiled and edited by Ronn Ronck, University of Hawaii Press, 1984) while in Hawaii. The first edition was published by the University of Hawaii Press in 1984 to commemorate the silver anniversary of statehood. We used this almanac as our statistical authority for the rest of this chapter.

The state of Hawaii is big! It is a chain of 132 islands, reefs, and shoals stretching 1,523 miles. There are eight major islands. In order of size they are Hawaii, Maui, Oahu, Kauai, Molokai, Lanai, Niihau, and Kahoolawe. These islands make up 99.9 percent of the total land area of 6,425 square miles.

The state of Hawaii is not the smallest of the United States. It is larger than Rhode Island, Connecticut, and Delaware. The Big Island, Hawaii, is three times the size of the smallest state, Rhode Island.

The 1980 census reported a resident population of 964,691 persons. The estimated population as of July 1, 1987, was 1,083,000, which rated Hawaii thirty-ninth in the United States in terms of size.

OAHU
∎ ∎ ∎

The hub of the state of Hawaii is the capital city, Honolulu. Retirement here would have all the opportunities that any big city offers. The Waikiki Beach area with its 33,000 hotel rooms is a mecca for tourists. The hustle and bustle of a stroll down Kalakaua Avenue is exciting but retirement in the Waikiki area could be exhausting.

We did locate a retirement complex about four blocks from Waikiki Beach. Nestled right in the middle of hotels, condominiums, shops, and restaurants is Laniolu Good Samaritan Center.* A twelve-story retirement residence with available nursing care. This center is a part of the Evangelical Lutheran Good Samaritan Society. Their brochure highlights "the heart of Waikiki . . . which provides opportunities for activity in the mainstream of life." It certainly offers mainstream activities.

This same organization has another facility on the other side of the island in Kanoehe. This is a large high-rise surrounded by cottages and is called Pohai Nani Good Samaritan Kauhale.*

We located a third retirement residence, Arcadia,* in a nice quiet area of Honolulu far away from Waikiki. This is a three-wing, high-rise, life care facility owned and operated by Central Union Church, United Church of Christ.

These three residences and the lifestyle associated with life care and continuing care residences will be covered in later chapters. We will include these as a part of Phase Two of retirement.

The climate is undoubtedly a major incentive to retire in Hawaii. At the Honolulu International Airport—a ground-level elevation of seven feet—the average temperature for the coolest month is 72.3° F. and the average temperature for the warmest month is 80.7° F. Honolulu rainfall averages twenty-four inches a year but in the interior of Oahu there is a rain forest. The average water temperature at Waikiki Beach in March is morning 75° F., afternoon 77° F, and in August is—morning 77° F. and afternoon 82° F.

There is much to do on Oahu. Aloha Week is a statewide festival in September. This is a week of pageantry showcasing the islands history and culture. There is the Honolulu Academy of Arts, Bishop Museum, the Honolulu Symphony, and a short opera season. Touring shows from the mainland come through Honolulu along with rock stars, ballet troops, and country music greats. There are twenty-two libraries on Oahu.

We have toured the University of Hawaii Manoa Campus and talked with faculty of the business school. The continuing education curriculum offers opportunity for additional study.

There is an abundance of parks, and they are used by everyone. Kapiolani Park is renowned for kite flying. We watched a record twelve-kite flight, controlled by one person!

Arts and crafts shows abound. At Aloha Stadium on Saturday and Sunday the flea market is always crowded.

There are clubs galore. All the service clubs are represented. There is a long list of fraternal organizations. All religions are represented, along with a number of "new religions" which combine Christian and Buddhist elements.

For sports fans there is the Hula Bowl, Aloha Bowl, and Pro Bowl, as well as the Hawaiian Golf Open at Waialae Country Club.

The Rainbows of the University of Hawaii have a large following.

Unfortunately there are also crowded highways. H-1 is the freeway thru Honolulu. During rush hour it becomes a parking lot. No different from any other big city.

What about living costs? Housing is the way it is on the mainland. You can check the papers, or talk to real estate people and there will be listings from low to exorbitant. The choice of a home or condo is yours and will be dictated by what you can afford. Needless to say, the lower the price the smaller the square footage. Price is also indicative of location and view.

We hesitate to quote housing figures because choosing a place is such an individualized decision.

Honolulu and closely adjacent areas are the most expensive. Smaller towns away from the big city offer the possibility of lesser cost. But it's all a matter of personal choice. What are you willing to accept concerning size and location?

An absolute minimum required would be $100,000, which would be a leasehold arrangement and would not buy very much—$150,000 to $250,000 will get you into the range of a decent size.

Of the total population of the state of Hawaii 80 percent live on Oahu.

KAUAI
■ ■ ■

The airport at Lihue on the island of Kauai, our favorite island, is 102 miles west of Honolulu International Airport. Kauai is a place where you could retire and really go Hawaiian. It's the least developed of the major islands but still has enough civilization to make it interesting. No crowded highways, or layer upon layer of tourists: there is still enough of "old Hawaii" left to offer you that true aloha feeling—if you want it.

Kauai was the first island in the Hawaiian island chain to form volcanically. It has a land area of 549.4 miles. The 1980 population was 39,082, of which 153 were military personnel. The largest town is Kapaa with a resident population of 4,467. A few miles south of Kapaa is Lihue, with 4,000 residents, the commercial center and the administrative seat of Kauai County.

The racial makeup of the island's population is: white, 11,147; Filipino, 10,237; Japanese, 9,775; Hawaiian, 5,704; Chinese, 520; and other, 1,699.

The highest point on the island, at 5,243 feet, is Mount Kawaikini. Nearby is Mount Waialeale, the wettest spot of all the islands, averaging 451 inches of rainfall a year. In 1982, hurricane Iwa hit Kauai with recorded winds of 117 mph and the rainfall on Mount Waialeale was 665.2 inches. Some say this is the wettest place in the world. The average rainfall at Lihue Airport is 44.18 inches and it has sunshine 56 percent of the time. The average temperature of the coolest month is 71.2° F. and 79.1° F. for the warmest month.

We found a retirement community, Sun Village,* a leasehold condominium complex of three four-story buildings, an activity center, and a swimming pool. It is located in Lihue, adjacent to the Wilcox Memorial Hospital.

Earlier in this chapter we made reference to Mrs. Elsa Holtwick's feelings about the cultural adjustments that are necessary in a move to Hawaii. The senior centers that she developed are most interesting. There are nine on the island with a part-time coordinator at each facility —a total of 220 members. We visited the Kapaa center and found a group of active seniors. There were few *haoles* participating that day. Quite a contrast to the AARP meeting that we attended at Kailua along the Kona Coast of the Big Island. That meeting was made up completely of foreigners.

Each year Mrs. Holtwick produces an extravaganza. A brochure with many pictures shows that there are a great number of *haoles* who participate. Part of the program reads:

Take me out to the ballgame . . . six softball teams.
Nippon Ichi Odori . . . Lihue Japanese dance class.
Lazy River . . . Kaumakani soft shoe dancers.
Oasioas . . . Kekaha Filipino dancers.
My sweet sweetie . . . eastside dancers.

There were eighteen events listed on the program as well as arts and crafts exhibits and homemade food.

Kauai has some turmoil. A First Hawaiian Bank report to the Kauai Chamber of Commerce envisioned 72,000 permanent residents and 21,000 visitors a day by the year 2005. A bank first vice president said, "If the people really desire growth the restraints of the past need to be adjusted to reflect that objective."

We sympathize with Mrs. Holtwick. She readily admits to a high resistance to change. In fact, she and others have marched on city hall!

There was evidence of lack of money for town purposes. We drove 75 percent of the improved streets on the island. The number of abandoned cars along these streets was startling! These, along with piles of refuse, didn't add to the beauty of the island.

Housing costs are high but probably slightly less than Honolulu. Princeville, about thirty miles north of Lihue, is a resort community with homes along the golf course and an area of condominiums. This is a beautiful development but would have a high percentage of vacation or second homes in the area.

In the many small towns housing can be found for less than $100,000 —no ocean view or looking onto a golf course.

The outer island prices are higher than Oahu because of the transshipment from Honolulu. We have been told that you make up for these costs by purchasing bread, rolls, etc., made on the island and by eating a lot of fruits and vegetables grown on the island.

Another asset is knowing where to buy. There is an underground group of stores that provides discounts for those with Hawaiian drivers licenses. Residents are also quick to point out that there are no heating costs and clothing expenditures are drastically reduced.

However, tire and shoe costs are high. Roads are paved with ground-up lava mixed with cement or black top. It cuts down on the skidding but chews up tires and shoe leather.

There is a medical center available on the island. We noticed that some specialists visit the various islands once a month. They place ads in the paper announcing their visits. However, a trip to Honolulu would be required for complicated medical services. Many airfares of this nature could become very costly.

There is some outstanding scenery. Waimea Canyon is a rift eroded to 1 mile wide, 10 miles long, and up to 4,000 feet deep—the Grand Canyon of the Pacific! The Na Pali Coast is world-renowned but requires a backpacking hike, helicopter, or boat excursion. After a while these beauty spots would lose some of their luster.

The big question looms. What would you do with your time? The size of the island and relatively slow development could cause restrictions on some retirement activities.

This would be a haven for a creative person who wanted to do some serious writing, sculpting, wood carving, or painting. The solitude would be fantastic. Gardening would produce some beautiful results as well as some great produce for the table.

Fishing is good but golf would be restricted as there are only four courses.

Anyone interested in helping people could find much to do. It might be through an existing agency, a church, or the development of a program as a result of an obvious need.

The slower pace, the international community opportunities, the possibility of much solitude if desired, and the true aloha spirit are available for a selected few who fit the profile—a profile that requires a 70-percent giving on the part of the *haole*.

HAWAII
■   ■   ■

We call it the island of extremes. At 4,034.2 square miles, it consists of almost two thirds of Hawaii's total land area, with extremes such as: Hilo, with an average rainfall of 133.52 inches, and Kailua-Kona, directly across the island (87 road miles), which averages 25.22 inches of rain. In between is Mauna Kea volcano (elevation 13,796 feet), with skiing available during some months. Nearby is Mauna Loa (13,677 feet) and Kilauea (4,093 feet). Both are active volcanoes that periodically add to the land mass. To the north at Waimea (2,670 elevation) is Parker Ranch, largest individually owned ranch in the United States. To the south is Ka Lae, the southernmost point in the United States. Along the coast are white sand and black sand beaches. All of this is located south and east of Honolulu Airport, 169 miles from the Kailua-Kona Airport, and 216 miles from Hilo Airport.

There was a total population of 92,053 in 1980.

Hilo

The capital, largest town, and commercial center had a population of 35,269 in 1980. It is definitely not a resort city. The main attraction along the downtown beach is the stark remains of a burned-out hotel.

There are beautiful gardens. Liliuokalini Park is fantastic. There are nice beaches and Hilo has an "old-time Hawaiian" flavor. But Hilo is wet! It's on the windward side—130+ inches of rain a year. Residents call it liquid sunshine. There is beautiful vegetation. The philodendron we grow in pots at home grow wild and appear to be trees! Naturally so —the soil is nutritious and they receive plenty of water. Why is Hilo so wet? Trade winds blow wet ocean air up the mountains where it cools and forms rain—sometimes in enormous quantities. That's why there are such beautiful waterfalls throughout the islands.

Land prices in Hilo are the lowest on the island. A land site 50 × 100 feet, with plenty of vegetation, can be bought for $15,000 to $20,000. Electricity is available, but no sewers or water. Every home has an arrangement where roof water drains into a very large cistern. A reasonably sized home could be put on one of these lots at a cost of probably $75,000, total cost around $90,000 to $100,000. But you'd better like rain!

The Kona Coast

A stretch of coastline about sixty miles long along Mauna Loa's western slopes is known as the Kona Coast; it is also referred to as the Gold Coast. The main town is Kailua village with a 1980 population of 4,751. This village is also referred to as Kona, so to clarify things most signs read Kailua-Kona.

It's here, along this coastline, that things are buzzing. Major growth is taking place. Fortunately the county of Hawaii is doing some planning and hopefully there will not be a hodgepodge of building.

Cattle Country

To the north and south is cattle country. Miles and miles of beautiful pasture land.

The town of Waimea is north. It reminded us of a company town since everything, buildings, malls, etc., seemed to have a Parker Ranch brand. A great place if your interests tend toward horses and cattle.

Once past the volcanoes, all the way to the southernmost tip of the United States, is great cattle country. There are 340 ranches on the island. While journeying to South Point we came upon a fairly large cattle drive.

RETIREMENT ON THE BIG ISLAND?
■ ■ ■

As usual that "question" comes up again. What would you do on the island of Hawaii? There is more diversity on this island than on Kauai. There are many activities. A few that we found include: The Kona Business and Professional Women's Club; AARP; Citizens Against Toxic Spray (CATS); West Hawaii Organists; senior citizens meetings; Kona Round Dancers; Senior citizens fitness classes; Hamakua Lions Club; Kona Shrine Club; South Kona Aloha Lions and Lionesses; International Order of the Rainbow for Girls; Sunset Promenaders Square Dance Club; Mauka Rotary Club; Barbershop Harmony Singers of West Hawaii; Girl Scout Council of the Pacific; Post 20 American Legion; Kona Elks Lodge; Waimea Exchange Club; Lea Lea Women's Golf Club; Kealakekua Toastmasters Club; Coast Guard Auxiliary; Big Brothers/Big Sisters; Kona Singles 35 Plus; Hilo Lioness Club; and the Hawaiian Scottish Association. This list could very easily be three times as long if we wanted to include everything we came across. There is much to do on the island of Hawaii.

REVERSE RETIREMENT—HAWAII TO THE MAINLAND
■ ■ ■

After thirty years of living near Honolulu why would you return to the mainland for your retirement? "Economic reasons," said Mr. and Mrs. R.D. very emphatically. When Mr. D. retired from a high-level position with the Department of Defense, they felt they had to leave the island. "Housing costs went up 25 percent in 1989 and the traffic continues to get worse" were their further comments. They wanted a warm climate and felt Florida was a "nothing area" so they chose Oaks North in

Rancho Bernardo, California. Even though California housing is high it is much lower than Hawaii.

We asked our son Larry, who lives in Aiea (near Pearl Harbor), about the 25 percent housing increase in one year. He agreed but felt that applied to the nicer residential areas. He also agreed with the comments about traffic. After twenty years on the island he will be moving to Wisconsin.

COMPARATIVE FOOD COSTS—JANUARY 1990

	Honolulu Area	Dallas
Nabisco Unsalted Crackers, 16 ounces	$ 2.05	$ 1.69
Campbell's Tomato Soup, 10 ounces	.63	.41
Growwheat Honey Wheat Berry Bread	1.99	1.69
Chicken, whole, per pound	1.19	.69
Salt, 1 pound, 10 ounces	.69	.39
Taster's Choice Decaf Coffee, 10 ounces	10.99	5.19
Rice, 20 pounds	3.99	1.19 (3 pounds)

Big-city living in Hawaii is expensive!

WOULD PAU HANA IN HAWAII BE RIGHT FOR YOU?

■   ■   ■

We have showcased three islands—Oahu, Kauai, and Hawaii—each different in what it has to offer. Maui would be somewhat like Hawaii. Much smaller but more developed. Molokai with only 263.7 square miles of land and a 1980 population of 6,049 is quite small, but probably the next island to undergo growth. The other three major islands would not be practical for retirement for most people.

Island fever has been brought to our attention by many people. A yearly trip to the mainland is the prescription that most people say cures this fever. It's brought about by a variety of causes: the confines of being surrounded by water and the need to reacquaint one's psyche with the old days, the old hometown, cherished old friends, and of course family, with a heavy emphasis on the grandchildren.

Everyone doesn't come down with the fever. The owner of a gift shop who came to Hawaii fourteen years ago doesn't miss the mainland. The last trip back was to his daughter's wedding. He was there for the wedding day and came back the next day. His wife who runs a boutique goes back three or four times a year. She expands buying trips to visit family and friends throughout the mainland.

A yearly trip or two to the mainland increases the cost of island retirement.

Once again, it is necessary to emphasize the cultural differences on the island. One Hawaiian word best expresses Hawaii: *Kipona:* Mixed, mingled; varying in color or texture, as of the sea, to add to, as something of a different character, as ferns to a lei (Pukui and Elbert, *Hawaiian Dictionary,* University Press of Hawaii).

In Honolulu at the very large and modern Ala Moana shopping center you might think you were in the Far East. On a Sunday morning in the multilayered parking area, we had to line up and wait for a parking place. The parking lot was very large, but the crowds were tremendous.

Extremes were evident throughout the mall. Sunday brunch at Liberty House was American correct and proper. Lyn's Deli was crowded by all races lined up to buy kosher corned beef sandwich and a beer.

Throughout the mall are multilayered ponds with huge goldfish lazily looking for a handout. Squatting on their haunches, using the pond rocks as a table, many of oriental descent were eating their rice and fish with chopsticks.

If you have a problem accepting cultural differences on a daily basis, staying on the mainland may be your best bet.

One other consideration, unfortunately on the negative side, is that wherever there are tourists there is more crime. It's a fact of life and Hawaii is no exception. The full-time resident doesn't have to be in the heart of tourist land but there will be occasions when it is necessary. There are constant reminders to be on your guard, but a word to the wise should be sufficient.

There are some other things that are a bit bothersome but can be handled. It seemed strange to watch the Dallas Cowboys play football at 7 A.M. on a Sunday morning! When there is a delayed sports broadcast, "Monday Night Football," for example, the six o'clock sportscasters have an interesting approach to announcing the score. Since the game has been played but will not be shown until after their broadcast, they announce, "It's close your eyes time." If you don't want to know who won the game that you will watch a little later you close your eyes and they put the scores on the screen but don't announce the score. It makes watching the game a lot more interesting! The mainland papers arrive a day late.

On the other hand there are ocean views. On the Kona Coast the supermarket parking lot had a view. We sat at a table overlooking the Pacific as we ate our McDonald's Egg McMuffin and in Oahu our Wendy's coffee and blueberry muffins were eaten as we overlooked a beautiful bay. Undoubtedly we were in the very first stages of island fever! At local-type restaurants, rice is served with *everything*.

If you are considering a move to a different location, and Hawaii is a possibility, spend twice as much time evaluating Hawaii as any other location. Maybe three times as much time. By all means an extended stay should be spent on the island of your choice before a decision to move is made.

It's terribly expensive to move things to Hawaii. Many treasured items will have to be left behind. They can't be replaced if you change your mind. Practice your retirement before making a big move of this nature.

If, after careful consideration, it's a go, you may well have before you the happiest days of your life. The true aloha spirit can give you that inner peace that so many people search for and never find. Another Hawaiian interpretation of Pau Hana is: a time to play, drink together. *Aloha!*

13

FOREIGN
RETIREMENT

∎ ∎ ∎

LIFESTYLE OPTION #10, FOREIGN LIVING

Retirement at the Buccaneer Hotel, the largest resort on the island of St. Croix—not bad! That's what George H. Baxel engineered for himself when he took early retirement from the presidency of Union County Technical Institute in Scotch Plains, New Jersey.

"Engineering a Dream Retirement" is the title of an article in the June–July 1983 issue of *Modern Maturity*. When Baxel decided to leave academia he wrote many letters to hotels and resorts suggesting he be a consultant in residence. He offered two or three days a week of his services managing departments such as personnel, training, plant engineering, and maintenance, in return for lodging, meals, and recreational privileges. He had four offers and chose the 140-room Buccaneer rather than larger hotels on the islands of Puerto Rico and St. John.

This is certainly an excellent example of preretirement planning, ingenuity, and creative thinking.

The Virgin Islands cannot be considered foreign; however, moving there represents a major cultural change that requires a great deal of adjustment in personal lifestyle.

Retirement in a foreign land has to be for the very adventuresome. Self-confidence, adaptability, a low boiling point, and a high degree of flexibility are other attributes required. These are necessary for both husband and wife, a 100-percent agreement on this lifestyle choice is an absolute must.

We have not had experience in international living. Our travels have taken us abroad and Fred has had corporate international experience.

Traveling abroad and living abroad represent vastly different situations. We pointed this out in the preceeding chapter on Hawaii.

Those who have lived overseas will know what to expect and adjustment to a new lifestyle will be easier. From here on we'll assume that the reader has not had an international career or experienced international living.

KEY RECOMMENDATION
■ ■ ■

From our research we have found that there is one recommendation that overrides all others. If you're considering a foreign retirement, *try it out before making the big move.* A "touristy" trip is not considered a tryout. An actual three to six months' living experience in an apartment or home among the inhabitants of the country is a must. This doesn't mean an apartment in a fancy hotel, it means living in the manner required when actual retirement takes place.

This all sounds very logical. The problem is that it's easy to get excited about a place as a result of a vacation, make a decision, and move a few months later. Practice this retirement lifestyle before making a full commitment.

Where? Look at a world atlas and take your pick. Needless to say, it's not that easy. Certain areas will probably rule themselves out. The Iron and Bamboo Curtain countries automatically are basically off limits. The Middle East, the emerging Third World nations, and certain countries in Latin America represent high-risk areas.

Your personal desires as far as climate and distance from home will be a prime consideration. Entry and residence requirements, as well as local law and taxes imposed on goods you bring into the country, will have a major impact on your choice. Stability of the country's currency in relation to the U.S. dollar and the stability of its government must be taken into account.

Availability of good medical services on both an everyday routine basis and a critical emergency basis will be of paramount importance, as are adequate sanitary services, usable water supply, general food availability, transportation, police/fire protection, houses of worship, cultural activities, and the list could go on and on.

Probably the biggest decision has to do with how far you want to vary from your present lifestyle. Living in a small interior village in Mexico and not being fluent in Spanish will be a problem. Whereas a flat in London could be handled quite easily, once you learned to drive on the left-hand side of the road.

A major study and evaluation are required. Just determining places to consider could consume a great deal of time. However, if you have the urge to really expand your horizons, making this type of study could be fun as well as a challenge.

GATHERING INFORMATION
■   ■   ■

We will assume that you want to live abroad and that you have determined certain basic requirements. What do you do next? The monthly newsletter *International Living** (published by Agora) is a treasure trove of information for anyone investigating retirement abroad. Of particular interest is their January 1990 issue, which contains a four-page Quality of Life Index. This is a summary of the world at the end of 1989. It is a collection and verification of thousands of statistics. Seven categories are analyzed:

Cost of Living—A comfortable lifestyle with most of the amenities Western societies consider necessities.
Economy—Gross national product per capita and growth rate.
Freedom—Political and civil rights.
Political Stability—The chances of political upheaval.
Health—The nation's health and health care.
Infrastructure—Communications and transportation.
Culture and Entertainment—Literacy, number of museums, newspapers, cinemas, recreational facilities, etc.

In descending order, the top ten nations are the United States, Canada, West Germany, Australia, Switzerland, Iceland, Italy, Luxembourg, Netherlands, and New Zealand. In descending order, the ten most affordable nations are Venezuela, Ecuador, Paraguay, Egypt, Mexico, Hungary, Costa Rica, Chile, Nigeria, and the Philippines. Iceland is the most healthy nation. Canada is the most cultured. Switzerland has the strongest economy but the cost of living is unreasonably high.

This issue also has a synopsis about retiring in British Columbia. It is interesting to note that Canadian houses are smaller and closer together than in U.S. cities but prices to buy or rent are double those in South Carolina or Florida. Clothing, food, and gasoline are more expensive than in the United States.

A catalogue of back issues at $3.50 each has a section on retirement. Some of the titles are "Guadalajara—A Low-Cost International Retirement Option"; "Beware of Pickpockets in Spain"; "Easy Retirement in the Caribbean"; "Retirement Community Building Boom in Europe"; "But What Happened to Costa Rica?" and "Retirement Havens—An Expert Chooses."

Locate a major bookstore in your town, a large full-service store. You will find guide books that cover most countries around the world. Very likely you will find helpful books for the countries that meet your initial requirements. These will be vacation- or tour-oriented but can also be useful in giving you an overview of the country.

For example, we found that *AA Illustrated Guide to Britain,* published by Drive Publications, Ltd., contained a tremendous amount of excellent material about Britain. This 543-page book, with good illustrations, maps, local lore, and helpful hints, would be a good basic reference book if Britain is on your initial list.

Another book that we have found to be very helpful is *Super Traveler,* by Saul Miller (Holt, Rinehart, Winston 1980). This contains a wealth of information on all subjects relating to foreign travel. Helpful hints are given for entry into many different countries. For example, did you know that there is a hair-length requirement for males entering Singapore? Front hair must not extend over the eyebrows, side hair not over the ears, and back hair not below the shirt collar.

Additional material on any country can be found in your local library. Some of this material tends to become out of date but will provide good historical background. The periodical section will have articles that are up to date.

There are many other good publications/books that will help:

■ U.S. Department of State*—Publication #9402: *Tips for Americans Residing Abroad;* Publication #8970: *Travel Tips for Senior Citizens*

■ U.S. Department of Health and Human Services*: *Your Social Security Checks While Outside the U.S.*

■ U.S. Department of the Treasury*—Publication #54: *Tax Guide for U.S. Citizens and Resident Aliens Abroad*

■ *Travel and Retirement Edens Abroad* (1988 paperback) by Peter A. Dickinson (AARP/Scott, Foresman)

■ *The World's Top Retirement Havens* (1989 paperback) by Marian V. Cooper (Agora)

Trying out a country by arranging an international home exchange is an excellent way to "practice" retirement. Organizations that can help in making an exchange are:

■ International Home Exchange Service*

■ Home Exchange International*

■ Hideaways International*

■ Worldwide Exchange*

■ Global Home Exchange and Travel Service*

Now comes the time for ingenuity. Anything and everything you can find out about your country of interest will be helpful. Many inquiries will produce little or no results but all are worth the try. You can't tell where you might really find a bonanza of information. Some places to check for information or leads on the country of your choice include: the nearest consulate; the nearest tourist bureau; The U.S. Departments of Commerce, Transportation, and State; your local travel agent; the International Studies Department of your local university; the International Department of a company with a subsidiary in the country; airlines that fly to your country of interest; your local bank, if it has a correspondent relationship with a bank in one of the countries you have chosen; country representative at a trade center, a moving company that handles overseas moves; and the information officer at a nearby military base. One inquiry can lead to another. This networking technique can prove very valuable.

There is another way to explore offshore retirement possibilities. Lifestyle Explorations* conducts tours for retirees to Uruguay/Argentina, Costa Rica, and Algarve/Costa del Luz (southern Portugal and Spain near the Strait of Gibraltar). A husband and wife team, Joe and Jane Parker, came up with this unique travel service. The cost, in 1990, of a thirteen-day tour of Costa Rica was $1,520, which included departure from Miami, double occupancy, and five dinners and lunches. The fifteen-day tour of Uruguay/Argentina was $2,390, and included the same benefits as the trip to Costa Rica. The fifteen-day tour of southern Portugal/Spain was $2,645 and included departure from New York, double occupancy, thirteen American breakfasts, and five dinners and lunches.

EUROPE
■ ■ ■

The February 1989 issue of *New Choices for the Best Years,** a magazine for those over fifty, has a five-page retirement article entitled, "Is Europe Worth the Big Price?" The article leads off with, "Take it from Americans who have been living in Europe: The bloom is off the rose."

A New York attorney then living in Rome—said, "Fat City is dead." Throughout Europe the American dollar has fallen, the cost of living has soared, tax benefits have narrowed, and real estate prices have gone through the ceiling. Not a very positive picture of retirement in Europe.

If there is interest in Europe, check the Appendix for the embassy address for the United Kingdom,* Ireland,* Spain,* Portugal,* France,* West Germany,* Italy,* Yugoslavia,* and Greece.*

Spain

We talked with Jane Parker concerning the dropping of the Costa del Sol, Spain, from the company's tours. She said, "Costa del Sol has become so expensive that it is prohibitive for the average retiree. It is terribly crowded. You might have a good view when you purchase a condo and then a sixteen-story high-rise goes up in front of you. Many Americans are moving out." She told us that if an area doesn't meet their company's standards she and her husband can't recommend the location.

Mr. and Mrs. J.R. went to the Costa del Sol area and came back very disgusted. They said "High-rise condos come right down to the water— there is very little beach—a minimal lunch costs $40, a pat of butter was itemized on the bill!" They heard horror stories about thieves breaking into car trunks and, at stoplights, smashing windows and taking whatever is on a person's lap.

MEXICO
■　　■　　■

There's no problem obtaining information about Mexico. Travel agencies and bookstores abound with material. Newspapers, radio, and TV keep everyone informed of the poverty, corruption, and economic chaos of the country. We have been to Mexico but only as tourists. You can't miss the primitive living conditions that the masses call home.

What would it be like to retire in Mexico? Our information search uncovered a book entitled *Choose Mexico—Retire on $400 a Month*, by John Howells and Don Merwin (Gateway Books, 1985). Will it be living in a geriatric ghetto (a retirement community) or starting a totally new life with new friends and experiences in Mexico? The authors are not talking about the tourist's Mexico; they refer to the Mexico that thousands of American retirees have discovered. A furnished two-bedroom apartment in Acapulco with a view of the ocean for $200 a month. Or a five-course dinner in Mexico City for $2.00, or a filet mignon and Caesar salad dinner in Guadalajara for $4.50.

The authors made a survey of hundreds of American retirees in Mexico, asking them about how they lived. Most reported that their food costs were around $150 a month. This included frequent dining in restaurants. In addition, hard-working household help is readily available, maids and gardeners wages are less than 60 cents an hour. The medium cost of house rental reported by those surveyed was $250 a month.

Adequate medical assistance is available, although some respondents said they would go to Mexico City or to the United States for an extremely serious illness. Incidentally, Medicare is not applicable outside of the U.S.A. Most prescriptions and over-the-counter drugs cost less than 20 percent of the U.S. price.

The nearly unanimous answer to the question, "What do you like most about Mexico?" was "the people." They are friendly. Although there is poverty, there is not misery. The people are happy and enjoy life. Related to this friendliness is the helpfulness of the people. They are almost always willing to stop what they are doing and help a stranger. They are steeped in politeness and love for their children, hence their children are well behaved.

All is not peaches and cream. When renting a home be sure it has a phone. It takes a year to have one installed. Patience is needed, it may be twenty minutes before a waiter takes your order. When the postage for an air mail letter to the United States went up to twenty pesos it was months before stamps in that denomination were available. Unpredictable shortages plague Mexico for months at a time. One has to ignore the constant spitting in the streets. It takes a while to become comfortable with "tipping" minor public officials. An occasional cultural fix in the form of a trip back home is strongly recommended.

The authors include chapters on Mexican law, covering each of the different regions, Mexican markets, and getting around in Mexico. They feel the country and the government are stable. It's a 185-page fun book to read and would be very helpful to anyone considering becoming an expatriate in Mexico.

We came across another interesting explanation of retirement in Mexico in the form of a one-hour video tape. We ordered the tape from Harold J. Fiedler, Box 9924, Spokane, Washington 99209. It's not cheap —$49.50—but it was helpful in understanding what it would be like to retire in Mexico.

It's a home video portrayal of the Fiedlers' life in Vista del Lago on the shores of Lake Chapala, the largest lake in Mexico. Their home is forty kilometers from Guadalajara. They make a couple of shopping trips a week to this large city.

There are about 2,000 Americans in their area. The various developments have been designed for Americans and built by Americans. After purchasing a home they contend that you can live for $500 a month. A tour through their home, room by room, was very impressive. It was a multilevel large house that cost around $60,000. Their house taxes for 1986—$12 American. They employ a caretaker and maid.

The video opened with scenes of their snow-covered home up north, and then switched to their Mexican home, highlighting a 72° F. average year-round temperature.

Since they live in a predominantly American community language is no barrier. They feel very safe in this country. In the smaller towns violent crime is rare and is treated very harshly by the authorities.

Mr. and Mrs. D.B. borrowed our film and became interested in Mexican retirement. In 1989 they drove to the Lake Chapala area and spent considerable time surveying the town of Ajijic. They discussed some pros and cons and gave us their general impressions.

The climate is excellent and the aura of romantic Mexico prevails. The atmosphere is pleasant and comfortable, inside the wall. They were concerned about the presence of black-shirted security guards with automatic weapons and their Doberman Pinschers, constantly patrolling the perimeter. Everything is walled with broken glass embedded in the top. This creates an ever-present awareness of two extremely diverse societies. Those cloistered within the walls and the very evident poverty outside the wall. Those within the wall are suspicious of those outside the wall.

This naturally drives those within the wall to constant interaction, shutting off those outside. Sensitive people would have to develop a calloused view of those outside the wall otherwise they would not be able to tolerate the environment. Those within the wall could very easily develop tunnel vision. Mr. B. mentioned that the constant party theme portrayed in the video tape would not satisfy someone's need for a meaningful purpose.

Mr. and Mrs. D.B. acknowledged that those they talked to were happy and liked the lifestyle. They were living very well with servants, gardeners, big houses, and club memberships on very modest incomes but it was not the kind of lifestyle that would give them real satisfaction.

Lifestyle Explorations also cancelled their tours to Mexico. We asked Jane Parker about this. She said, "Lake Chapala is drying up and polluted and the air pollution in Guadalajara during the winter when there is no rain or wind is worse than Los Angeles. . . . Since 1980 there has been no appreciation in homes so we recommend people rent not buy. We don't consider the government to be stable."

Another view of Mexico and Latin America is portrayed in an article entitled "Latin Crisis" which appeared in the June 12, 1986, issue of *The Wall Street Journal* provides a lot of food for thought for those considering a retirement anywhere in Latin America. In Mexico, because of economic crisis, what once was the middle class is rapidly moving toward poverty. Those who were once the poorer class now live hand to mouth. This article cites increasing hard times throughout Latin America. Bolivia, Chile, Venezuela, and Costa Rica had two to four times as many jobless in 1985 as they did in 1970. It is estimated there are 40 million unemployed in Latin America.

The article quoted Lourdes Arizpe, a Mexico City anthropologist. Referring to Mexican unemployed, he said, "If there's anything that's explosive and dangerous it's these 4 million people. They have left the land. They have no hope of education, training, promotion. They have nothing to lose."

There is undoubtedly much to consider when contemplating a retirement anywhere in Latin America.

COSTA RICA
■   ■   ■

An article in our local paper touted the advantages of living in Costa Rica; 30,000 Americans now live there, of which 6,000 are *pensionados* (retirees). Costa Rica is located between Nicaragua to the north and Panama to the south.

The attractions of Costa Rica are a high standard of living at a relatively low cost, a climate that requires neither heating nor air conditioning, with an average temperature of 72° F.

The locals look upon *gringos* as their friendly brothers to the north. Costa Rica abolished its army in 1948. Teachers outnumber police officers and the literacy rate is 90 percent. It is considered Central America's most stable democracy. Legitimate elections are held every four years and voter turnout is more than 90 percent. The San José metropolitan area hosts numerous theaters, art galleries, three Spanish dailies, and one English-language weekly newspaper. A good life, including live-in maids, gardeners, and a three-bedroom house with a pool, can be had at a fraction of the cost in the States.

Sounded good, so we wrote the Costa Rica Tourist Board in Miami, Florida.* We received an abundance of material. Included was a brochure containing information on *pensionado* or *rentista* status. Some of the rules and conditions that must be met in order to retire in Costa Rica are a monthly income of $600 U.S. with yearly proof of this income; a valid passport, birth certificate, marriage certificate, and a police report from the city of residence for the last six months; you are not permitted to be employed earning a salary by a Costa Rican company;

you will obey the laws of Costa Rica; you will reside in Costa Rica for a minimum of four months each year; your identity card must be renewed every two years; you must inform the Pensionada Department of any change of residence, telephone number, or post office box; on a one-time basis and for your own use only, you can import unlimited household goods duty free. You can import only one freezer, refrigerator, stove, microwave oven, washer and dryer; you can import or purchase one automobile of a value of $16,000 U.S. Taxes on this are 15 percent. If the value exceeds $16,000 U.S. you will be charged all taxes. If you sell the car within five years to a Costa Rican you must pay all taxes. This doesn't apply if you sell to another *pensionado*. There are many subconditions to each of the above. This brief of the rules will give you some insight into what is involved.

We sent away for the book *The Costa Rica Traveler*, by Ellen Searby (Windham Bay Press, 1985), which proved to be very interesting. The author lives in Alaska and has worked on the Alaska state ferries since 1975. She has traveled in thirty-eight countries. A real adventurer.

Her book is 208 pages and contains a wealth of information about getting around in Costa Rica. In each town she visited she lists accommodations from the very inexpensive to deluxe, and gives her impressions of the locality. All told she evaluated 160 hotels throughout the country, priced from $0.75 to $150.00 per night. Her description of living in Costa Rica is compatible with the other material we read. She said, "Meeting the Costa Rican is as much a privilege as traveling in the beauty of their country."

There are thousands of North Americans who have retired in Costa Rica. Some are having a wonderful time enjoying the friendly people, climate, low cost of living, and a new way of life. However, as in any locality, all retirees aren't living life to the fullest. The author commented on a retired aerospace engineer who used his slightly impaired hearing as an excuse not to learn Spanish. He spends his days in his apartment watching TV. She commented, "He hasn't thought to walk over to the university and volunteer to teach a physics or engineering course in English to keep his brain cells alive."

Ellen Searby sums up this type of retirement accurately: "I think retiring here, or perhaps anywhere, is like the fenceposts you'll see along the road. . . . If a dead log is set, it soon rots in the tropics. . . . Costa Ricans plant live poro tree trunks with the bark left on. . . . They grow into trees that work as fenceposts for a lifetime. . . . You keep living and growing or rot." There is much truth to her observation.

She interviewed Edwin Salas, the head of the Pensionada Department, who had some good advice for those contemplating retirement in Costa Rica: "When you're deciding to retire here, think about your attitude toward foreigners at home and then toward Costa Ricans. You'll find the villagers kind and generous as long as we don't feel rejected. . . . Costa Ricans are very sensitive."

We enjoyed reading this book. It contains a great deal of "inside" information that would be invaluable to anyone going to Costa Rica.

We were intrigued with the material we received about Costa Rica. Why not a two-week stay in this country? Eastern Airlines has a direct flight out of Miami and the cost is not prohibitive. There is a Costa Rican Counsular Office in Dallas and Fort Worth. These would be very helpful in opening doors for us to get acquainted with retirees. Our schedule could be adjusted to free up two weeks.

We started becoming excited. We studied the map to determine what towns we wanted to visit. At first the large frontier with Nicaragua didn't bother us. But the big push for millions for the Contra forces in Nicaragua caused us to look a little closer at the border.

We attended a meeting where two refugees from Nicaragua described their terrible ordeal. The worldwide boulevard of terrorism is constantly brought to mind by the media. Watching a hijacking and the taking of hostages unfold on TV gave us heartburn as we contemplated the trip. We also pondered the fact that Costa Rica gave up its army in 1948.

As you have probably guessed, we chickened out!

Jane Parker told us that Costa Rica is booming again. All the hotels are full.

During her last tour to Costa Rica two Canadians were part of the group. A Canadian TV station sent along a crew to chronicle the tour and especially the Canadians' involvement. The story was shown in Canada and she has received numerous inquiries from Canadians wanting to know when the next tour is scheduled.

She feels a retirement community in Costa Rica would do very well and has made inquiries, but finding investment capital for a foreign venture is a complicated process. She still has hopes.

EXCHANGE RATE
▪ ▪ ▪

The most volatile aspect of foreign retirement is the value of the dollar. An individual has no control over this. A sharp decline in the dollar is automatically reflected in the amount of money available to buy the necessities of life. If you have purchased a residence, you are at the mercy of the exchange rate. If the rate is negative, selling your house would result in a loss. This is international in scope and applies to any foreign currency.

CANADIAN RETIREMENT
IN THE UNITED STATES
▪ ▪ ▪

Their concerns were brought to our attention as we talked to many Canadians in the United States. They constantly monitor the value of the Canadian dollar in relation to the American dollar. Every "swing" affects their standard of living. We were told this is why there are very few Canadians as full-time retirees in the States.

We surveyed thirty retirement communities and where figures were available only 2 or 3 percent in a community were Canadians. For example, Bristol Village in Waverly, Ohio (Chapter 11), a community of 395 homes, has two Canadian couples.

Canadian snowbirds tell us it is not a major concern to them since they can go back if the rate becomes prohibitive. They adjust their snowbird time schedule on the basis of the strength of the Canadian dollar.

Phase One of retirement in a foreign country could be interesting, exciting, challenging, and probably at some times frustrating. A desire to see and experience another country could be satisfied by offshore retirement.

Without a doubt it's not for everyone. For those with a pent-up desire to see and do something different during their freedom years, foreign retirement could be the answer to their dreams.

As Phase Two of retirement approaches, the time when aging takes its toll, a move back to the homeland would seem to make a great deal of sense. A logical move would be to a retirement community with health care facilities.

Adventuresome singles would have a rare opportunity to establish a residence and then use it as a base point for seeing that part of the world. Married folks have the same opportunity but both parties must be 100 percent in accord on this lifestyle.

If you have always had a dream to see faraway places, then foreign retirement is the opportunity of a lifetime—go for it!

14

SPECIAL INTERESTS

■ ■ ■

LIFESTYLE OPTION #11, OPTIMUM
FULFILLMENT

We chose a very strong title for this lifestyle. A title that will probably raise some questions. Such as, Can human beings ever achieve optimum fulfillment? How? When? This gets into some deep underlying human needs. Too deep for us to explore. But since each person is unique and retirement brings freedom time, maybe the optimum fulfillment can be found.

The following lifestyles may come close. Perhaps one of these will lead you to your optimum dream.

COLLEGIATE

■ ■ ■

Visualize a retirement community on or adjacent to a college campus that gives you the opportunity for intellectual stimulation through auditing college courses and being a part of student discussions; to work toward a first degree or advanced degree; to be a part of special courses designed for adults and in some cases just for retirees; to attend very easily debates, lectures by outstanding speakers, university symphony/choral presentations, student dramas, and special interest groups addressing current issues such as the environment, economic and political conditions, as well as the entire spectrum of international affairs; to become a supporter and follower of the football and basketball teams or other sports activities; if you were a graduate of the college, to become active in alumni activities at the grass roots level; if in your collegiate days you belonged to a sorority or fraternity and there is a chapter on campus, to become active in alumni activities; and, if you want to establish closer ties with students and faculty, there is an opportunity to become involved.

Being in proximity to a campus, in many cases within walking distance, enables the spirit of the students to become contagious. We experienced this during the week we spent at an Elderhostel program at Clemson University. Being with students in the cafeteria, meeting many of them as part of the Elderhostel program, shopping in the stores full of Clemson insignia merchandise, and talking/listening during informal chats, has to add zest to life. On a sustained basis, years may well be added. If you have always had a yearning to be a part of an academic environment, this type of lifestyle may be the answer to that long subdued need for academic involvement.

We have found ten communities of this nature. They present a vehicle for involvement but academic associations are not automatic just because you live in an adjacent retirement community.

There is a parallel here to the integration into the "true Hawaiian spirit" that we discussed in Chapter 12. You have to earn your way into an academic environment.

An "I used to be" or "I know how it really is" or "Let me tell you" approach will shut the door to involvement. Using finesse, as in a bridge game, is required. Finding your way must be done very slowly and carefully.

College Harbor*

This is a continuing care retirement community on the campus of Eckerd College* (enrollment, 1,325) in St. Petersburg, Florida. (See Chapter 18 for a detailed description of continuing care/life care communities.)

There are two adult education programs: a degree curriculum called Program for Experienced Learners (PEL), and the Academy of Senior Professionals at Eckerd College (ASPEC)—a group of 216 retirees and spouses who attend classes, council students, and form study groups.

We surveyed this unique campus environment in mid-1989 and again in early 1990. Innovative has to be the best word to describe this complex.

The location is excellent. The 281-acre campus is on the shoreline of Boca Ciega Bay. This is at the southern extreme of St. Petersburg, adjacent to the Pinellas Bayway (Fifty-fourth Street) leading to St. Petersburg Beach.

The retirement community is a 5-story, 140-apartment building fronting on the bay. A new apartment wing will be built. A 60-bed Medicare-approved nursing facility and a 25-suite assisted-living floor are located in an attached Health Pavilion.

There is a redeemable bond program which provides 22 days per calendar year, up to a lifetime maximum of 360 days of in-patient care. The bond varies from $45,000 for an alcove apartment to $174,000 for a 3-bedroom apartment. There is an additional monthly service fee varying from $660 to $1,575. A second person pays an additional $325 per month. A yearly lease program that does not include health coverage is also available. Florida has a law that protects residents of continuing care facilities.

Included in the above costs are one meal a day, weekly maid and linen service, utilities, local transportation, and amenities such as lounges, heated pool/whirlpool, lecture room, library, exercise room, and services of an activity director.

Our first visit was during a water restriction imposed due to an extreme drought. The campus showed the lack of water during the summer. On our second trip we saw an improvement. Campus buildings are Florida style. No more than two stories, not crowded, light and airy.

The ASPEC has its own building and is run as a separate entity, but is an integral part of the college. The center is on the shore of the bay and includes staff offices, a common room, conference area, meeting rooms, exhibition areas, study rooms, dining and snack facilities. The ASPEC program has had a lot of national publicity and representatives from many retirement communities have visited to learn more about it.

Mr. W.W., a retired chief executive, resident, and a member of the ASPEC, spoke in glowing terms of his involvement. In fact he urged Fred to "come on down and join us."

The opportunity presented itself to spend some time with a lady who has been a resident for one year. We were chatting in a small lounge area near the entrance. Three times Fred went to the door to assist residents with cane, walker, or in a wheelchair. Our newfound friend said, "That is something you have to get used to" (indicating the elderly disabled). She said, "When I first arrived I became very depressed because of that."

This delicate subject needs to be surfaced. The young old or still very active old will have a daily reminder of what's to come as they participate in community activities. Each person has to find his or her way of living with this reminder.

Louise Hullman, a resident and our guide, told us as we walked around that the noted author James A. Michener would soon be joining the community. She glowed with pride as she gave us this news.

Meadowood*

It is difficult to differentiate the boundaries of the town of Bloomington, Indiana, from those of the University of Indiana with its enrollment of 25,000. Suffice to say, this is a university community.

Located near a university facility is the retirement community of Meadowood, for those sixty and older. There is an assisted-living and skilled nursing facility on a pay-as-you-use basis. This is a beautifully landscaped community of ninety-two garden homes and ninety-two mid-rise apartments, a community building, and a health center set on thirty rolling acres, bordered by heavy woodlands. All of the roads are named after trees—Sassafras, Juniper, Linden, etc.

Apartments or garden units vary in size and monthly rental is from $600 to $1,000 a month for a single. The cost for a second person averages about $350 per month. This includes one meal a day, monthly housekeeping, planned activities, van transportation within the complex, and scheduled transportation for shopping, doctor appointments, etc.

Because of the size of the university there are numerous events every month. Here is one month's schedule. In the auditorium the stage version of *Singing in the Rain*, Scotland travel film, the IU Ballet Theater Spring Show, and the "Bandorama" put on by the combined symphonic, concert, and university bands. In the Sports Arena men's and women's track meet, and ten basketball games. Other productions on campus include the presentation of *Orfeo* and the flapper-era production, *The Boy Friend*.

In addition, there are dozens of intellectual opportunities in the various schools that make up the university. All of this available in "your own backyard."

Henton at Elon*

Exactly opposite from the large campus of the University of Indiana, is the charm of the small campus of Elon College. It is located in Elon, North Carolina, which is twenty minutes from Greenville and mid-state, halfway between the mountains and the Atlantic Ocean.

We were captivated by the campus and town. This liberal arts college of 3,300 students, affiliated with the Church of Christ, has been built making extensive use of classic columned buildings. In 1989 it celebrated its one-hundredth anniversary.

Brick walls and wrought-iron fences follow the red brick walkways as they wind through the tall oaks. The name of the college—Elon—is a Hebrew word meaning "oak."

We were impressed with the weekly Thursday morning ritual. Around the Fonville Fountain and Scott Plaza tables are set up and the entire college community meets for coffee and informal conversation.

Their cultural calendar includes Collegiate Gospel Music Festival, Songs and Stories of the Dust Bowl, Drama-Triple A Plowed Under, a recital, spring concert, Festival of the Arts, and many more activities.

There is a football and basketball team. They don't compete in the Big Ten but have won many championships.

Mr. John C. Ketcham of College Communities started Henton at Elon with the express purpose of ". . . an alternative to the traditional retirement community which focuses on recreational facility and empha-sizes play . . . we want our people to participate in sports and maintain their hobbies but we want to put before them the opportunity to partici-pate in the life of a college . . . we really want to interweave people."

Within a short walk of the campus is the community of thirty acres that will eventually have 100 homes. The initial grouping of homes has them facing into a commons with a large brick patio which serves as a gathering place for the neighbors.

There is an age restriction of forty-five and up. The homeowners asso-ciation reviews architectural plans with a right to veto. Homes range in size from 1,000 to 2,000 square feet and cost from $90,000 to $150,000. There are wooded lots available since the community is still in a develop-ing stage. We feel it's an excellent idea in a great location.

College Walk*

The name of this retirement community identifies its closeness to Brevard Junior College. Located in the southwestern tip of North Carolina is the town of Brevard. Its population was 5,323 according to the 1980 census. This small mountain town is in the heart of the Blue Ridge Mountains at 2,230 feet.

The walk to the college is over a bridge and enters the rear of the 140-acre campus. The college has an active continuing education curriculum. Currently it offers 100 courses annually with an enrollment of 1,500 participants. According to Ms. Jacolyn Campbell, Assistant Director of Continuing Education, most of these are retirees.

At College Walk there are two living choices—apartments or cluster homes. There is also a personal care unit. Apartments are leased and require an entrance fee varying from $13,000 to $23,000, plus a monthly fee from $675 to $950 for one person. Add $350 for a second person.

Cluster homes are purchased, starting at $105,000 and a monthly fee of about $400 per couple. All residents receive one meal daily, bi-weekly housekeeping in the apartments, a flat linen service, and use of the social and recreational areas.

The gateway to Pisgah National Forest is nearby. Bordering the forest is Great Smoky Mountains National Park. This is hikers', skiers', and explorers' country. It's beautiful country but you better like mountain driving!

Clemson Downs*

This modified continuing care community is located on thirty-seven acres in the northwestern corner of South Carolina, adjacent to the Clemson University campus. The setting is beautiful and if you want a university town of 8,000 that is truly fanatical about the sports program, this would be the place for you. The football stadium holds ten times the number of residents in the town. Every game is sold out years in advance.

Austin Manor*

On the campus of Ohio Wesleyan University in Delaware, Ohio, a university residential hall has been remodeled into sixty-two apartments with lounges and meeting areas. This is truly an intergenerational living and learning environment. Retirees, university alumni, faculty, and honor students are welcome. The National Church Residences manages Austin Hall.

Providence Point

This community in Issaquah, Washington, was included in Chapter 11. Adjacent to this 180-resident community is the Lutheran Bible Institute and Marianwood, a total health service including skilled nursing.

Communiversity is the title of the education program for residents at Providence Point. A Program Planning Board is comprised of homeowners from Providence Point and staff from Marianwood, Providence Point, and the Lutheran Bible Institute. This board assists in the development, evaluation, and carrying out of classes and programs.

The communiversity concept will continue. When the property was sold by the Lutheran Bible Insitute a condition of the sale was a $10 a month homeowners' fee, which provides the funding for the nonprofit corporation.

The courses offered are small, wide ranging, and informal. The emphasis is on learning, growth, and social interaction. There are no tests or grades. A small fee is charged. Course titles include: Health and Physical Fitness, History, Current Events, Creative Writing, Literature, Geography, Art, Recreation, Bridge, and Religion. Most classes are held on the Lutheran Bible Institute campus.

The Village*

In Indianaola, Iowa, twenty-two miles south of Des Moines, ground was broken in November 1989 for the thirty-five-acre Village Retirement Community. This will be the fourth facility sponsored by the Wesley Retirement Services (WRS)* of Des Moines. WRS is related "in faith and love" to the Iowa Conference of the United Methodist Church.

The Village will be a modified continuing care facility and will have a close association with Simpson College, which is a few blocks from the

Village. Enrollment at the liberal arts college is 1,700. The vice president of Development and College Relations, Dennis D. Hunt, said, "We eagerly await the completion of the Village so we can present opportunities for Village residents to stay educationally active." He was featured in an article in *The Voice,* the Village newsletter, entitled, "The Village + Simpson College = A Perfect Match."

Also in *The Voice,* a 1925 Simpson graduate, George Woolson, said, "Consummation of the Village cannot come too soon for me . . . I am doing well in my apartment living but there is still something I lack—the assurance of health care in the next few years."

The Colonnades*

At the University of Virginia (UVA) in Charlottesville, the Alumni Association, University Real Estate Foundation, and the Health Services Foundation set out to develop a life care retirement community that was superior in every way.

To accomplish this they solicited proposals from developers. Fifteen were received and the Marriott Corporation was chosen to build the Colonnades; 5,000 Charlottesville residents were surveyed as to senior needs and wants. Plans were developed and a fifty-seven-acre site on UVA property west of the city was chosen for the 180 apartments, 40 cottages, nursing home, and recreation area. In mid-1989 there was a *900-person waiting list.* The opening is slated for late 1991.

In the July 21, 1989, issue of *The Wall Street Journal* there was an announcement that Marriott will build 150 retirement sites at a cost of $1 billion in the next five years. Coupling together the life care concept, the sponsorship of three university foundations, an on-campus location, and the Marriott Corporation has ensured initial success. We would speculate that it will be a lasting success.

The August 1988 *Mature Outlook* Newsletter devoted a page to "Retirees Head for College Housing." The article included mention of officials at Cedar Crest College in Allentown, Pennsylvania, who visited Eckerd College to obtain information about its program. They want to add a retirement residence to complement their five-year-old Learning in Retirement Program.

At the University of Michigan in Ann Arbor there is an alumni program that offers a lecture series, travel program, and social events. They have no on-campus housing for seniors but according to the director of Alumni Enrichment Programs developers have built four or five apartments and condominium buildings near the campus that are marketed to the alumni returning to campus.

A lifetime of learning—an appropriate way to end this section.

RELIGIOUS
▪ ▪ ▪

Everyone has a conviction about religion. It may be "I don't believe." Others who believe have varying degrees of belief. Those with deep convictions about their faith and a need to search continuously for greater understanding have a unique opportunity in retirement. Entering the priesthood, joining a convent, or studying for ordination will give satisfaction to those who have heard God's calling.

But there are still many, with a lesser degree of persuasion, who would like a religiously oriented community—a facility where the surroundings are compatible with their personal sentiments.

Alexian Village* of Tennessee

Since 1938 the Alexian Brothers have been providing health care high atop Signal Mountain in Chattanooga, Tennessee. The order was born in 1334 in Aachen, Germany, and took its name from St. Alexius, a Roman nobleman who gave up his wealth to work with the sick several hundred years before.

Today, world headquarters, the monastery, and 302 retirees 62 years of age and older live in the 235-unit life care retirement community. A 124-bed health care center is also a part of the community. The entry fee ensures health care privileges for life.

The monthly service fee covers twice-monthly housekeeping, flat linen service, and the main meal of your choice in the Evergreen Room.

There are the usual activities found in a retirement complex but here there is an addition—daily mass at St. Augustine Chapel.

An article in the *Chattanooga News-Free Press* featuring the fiftieth-year anniversary went to great lengths to point out that the order is well rounded. For example, Brother Cajeton Gavranish is activities coordinator, teaches tennis at Notre Dame High School, and plays in a jazz quartet. On the first Wednesday of the month the sweet tones of his saxophone can be heard at J.P.'s. That's the night on which the Catholic Social Services receive a cut of the gate.

Mr. R. Kilgore, marketing director, wrote us that among the present residents is a former head of the White House Press Corps, a Criminal Court judge, nurses, professors, and retired senior military officers.

Alexian Village is a way of life with good neighbors, good friends, and good times. There is an added ingredient not present in many retirement communities: the opportunity for peace and tranquility that is found only in very special surroundings. Perhaps Alexian Village would be that special place for you.

Martins Run

"The only Jewish-oriented life care community in the United States" —so says Joan Sterrett, Director of Marketing and Public Relations at Martins Run. One other distinction is that it has been accredited by the Continuing Care Accreditation Commission.

It is located fourteen miles from downtown Philadelphia on twenty-two acres adjacent to the Paxton Hollow Golf Course. There are 198 garden apartments and a 60-bed medical center. Browsing through press releases and local newspaper articles was enlightening. For example, Mr. L.S., a resident, is doing research for a paper he must submit in order to keep his membership in the Retired Executives and Professionals organization. His subject is " 'Quirks'—the What and Why of Human Eccentricities."

Mr. and Mrs. S.P., ages seventy-six and seventy-eight maintain a busy exciting life. He teaches at Widener University two days a week, substitute teaches in Delaware County schools, and teaches homebound students on weekends. Mrs. P. wrote a book entitled *Retire, Refired.* She espouses multiple retirements: "Retire many times." She travels to Washington, D.C., and gives seminars for government employees, using her book as a guide to dynamic retirement.

Mrs. E.R., at age eighty-four, travels. So do many others, but she is a globetrotter to places such as Iceland, New Guinea, a trip down the Amazon, and a river float in Mexico.

About 10 percent of the residents are survivors of the Holocaust. All Jewish holy days are celebrated and there are Friday evening services.

Kosher cuisine is served. The weekly activity schedule is crowded with cultural, social, and religious activities.

Undoubtedly there is deep meaning and satisfaction in this community.

Martins Run Trivia. Brown Elementary School was closed for several years. In 1980 the property was transferred to Martins Run and the school building became the activity center—the hub of Martins Run. A fantastic utilization of surplus schools!

Tri Vista Villas*

The entry road to Lake Junaluska suddenly unfolds from a knoll overlooking this 200-acre lake. A large cross on a stone marker base sets the atmosphere. We savored the view. Many structures were on the shoreline with patches of fall colors interspersed and in the background were the Great Smoky Mountains of North Carolina. A half hour earlier we had come off the Blue Ridge Parkway. We were now twenty-six miles west of Asheville.

The lake is surrounded by 1,200 acres and comprises the Lake Junaluska Assembly, Conference and Retirement Center of the Southeastern Jurisdiction of the United Methodist Church. This is a place for worship, leadership development, family enjoyment, personal growth, meeting new friends, strengthening old ties, and for rest and recreation.

The Junaluska Assembly Housing, Inc., developed a condominium complex of fifty-six units in 1986, a short five-minute walk from Stuart Auditorium, the chapel, and other activity centers. They blend in very nicely with the surroundings.

Being a Methodist is not a requirement for purchasing a condo but it is stressed that a buyer be "in harmony with and supportive of the Assembly and its purposes as a Christian Conference and Retirement Center." A monthly maintenance fee includes the assembly membership fee, which covers free registration for many events, discounts on meals in the assembly-operated dining rooms, and many additional benefits.

An interesting way to try out this lifestyle would be to attend an Elderhostel program on site. In the spring of 1990 Western Carolina University held *five* one-week courses on the assembly grounds.

Mountain and lakeside living with a purpose best describes this lifestyle.

COLLEGIATE AND RELIGIOUS
■   ■   ■

In Madison, Connecticut, on a 125-acre property called Mercy Campus, are the McAuley*—a continuing care retirement community of 250 apartments; St. Mary Home—nursing care; St. Joseph College—a four-year women's college, also offering graduate studies to men and women and a weekend program for adults working toward a bachelor's degree; Connor Chapel—where mass is celebrated daily; a convent for the Sisters of Mercy; and access to Mercy Center—a conference facility overlooking Long Island Sound.

All of the above are three miles from downtown Hartford and Bushnell Memorial Hall, the performance home for the Hartford Symphony Orchestra, the Connecticut Opera, the Hartford Chamber Orchestra, and the Hartford Ballet. In addition, theatergoers enjoy the nationally known Hartford Stage Company. Bradley International Airport is nearby.

Sister Margarie Boyer, coordinator of Adult Education Programs at St. Joseph College, keeps McAuley residents regularly informed of relevant programs at the college. She also told us, "We hold two special events just for the residents of the McAuley in the fall and spring. I work closely with their academic liaison committee and attend all their meetings."

In July 1990 there will be three weeks of Elderhostel programs on campus and McAuley residents can attend on a commuter basis.

Combining a collegiate and religious environment may come very close to the optimum retirement fulfillment!

RETIRED MILITARY
■   ■   ■

Why would anyone want to live in a community exclusively for retired military? We asked retired colonel D. Currin, a twenty-one-year veteran of the Army Airborne, with eighty jumps and two tours of Vietnam, this question. He replied, "To be with people of similar interests, background, and experiences. Everyone in the military is on duty twenty-four hours a day, seven days a week. Moves are very frequent and in many cases to less than desirable conditions. Your assignment comes first and the family must adjust. In addition, the constant threat of conflict and possible combat adds more stress. A strong kinship among career military develops. Whenever there is a need there is always a response from a member of the unit. Many want to continue this closeness and a retirement community fills that need. It is not for us. We feel a cloistered environment would be too narrow in scope."

But there are a lot who find this kind of living to their liking. Here are six military retirement communities that we know of.

Air Force Village I*

Set in San Antonio, Texas, Air Force Village I is a high-rise garden apartment life care facility. Built in 1970, there are 379 apartments and a 68-bed nursing home available for retired air force officers, their spouses/widows, young air force widows, and their dependent children. When we first visited the complex in 1985 there were 1,700 people on the waiting list—a three- to four-year wait. This facility has been accredited by the Continuing Care Accreditation Commission sponsored by the American Association of Homes for the Aging. A 44-bed expansion in the nursing home is under construction.

Air Force Village II*

Five miles from Village I is Village II, which was opened in 1987. This 316-apartment and cluster-home complex, with a 63-bed nursing home, is for the same retired categories as listed above. Plans call for an additional 90 garden homes.

Both villages are under the auspices of the Air Force Village Foundation. Mr. F. Muise, Director of Admissions and Marketing, told us, "The villages remain dedicated to our charitable mission and widows in need of assistance retain first priority for village residency."

Air Force Village West*

This $60 million life care facility is available to *all* retired officers, regular, reserve, National Guard, and warrant officers of the U.S. military services or their widows.

It is located on 153 acres adjacent to March Air Force Base in Riverside, California. Entrance fees range from $62,000 to $250,000, plus a monthly service fee. There are 304 living units in this village, which was officially opened in February 1990. It is 80 percent sold. There is no affiliation with the two San Antonio Air Force Villages.

The Fairfax*

A life care retirement facility for retired army officers, built by the Marriott Corporation in conjunction with the Army Retirement Foundation-Potomac, the Fairfax was completed in February 1990. It is 80 percent sold. There are 382 independent-living residences, 55 assisted-living units, and a 60-bed nursing care center. It is located adjacent to Fort Belvoir, Virginia, just south of Washington, D.C.

Final county approval for Falcons Landing* is expected in May 1990. The Marriott Corporation, in conjunction with the Air Force Retired Officers Community, will build this facility along the Potomac River south of Washington, D.C. There will be 350 units and 1,300 retired air force officers have made down payments in order to have a priority number.

Bob Hope Village*—Teresa Village*

The Bob Hope Village* in Shalimar, Florida, and Teresa Village* in Fort Walton Beach, Florida, are guided by the Air Force Enlisted Widows Home Foundation, Inc.* Marvin Hicks, Director of Communications for the foundation, emphasized that these two villages were the only retirement communities for enlisted personnel in the country. Entrance is limited to retired air force personnel and is primarily for those in "dire need." Residents take care of their own meals and there are no medical services available. No government funds are received.

Bob Hope has been a major benefactor and the village bearing his name is well planned and very attractive. There are a total of 379 units in both villages and they are fully occupied. Needless to say, they are always in need of funds.

Aldersly*

The Danish royal family has made many visits to Aldersly,* where Danish descendants and their friends enjoy retirement. Located in San Rafael, California, the first building was dedicated in 1921. Today there are ninety-three residents of which 50 percent are Danish. The oldest resident is 107 years old and still has all his meals in the dining room. This community, which provides a continuum of care, is a bit of Denmark in California even though the stone marker on the grounds says 7,174 miles to Denmark!

Fraternal

All fraternal organizations regardless of their makeup, a sisterhood or brotherhood, are grounded on solid moral principles. Throughout the nation there are retirement communities for the seniors of these fraternal organizations. This special-interest category is mentioned to remind those who have the membership qualifications of this possible close connection with elders of like interests.

Very Special Interests

For sunworshipers, we found Cypress Cove near Kissimmee, Florida (Orlando area), a nudist retirement community. We did not do an indepth survey of this community!

A thirty-six-room home, in Los Angeles, California—for retired radicals—elderly Communists, religious liberals, and social reformers—is being sold. Of the fourteen residents aged seventy-seven to ninety-nine, eight have no place to go. Finding new accommodations undoubtedly presents a very special problem.

Dr. Ken Dychtwald in his book *Age Wave* published by Jeremy P. Tarcher, 1988, describes some unique retirement communities being contemplated: in Frederick, Maryland, Wormens Mill, an old-fashioned farming village; in Grand Rapids, Michigan, Heritage Village, a museum of the history and culture of Michigan; in Providence, Rhode Island, William Hill, a New England village of the mid-eighteenth century; and in Walnut Creek, California, Byron Park, an eighteenth-century English country inn.

We talked to a developer who is planning Friday Mountain in Austin, Texas, a community with a conference center and continuing education facilities. A similar complex is being considered in Kennebunkport, Maine.

The possibilities are unlimited!

Visualize a retirement community for amateur and professional thespians, photographers, video producers, dancers, musicians, writers/editors, artists, and scholars from a special discipline.

As the new generation of retirees searches for later life fulfillment the need for special interest communities will produce many more lifestyle options.

Exciting!

15

ENTERING PHASE
TWO RETIREMENT

. . .

The preceeding fourteen chapters have been concerned with an active retirement. The premise has been that your health and, when applicable, the health of your spouse are good enough to allow you the freedom to do what you want. We call this Phase One retirement.

As night follows day, aging, and possibly disease, will take its toll. Dr. John W. Rowe, Director, Division of Aging, the Harvard Medical School, at a Conference on Aging sponsored by Travelers, said ". . . old people aren't aging any faster than young people—they've just done more of it. They've lost functions; they have less reserve."

What to do about this slowdown is perplexing. It could be depressing, but the doldrums will accomplish nothing. In fact they will accelerate the process. Approaching this stage of life in a realistic positive way allows the individual more happiness.

We call this Phase Two retirement. The chart on page 219 portrays Retirement Transitions. There are three normal transitions, each with a beginning and ending.

1. Work life starts in our much younger years and ends on retirement day.
2. Retirement day is the beginning of unencumbered freedom and ends when aging and/or health matters cause restrictions.
3. Phase Two starts when a lifestyle change is required and the ending is the journey to the "great unknown."

Those who continue work life up to the beginning of Phase Two will have two transitions, Numbers 1 and 3 above.

The adjustment required at retirement day is well defined. Work stops and freedom starts. Transition to Phase Two is slow moving, not well defined. Accordingly, there can be differences of opinion among all concerned, self, spouse, relatives, as to when Phase Two is actually reached. It's extremely important for each of us to accept the reality of these changes, retain control, and take positive actions.

Realistically accepting the future and planning for this lifestyle change will be best for all concerned. Unfortunately, everyone doesn't plan. The "what will happen will happen" types can back themselves into a difficult corner. Those who put off thinking about all aspects of the future can also find themselves in the same difficult corner.

This can be best illustrated by a case study.

Case Study
Eighty Versus Sixty-three
or
I Can't Do that to Mother

This case is completely factual. Names and places are fictitious.

The setting—a modest two-bedroom, three-bath retirement home on a golf course in a small city. A year ago this family moved here from a large house in a big city about 650 miles away.

The people involved:

■ Ann—a quiet sixty-two-year-old woman with severe diabetes. Her life has centered around being a full-time wife and mother of two sons.

■ Carl—a sixty-three-year-old recently retired executive. A strong personality. A charger who was burning out and retired at sixty-two to play golf.

■ Nora—Ann's eighty-year-old mother. Widowed for many years. Has been living with Ann and Carl for about seven years. Prior to the move at Carl's retirement she was very active in a senior citizens' center. Through this affiliation she had many friends, played a lot of cards, went on trips, and was excited about life.

RETIREMENT TRANSITIONS

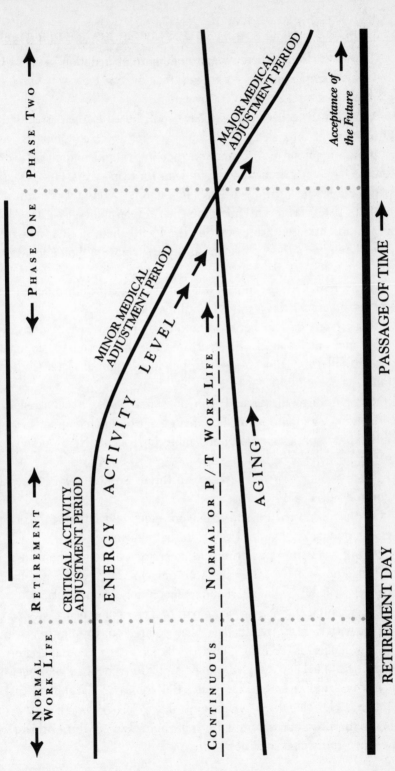

Prior to the move there was an undercurrent irritation between Carl and Nora. Carl confided to friends that all was not well but it was tolerable.

A great many other upheavals have contributed to the current unrest. One son went through a very difficult divorce, which still impacts on the relationship among Carl, Ann, and their two grandchildren. The other son has had major occupational problems for many years. However, he is settling down now. Ann's diabetes problem is a constant concern.

Carl's sister has recently become their responsibility. She has Alzheimer's and Parkinson's diseases. She lived with them in their new retirement home for a short while and is now in a nursing home in a nearby city.

Carl is now one year into retirement. He has a health problem. Corrective surgery has been put off until his ulcer heals.

Today Nora stays in her room and reads Harlequin romance novels. She comes out for meals. Most of the time she doesn't get completely dressed and many times forgets to put in her partial plate. Carl can't stand this.

Nora no longer drives and Ann does errands for her. Occasionally, perhaps once a month, Ann and Nora go out to lunch or an affair at the club. These outings are becoming more infrequent. Nora doesn't have the stamina she once had.

When friends visited who knew all three very well, Nora closed her door and never said hello.

Carl has suggested to Ann that Nora move to a retirement home. A very emotional Ann said, "I can't do that to Mother!"

No one has visited any retirement complexes, although there are three nice facilities not too far away. According to Carl, Nora has sufficient finances available to handle requirements at any of these places.

The advantages of Nora's being part of a group and being with people her age with similar interests have been pointed out to Ann. In addition, the advantages of reducing the stress factor in the household are very evident. Ann acknowledges this logic and also recognizes her obligation to her husband of forty-three years. But she says, "I can't do that to Mother." Her quandry is understandable.

As a short-term compromise, Ann has agreed to go with Carl and visit the three retirement facilities.

1. Who's at fault?
2. Why did this happen?
3. How can it be solved?

Before Reading on, Come Up with Your Answers to the Three Questions.

1. As we see it, all three are at fault.

2. Little or no planning is at the root of why this happened. Moving to a house about half the size of the previous house must result in territory problems. Expecting an elderly person to take initiative to find new friends in a new town hardly seems practical. Nora's succumbing to the easy way out—reading novels—is a most logical reaction. These kinds of problems could have been anticipated and talked through long before the move. Ann's image of a retirement facility is understandably shaded by her visits to Carl's sister, who is in a nursing home. In addition, her experiences with older people didn't include retirement communities. These complexes are relatively new. Ann's somewhat sheltered life has been based on close family ties and the obligation of taking care of one's parents.

3. Obviously a move to a nice complex would be best for all concerned. A try at selling Nora on a move to a retirement complex, through a carefully planned campaign, would be the best approach. However, this takes time. Emotions are controlling the situation, not rational thinking. It's a very mixed-up problem. Everyone has been backed into a difficult corner.

NOTE: We were the visitors from the big city. We never saw Nora during our visit. Carl asked us to put something in our book about parents not living with their kids.

What can be learned from this case study? Obviously a great deal. Accept the fact that you will get old and at some time or other need some help.

Who will provide that help? Your kids or other relatives? In our case study Carl would urge you to not burden your kids.

Will you be self-sufficient and make certain that when time for help comes, provisions for help will have been made? The kind of help and in the environment that you want. In other words, on your terms, with you making the decisions and being in full control.

This can be done. It will require change and the ability to adjust to change. You need to accept that before you need help you will plan and make whatever arrangements are necessary, move if it is required, adjust, and go on with a full life.

It's part of the philosophy of not retiring from life. You need to live life aggressively to the fullest within whatever limitations have been imposed by health considerations, or just plain slowing down because of aging.

Positive mental attitude (PMA) is vital at this stage of the aging process. To give in, to take the easy way out—reading love stories all day —is self-defeating.

We would urge you to broaden your understanding of aging. A new field of study has emerged. There is a medical specialty called Geriatrics which deals primarily with the diseases of old age. The emerging field is Gerontology. This scientific study of aging examines specific changes in older individuals as well as the various social issues confronting older people. Today there are many universities that have research on aging in process.

The goal of this discipline is to determine ways to enhance the quality of life in the later years. Medical advances have added years to life—the question now is, how to add life to those years.

We had a long conversation with Reverend Don R. Renshaw, who has a Ph.D. in Social Gerontology. Our meeting centered around the question: what can a person do to prepare for and handle the changes that Phase Two brings?

Reverend Renshaw's immediate answer was: "A person's authentic response that their physical facilities will become less dependable due to aging. Being honest with one's self is of paramount importance." He illustrated this by citing the person at sixty-five who says, "I'm just as good as I was at thirty-five." That's not being honest, it is self-delusion. This is not an authentic response, it's wishful thinking, a nonacceptance of the facts. On the other extreme, an attitude of it's all over at sixty-five or retirement time is also not an authentic response to the change.

He further said, "The hardest thing is the emotional coping and compensation necessary to be able to offset the loss. . . . For example, any form of communal living is giving up some level of independence— having to be at the dining room at 5 P.M. for the evening meal is a loss of self-determination of when I want to eat."

Unless a person recognizes a loss he or she will not be able to accept the coping necessary to make up for the loss. In all of life coping is essential; it is especially important in the winter of our lives when there is a definite ending point somewhere over the horizon.

Honesty—an authentic evaluation of our personal status—is critical if we want to cope successfully with any change. Reverend Renshaw said, "The heart of retirement is lifestyle, the heart of aging is compensation."

Reading his doctoral dissertation on aging was a challenging intellectual exercise. There was a tremendous amount of relevant material. We could go on for several pages but that's not practical. Reverend Renshaw's definition of successful aging summarizes this view:

> That emotional response to later life which is characterized by the individual's ability to cope with changed status, reduced physical ability and decreasing mobility, without losing feelings of self-worth and the ability to compensate for these losses in meaningful ways.

Our readings and gerontology programs we have attended have been extremely helpful in writing this book. Did you know:

■ Chronological age is a poor predictor of behavior.

■ Aging and memory loss do *not* go hand in hand.

■ Researchers are finding increasing evidence that each person's *attitude* toward learning and memory is a vital part of the ability to learn and remember in later life.

■ Senility is *not* inevitable and a normal consequence of aging.

■ Today's retirees are gerontological pioneers. This group is establishing norms that others may follow with regard to leisure, learning, and activity in retirement. They are pathfinders.

Check the adult classes curriculum at your local college, church programs, and library for sources of information on aging.

Phase Two of retirement is inevitable. We asked Mr. F. K. of Wheeling, West Virginia, a seventy-four-year-old retiree, what he had been doing lately. He replied, "Just going from doctor to doctor!"

Another retiree said, "We're at that age when we meet all our friends in the doctor's office."

THE SANDWICH GENERATION
■ ■ ■

You might think we are talking about the generation that seems addicted to the fast food sandwich! Not so! Years ago having aged parents live with one of the kids, usually the oldest daughter, was a way of life. Today it happens, but many people do not consider it a "good" way of life. When it's necessary, many times it creates a sandwich. The kids are sandwiched in between their live-in parent(s) and their own kids. Complicating the situation is the working mother. Where can the time be found to be a nurturing parent to the children and a caregiver to the aging parent(s)?

A Dallas columnist wrote that the traditional family went out with Ozzie and Harriet. Today, time is the most precious commodity and if it's difficult to find quality time with children there will be no time for the old.

We agree with these sentiments and urge Phase Two retirement planning. It's not necessary to be a burden on the kids. You can be self-sufficient in an environment of help and in the company of friends with similar needs and circumstances. Give serious consideration to the next three lifestyle chapters as you develop your total retirement plan.

PHASE TWO AND
THE SINGLE PERSON
■ ■ ■

Obviously, Phase Two retirement has to be a very critical consideration for the single person. Mr. B.D. at age sixty found himself a single again—the result of a divorce. The why or who was at fault makes no difference. In a period of a year what was a happy marriage deteriorated into a divorce and a new marriage for the former wife.

Mr. D., who thought a happy retirement was assured, now faced a quandary. He was a long service employee with a good company so his retirement finances would be adequate. That was not the problem. As he tried to do his retirement planning, it was now a case of where, when, and maybe with whom?

He found that he was a highly desirable commodity. There were many women in their later years looking for companionship, some very aggressive in their search. His stories were too intimate to include in this book.

We have had many discussions with Mr. D. and various options have been determined. Fortunately there was no immediate retirement action required, although everyone after age fifty-five is a candidate for an early retirement golden handshake.

Trying to determine a course of action was very difficult. In reality Mr. D.'s world blew up. He had faced cancer and two other serious health problems in the past but there had always been a spouse to offer encouragement and love. Today he was alone in a new town house. Friends were still assisting but he will soon be on his own.

There were no pat answers. Find a new avocation, find new single friends, take advantage of your new freedom—these and many more suggestions had been offered. He had heard them all. It was his call and it was not easy to make.

PHASE TWO—LOSS OF A SOUL MATE
■   ■   ■

The loss of a soul mate presents an even more difficult adjustment— the toughest that we will ever have to handle.

Liz Carpenter, former Press Secretary and Staff Director to Lady Bird Johnson, wrote a very perceptive book entitled *Getting Better All the Time* (Pocket Books, 1987). She starts Chapter 2, "Coming Home," with a vivid description of a phone call, "It happened, that moment all couples fear the most, dread the most. Suddenly one of you is gone. Such a simple thing as a phone call in the night and your whole life is changed."

Her writing style, honest and to the point, takes the reader through the turbulent emotional upheaval and finally to the awakening of a new day. After her move from Washington to Austin, Texas, she accepted that God had given her a chance at a second life.

One day while talking with her editor in New York, a scene outside her window caused her to say, "I'll call you back." A baby deer was lazily sniffing at the geraniums, in the background was the pink granite dome of the Capitol of Texas. For five minutes she took in the wonder of it all.

Then the awakening—she had learned how to move from loneliness to solitude. There is a vast difference.

We met with Rachel Edwards, MEd., a licensed professional counselor. She has a full-time counseling practice and is associated with the Dallas Christian Counseling Services.* Her Master's Professional Paper concerned bereavement and evolved into a training program and support group on bereavement and loss recovery.

We explored with her what is present in the lives of those who have made a successful adjustment to losses in Phase Two. She had written out four primary considerations:

1. A faith in God. In life, purposes and meanings beyond yourself and beyond a partner. This allows for expansion of the ͻpirit during times of diminishing physical health and losses.
2. Someone to share with. Many who suffer a loss do so in silence. They have found no way to express their loss. This is especially prevalent among those who have prided themselves in "keeping it together." Sharing will seem unfamiliar and possibly shameful at first. But the pain that is being felt is part of the flow of life. Give yourself permission to be comforted. At times a licensed professional will be the best person to share feelings with.
3. An appreciation of life. Wisdom that has been accumulated and the past experiences of learning to change will provide a foundation to reflect on when coping with a new loss.
4. Life has its seasons. Moving from one to the other is difficult to face. Accept the natural pain of the loss and move on. Losses have happened many times in everyone's life.

In preparation for losses she feels everyone should have a plan that has been discussed with significant others. Educate yourself about the grief process, have a confidant to share losses, and have interests and activities.

Regardless of the preparation, the phone call in the middle of the night will be devastating, but preparation will help you climb up out of the deepest of all valleys.

Mr. Lawrence A. Appley, retired president of the American Management Association, and Fred's former boss, sent us a pocket-sized mini-white paper entitled, "Aging Yes—Growing Old No." He closed with some suggestions from an octogenarian:

- Constantly exercise the mind. Write something every day—an essay—a valued thought. Cut down on time in front of the "boob tube"—strive to increase your vocabulary. Continually review and update your basic philosophy.

- Work with young people.

- Avoid phrases such as: "This is the way I [or we] used to do it"; "I remember when"; "The good old days."

- Have a job—a career—regular responsibilities to be performed.

- We were given the raw material and the tools with which to shape our lives . . . the power to judge between right and wrong.

A comment by Odi Long, eighty-one years of age, who has served longer in the Peace Corps than any other volunteer, ties right in with Mr. Appley's philosophy: "When you have idle moments, when your mind is not occupied you start feeling your age. I don't have idle moments."

Our destiny is in our hands. Whether it's as a teenager, young parents, or a senior in Phase Two, we can mold our lives.

The National Mental Health Association* in its "Coping" series—Pamphlet #4 *Coping . . . with Growing Older*—give us some thoughts to ponder. "The key ingredients in coping with growing older are your outlook, lifestyle, and ability to anticipate and plan for change."

How will you approach Phase Two? Will it be dreaded? Or, as with any other life change that has been experienced—marriage, family planning, career change, or a move to a new city—will you face it with a positive attitude and a plan of action?

Approach the future with dread and it will be a dreaded experience. In many cases destined for failure from the beginning. What will be will be. Make the most of it and work hard at maximizing every bit of pleasure available.

Granted, Phase Two is on the downside of the mountain. We don't know how far we will go down the mountain—perhaps a long way.

Live that trip down the mountain to the fullest!

16

RETIREMENT
RESIDENCE

■ ■ ■

LIFESTYLE OPTION #12, PHASE TWO
CAREFREE LIVING

IF YOUR MOTHER IS OVER 70 THERE'S A 90% CHANCE SHE'LL FEEL AT HOME IN A RETIREMENT INN. This is the headline of a quarter-page ad that appeared in one of our Dallas papers. It was followed by other eye-catching ads. At the same time a TV commercial blitz featured Harry Morgan (of "M*A*S*H" fame) as the spokesman for the newly opened Retirement Inn at Forest Lane.*

This same approach was undoubtedly used throughout the country wherever a Retirement Inn has been built. There are currently eight in California, one in Oklahoma, in Utah, and in Texas. Their goal is to have a Retirement Inn in every major city. They feel there is a large market for comfortable nonmedical retirement facilities. We agree.

The premise behind this lifestyle is that active elderly who want to get away from the responsibility of a big house, but don't want to leave friends and family, have need for a comfortable "local" residence.

In 1980, SAFECO (the insurance company) purchased Retirement Inns from its founders. Things changed from the initial thoughts that SAFECO had in developing a major chain of retirement residences. They worked out a sale with Southmark. Difficulties arose within Southmark and bankruptcy ensued. SAFECO has the Dallas and Fort Worth inns and has worked out a management contract with Leisure Care,* a company started by Charles Lytle, a former SAFECO executive.

The Retirement Inn facilities that we have surveyed have three floors and remind one of an English inn. Each resident has a comparatively small efficiency apartment which he/she furnishes with his/her own furniture and decorations. Lounges are placed throughout the building to encourage conversation and companionship. There are usually about ninety apartments, each with an outside view.

No medical facilities are available. Each person must be in reasonably good health. If nursing care is required, a person would be forced to leave the inn. An alert call system has been installed in each apartment for use in the event of an emergency.

Three meals are served each day in a central dining room. Weekly housekeeping, linen service, and scheduled transportation are provided. Also available are a beauty/barber shop, a general store, a small theater, a billiard room, and an arts and crafts center. A full-time activity director keeps things humming.

A one-bedroom apartment (450 square feet) costs $1,475 a month. Two people can share an apartment for an additional $250, i.e., $1,725 for two. The only additional costs would be for a private telephone, purchases at the store, and use of the beauty/barber shop. Some planned outside activities have a small fee. Renter's insurance and medical insurance are not included. Parking space is provided. There is no additional storage space for extra mementoes. Pets are not allowed.

The monthly activity calendar at the various locations appears full with such things as: Bible fellowship every Thursday; Creative cookery every Friday; a monthly birthday celebration; social hours/happy hours; senior stretches; Casino nights; special occasion parties; door-decorating contest at Christmas; Bingo; Films and speakers; first run TV movies; field trips; dancing lessons; lunches out; swimming at a recreation center; and prayer and share.

The mother of a friend of ours decided against a Retirement Inn. She thought the apartment was too small. This is always the problem when any kind of down-sizing takes place. It's extremely difficult to dispose of lifelong treasures.

One of the basic concepts is that residents should spend only a minimum amount of time in their apartment. There are six lounge areas on the first floor and four on the second and third floors. They are decorated in a traditional Queen Anne style. The lounges take the place of the normal living room. Another objection our friend's mother had was the number of people using walkers and canes. She didn't like that environment, even at age eighty-five!

One problem we noticed at the Dallas Inn was the lack of outside walking area. Perimeter parking would allow for walking around the site but there were no sidewalks outside of the site. It was located near the intersection of two eight-lane highways, some stores and restaurants. There was not an immediate adjacent residential area. Outside of the building it was very noisy and not at all conducive to much outside activity.

The Retirement Inn at Quail Run* in Oklahoma City, Oklahoma, was in an excellent location. It was within walking distance of a nice shopping center and adjacent to some attractive apartments.

We had a fine talk with Mrs. M.M., a resident at the Dallas Retirement Inn. She was one of the first residents to move in back in 1982. A delightful widow of eighty-one, originally from Indiana where she was a grade school teacher who quit teaching, when she married. Her husband, a railroader, was transferred to Texarkana, Arkansas, and they lived there for thirty-one years. She didn't like the town but the move went with the job so she made the best of it. Later she moved in with her daughter in a suburb of Dallas.

Eventually a slight stroke and her daughter's and son-in-law's extensive travels dictated a move to a residence where there were other people nearby. She has made the best of the move and was happy in her surroundings except for two instances. She said, "Twice I got bitterly mad around here, but twice in all these years isn't too bad, is it?" There again, that positive attitude surfaced—a requirement if one doesn't want to become a grouchy old person.

One of the highlights each month was accompanying her daughter to the meeting of the "Stitch and Bitch Club," a group of neighbors who still met even though they had all moved from the old neighborhood.

Other times she kept to herself. She would not turn on the TV during the day, so she wouldn't become addicted to it. A fine person who was handling aging in a straightforward, honest, well-adjusted manner.

There is a major need for this type of "home away from home" and it represents a developing business. This is referred to as a congregate living environment. Throughout the country there are hundreds of these separate (your own small apartment) and together (scheduled activities, dining, and lounge area companionship) facilities.

They serve a need that in the past was filled by the family—living with the kids during the slowing-down years. To many seniors this isn't an acceptable lifestyle. Even when the spouse passes on, a person's need for independence and dignity remains strong. A retirement residence—adult congregate living facility—is a good lifestyle for a lot of people.

Burgundy Place* in Tulsa, Oklahoma, is a ten-story building in a nice neighborhood very near the campus of Oral Roberts University. All units are rentals but there is an option—you don't have to sign up for the meals. A one-bedroom apartment (740 square feet) is $740 a month. The meal charge for three meals a day is $195 per person—total $1,130 a month for a couple. Normal amenities are included, plus one special not found at other places. The two large meeting rooms on the ground floor have been reinforced with concrete and steel and serve as a tornado shelter. Living in the vicinity of Tornado Alley makes this a desirable addition to the building.

Westwood Horizons* in Los Angeles is another high-rise. The four-teen-story building is in the heart of Westwood Village, adjacent to Bel Air and Beverly Hills. UCLA's medical center is one block away. This is a rental facility with three meals included. One difference from other places is that there is daily maid service and you can bring your own furniture or use theirs. No cooking is allowed in the rooms and pets are forbidden.

All Jewish and Christian holidays are celebrated and Jewish religious services are conducted by a rabbi each Saturday morning.

A standard suite—living room, bedroom, and bath—is $1,895 a month, plus $475 for an additional person—total, $2,370. There is one other nominal charge for a space in the secured underground parking lot.

Madison House in Totem Lake, Washington, is an example of "Ca-tered Living," the byword of the various Madison House facilities around the country.

This rental, 146-apartment complex, is located in the outskirts of Seat-tle. Amenities are comparable to other facilities of this nature, including three meals a day. A one-bedroom apartment is $1,995 for a single, $2,195 per month for a double.

In August 1989 the Madison Club, an assisted-living wing, was opened. This addition provides twenty-four-hour staffing by nursing assis-tants supervised by a registered nurse; afternoon snack and teatime; es-cort to and from the dining room (three meals); supervised bathing and medication supervision; room service, and special social and activities program. A one bedroom unit is $2,395 for a single and $1,395 more for a double.

There are a total of 165 residents at Madison House, including an Alaskan pioneer bush pilot, a *Titanic* survivor, and a well-published author; 90 percent of the residents are single.

As indicated above, "Catered Living" is expensive.

Winstead* in Cape Cod, Massachusetts, is built in the traditional Cape Cod architecture. This inn has atmosphere with its Victorian parlor and fireplace. Visualize a roaring fire during the winter: to us it is New England personified. A greenhouse and landscaped atrium for recreational and social use blend in appropriately.

Winstead is located in the historic district of the village of Harwich Center, one block from the Albro Senior Citizens Center, village shops, and across from the library.

A one-bedroom suite with kitchenette is $2,600 monthly for two. Three meals a day, housekeeping, and laundry are included. It is stressed that this is a small retirement community unlike any other where a select few will enjoy superior personalized attention.

Kings Row* in Middletown, New Jersey, is located in the shore area of New Jersey. This community is now managed by the Marriott Corporation Senior Living Services Division. It is a traditional rental retirement residence. Amenities include three meals, daily housekeeping, and the other usual services. A one-bedroom apartment is $1,930 a month for one person; $2,650 a month for two.

Carlyle On The Bay* in Miami, Florida, overlooking Biscayne Bay, is a high-rise (ten-story) apartment building. Two kosher-style meals are served each day. There is weekly maid service, a licensed nurse on the premises, transportation to shopping and doctors, a twenty-four-hour doorman, and a full-time activities program.

A one-bedroom is $1,495, single; $1,745 for two persons. They have recently converted some floors to assisted living. An Alzheimer's Dementia Unit has also been established.

Share Our Home

Our most interesting retirement residence came from an ad we answered in *The Wall Street Journal.* The ad described a small retirement facility in a suburb of Orlando, Florida. We received a two-page well-written letter describing what was available. A couple has a 3,010-square-foot one-story brick home on a two-acre plot of land. It is located in one of the most exclusive residential areas in the suburb. They rent out rooms to elderly persons. Meals are "Pritikin" style: i.e., low-cholesterol foods, no fats, and low sugar. Their home is described as being tastefully furnished with quality pieces in a manner to which one of gentile background is accustomed. Two bedrooms sharing a bath were available and described, "like coming home and using your daughter's best guest room." Guests should be ambulatory and able to tend to their own needs. A doctor's written evaluation is required.

A price was not quoted and we did not pursue the matter. It sounded real good, but then could it be too good?

In the well-run retirement residence a very definitive lifestyle emerges. As the "slowdown" progresses the built-in companionship and services of the retirement residence are of great assistance. This becomes an extremely valuable support system. Loneliness isn't a problem. A resident would not become one of the invisible elderly.

You are probably wondering just who are the invisible elderly. They are the individuals who are still in their homes and limited to some degree by the "slowdown." In many cases their kids are in other cities, and most of their old neighbors are gone. Occasionally a compassionate neighbor stops by or assists with the shopping.

Alice has seen many folks in this predicament as she has delivered meals on wheels. Often it's extremely difficult for her to leave because these people are lonely and want to talk.

One of the invisible elderly is the Dallas widow who needed medical help but not severely enough to call an ambulance. She had no one to call. Finally a name came to mind—her automobile mechanic. He drove over in his tow truck, took her to the hospital, waited two hours, then drove her home.

Also among the invisible elderly is the friend of ours who lives alone in a residence hotel in New York City. For years she would not see us when we were in New York. She used to sleep all day and watch TV movies all night. Finally she consented to see us.

She met us at our hotel and marveled at the blue sky as she looked out the window. Her one apartment window looks out on the window of another apartment. Her relatives are gone and there are no friends. She is alone.

A happy note. We continue to try to assist by visits and frequent phone contact. She has an arthritic condition and requires around-the-clock nurse's aides and now leads a much more normal life.

THE OTHER SIDE

▪ ▪ ▪

There are a couple of downsides to a retirement residence. The mother of another friend of ours has great difficulty with the continual loss of friends. She is one of the youngest at the residence. Being a compassionate person she quite naturally became confidant, helper, big sister, and hand holder to those who were older and in need of help. She developed close relationships which were severed when age took its final toll.

An additional downside is the high probability of another move. As the slowdown continues much more personal care will be needed. Practically all places require a reasonable degree of good health, age taken into consideration. But all places require the person to be ambulatory. Therefore, if a person needs a great deal of care or is highly limited in personal movement, a nursing home is the only answer.

Unfortunately this means the loss of the support system. At a time when physical deterioration is accelerating, friends and pals are left behind. It can be traumatic.

New faces, new surroundings, and an environment of illness are thrust upon a person. Unknown medical personnel become an integral part of everyday living. All these major changes coming in a short period of time could very easily cause depression.

Prior to 1980 there were few retirement communities of any kind. This business expanded rapidly and many of the facilities established in the early eighties have residents who are now in their late seventies and early eighties.

Many of these people need some help. Assisted-living facilities answer these needs; however, all resident-type facilities can't convert to assisted living. For example, Retirement Inn in Dallas investigated this possibility and couldn't meet the regulations. This doesn't mean there is anything wrong with the inn but government regulations come into play and become impossible to meet.

What is emerging is home health care provided by an outside care company. This allows the person to stay in his or her apartment for a much longer time.

You can get some of these services which provide that little extra help. The retirement home resident and the company providing the services enter into an agreement.

RISE AND SHINE— $2.00 a trip, wake-up call, morning dressing assistance, and reminder to go to breakfast.

BUTTONS & BOWS— $2.00 a trip, checkup to inspect and assure proper attire, grooming, and accompany to/from activities.

TUCK IN— $2.00 a visit, assistance with nighttime chores such as undressing, turning down bed, denture care, and back rub.

DINNER BELL— $6.00 a day, three meals, assistance to/from all meals.

FANCY FINGERS— $12 a session, basic nail care, filing, and polish.

TRAY SERVICE— $2.00 a trip, meal delivered and set up.

POWDER ROOM FOR LADIES— $6.00 a session, bathing, skin care, wardrobe assistance.

FIT AS A FIDDLE FOR MEN— Same as Powder Room for ladies.

THE APOTHECARY— $8.00 a day, medication management program set up by a nurse once a week and up to four reminders to take medicine each day.

Service such as the above will help an individual retain his/her independence and keep that all important self-esteem at as high a level as possible.

17

RETIREMENT COMPLEX— AVAILABLE HEALTH CARE

∎   ∎   ∎

LIFESTYLE OPTION #13, PHASE TWO HEALTH CARE WHEN NEEDED

"An active retirement community where your every need—every wish —has been anticipated and planned for"—". . . served by our adorable uniformed waitresses"—"Listen to the soft laughter from the club/fitness center"—"Stirs the imagination, heightens the senses, and inspires the youthful at heart"—"The perfume of orange blossoms wafts the air"—"Our competent staff will handle all these tiresome (and sometimes dangerous) chores for you."

These inspiring phrases have been taken verbatim from the brochures of many retirement complexes. They are the product of an ad agency and designed to stimulate interest in a particular facility. Another of our favorites is, "I'm ready to be pampered."

There's nothing wrong with these advertising pitches. All our life we have been bombarded with magical words that will hopefully produce an image that will satisfy a need.

But all brochures aren't full of glowing fun-type phrases. Some statements are disturbing. They hit hard at potential problems that we would prefer to defer—to face at some other time. For example: "The future should not be left to circumstances and chance." "Plan for the future rather than depend on family members for daily support." ". . . Big difference between asking an occasional favor and being dependent upon family and friends for daily assistance." ". . . Children or other relatives or friends to take care of you, placing an undue hardship on them and taking away your independent way of life." "Meeting the anticipated problems of advancing age with comfort, security, and dignity."

Some retirement communities have programs and facilities to assist with the problems of advancing age.

True Life Aging

"Mother, we think it's time for you to move to a retirement home." Jane Smith (not her real name) heard her two daughters make this request. Her thoughts included, "I'm not ready for this—all old people— no more freedom—it's the end, why?" A rash of serious nondisabling medical problems had prompted the two daughters to have this heart-to-heart talk with their mother.

The above discussion was related to us by a retirement community resident age seventy-nine. This was followed by an in-depth discussion with an executive who had just taken over the community. The original management had gone into bankruptcy. As this story unfolds it will be very evident why all names, including the names of the facilities, have been changed.

The setting is a progressive city of about 1,300,000 people located in the Sunbelt. During our research we made three survey trips to this city and had surveyed the two retirement communities concerned in 1985 and 1990.

Jane Smith is a feisty senior. Expressive and easy to talk with. After her daughters' request they visited a not-too-distant retirement community and she was given two weeks to make up her mind. "I didn't want to be a burden to my girls; I love them very much but don't want to live with either of them; I wanted my freedom" were her thoughts. So she decided to lease an apartment in Retirement Community A.

Included in the rent were a daily main meal, weekly maid service, weekly bed linen service, utilities, scheduled transportation, full-time activity director, and adjacent health care facilities on a pay-as-you-use basis.

She became dissatisfied with the management. Her words were: "The director was an S.O.B." He wouldn't increase the temperature of the pool to 85° F.

She and seven other widows (two were past presidents of the residents' association) and a widower moved to Retirement Community B in the same town—a community with similar services that had just gone through reorganization.

After many cups of coffee we were joined by the executive who put the reorganization together. We will call him John Doe. Jane was most enthusiastic about John and his method of operation. Perhaps a case of a "new broom sweeps clean."

Many residents stopped by our table in the lounge including the widower who had also moved to this community. A distinguished-looking gentleman, nattily dressed for the dining room, using a cane, and referred to as "the colonel."

Jane has become very active. Every day she teaches a water exercise group which ends with a sing-a-long. She has written articles for the newsletter and wants to write a humerous human interest book. She belongs to the XYZ Club (Xtra Years of Zest). "I am never alone, God is always at my side," she said.

She left to join her gang for lunch, carrying her mini-shopping bag. She uses this for leftovers, providing her with her evening meal. She was very well dressed and walked away with a confident stride. A real joy to be with.

John Doe has been in the retirement community business for over ten years. At one time he was associated with Dr. Berg. (See reference to Dr. Berg's conviction in Chapter 18.) He discussed the financial problems that emerged and hence his involvement with retirement communities today. Some of the problems involved poor planning. The kitchen and dining room were not large enough to handle the total resident population once it was full; they had only 60 percent occupancy now. The kitchen for the ninety-bed health center was too small. A van was bought to "ferry" meals from the main kitchen to the health center.

Originally, a religious-affiliated foundation was formed to do the initial organization. The planning, building, and administration of the community were contracted to others. During his financial evaluation he could identify where $17 million was required. A total of $27 million was spent. The original ownership will get $0.20 on the dollar. Mr. Doe was aggressively marketing the facility and felt it will be filled in six months.

Good resident relations are the key to a successful community. John Doe felt it was essential to be compassionate, fair, and firm. For example, a resident wanted the van to take her to see a relative 200 miles away. Normally the answer would be, "No, we can't tie up the van for that long a time." He insisted that the staff inquire about finding an affordable way to get her to her relatives. He said, "Many older folks don't have the mental dexterity to do this on their own and need help. Offering a solution rather than a 'no' goes a long way toward good administrative/residence relations."

We gained many insights into retirement community administration. Dealing with the needs, feelings, and insecurities of the elderly requires a delicate touch.

Many communities have doctors' offices on site. The Lawrence Welk Resort (Chapter 8) has a Scripps Clinic located in the shopping area. This is a general medical office and assists anyone who comes in. It is a convenience rather than an integral part of the services of the retirement community.

Villa Del Ray Retirement Inn* in Escondido, California, has a registered nurse come in once a week to take blood pressure, weight checks, etc. This service is completely voluntary.

Eagle Towers* in Stamford, Connecticut, has a registered nurse on duty at all times. This is helpful to the residents but doesn't take the place of a health care facility. Known as a vertical retirement community, this fifteen-story facility offers residents a great view of Long Island Sound or the beautiful New England countryside. The residents call themselves Eaglets. We were particularly impressed by the fine paintings in the first-floor lounge and dining area.

Meadowstone Place in Dallas (included in Chapter 11) has their emergency medical response system tied directly to Medical City Hospital. This means that the hospital is immediately alerted if you have a problem. Swansgate, another community that we included in Chapter 11, has the same type of association with the hospital next door.

These are nice services but they are not a part of on-site health care. The advantage of a health facility that is part of the community means a relocation to an unfamiliar nursing care complex would not be required.

The support system developed within the community remains close at hand to offer continuous support. The possibility of frequent long trips by a spouse and others to a care facility could be avoided. The nearness of friends and loved ones is of incalculable value during a health crisis. If the crisis evolves into a more permanent need, the nearness factor becomes even more important.

Another major advantage of on-site health accommodations is being among friends and acquaintances who are also in need of medical services. This would be much more comforting than moving in among strangers.

Writing this section has been difficult. The subject of health problems in the declining years is not full of joy and happiness. We have been unable to find a way to portray this in an up-beat manner. An increasing frequency of health problems does occur in advanced age. It's a fact of life and we must deal with it in a straightforward manner.

Therefore, preparing for this eventuality would seem to make a great deal of common sense. Our purpose is to acquaint you with the various approaches taken by communities that offer on-site health care. This will help those who want to consider this lifestyle option.

Castle Ridge*

We surveyed Castle Ridge, on the outskirts of Minneapolis, right after a howling Minnesota snowstorm. The snow was piled high and the roads were gutted with icy ridges. But we came away with a warm feeling. This is a very nice well-designed condominium complex with an attached sixty-bed skilled nursing care facility.

A total of 240 condominiums branch off a two-story commons building. All of the units were not complete when we were there. The first level of the commons building contains a pool, whirlpool, sauna, exercise room, lockers, wood and metal shop, game room, convenience store, two lounges, resident mailboxes, guest suite, activity director's office, and administration offices. A greenhouse adjoins the corridor to one bank of condominiums.

The second floor has a restaurant, library, lounges—where three feature films are shown each week on large screen TV—private party room, arts and craft room, beauty/barber shop, chapel, and chaplain's office. We were told there was a patio and the grounds were nicely landscaped.

The commons or community center is reached from all four condominium buildings by a short indoor walk. The care center, a facility of Twin City Christian Homes, which is a ministry of the Minnesota Baptist Conference, is also accessible from the commons.

There are seven different styles of condos with base prices going from $60,000 to $160,000. Monthly fees vary from $110 to $325. This does not include any medical services.

Enclosed with the material that was given to us was a one-page letter from a single resident. Naturally it extols the virtues of Castle Ridge but it's written from the heart and brings out some good points:

At Castle Ridge we know and care for each other . . . having recently experienced my husband's death, I can truthfully say I had much support from my neighbors, staff, guards—both prior to and following his death . . . after a lifetime of yard work and housework it is so pleasant to come home from a day's work and have the freedom to do as I wish . . . why wait until I am past my working years to have these benefits when I can start to enjoy them at fifty-five . . . I can traverse the halls, ride the elevator, or use the common areas late at night without fear . . . being a new widow I find this especially important . . . I can lock my door and take a trip knowing I have nothing to fear . . . I prefer being where I know the neighbors have a somewhat similar preference for music . . . had I a young neighbor who had their stereo turned loudly to contemporary music, it would be difficult to endure. I prefer being in the Twin Cities area—my home —my friends—my family—activities—credit rating—banks—all familiar.

There is an opportunity in this complex to become a part of the community while still working; then continue on at retirement and pursue activities at your convenience. If advanced age requires health care, one knows that hourly housekeeping, limited food tray service, along with assistance in living and adjacent skilled nursing care are readily available.

Olds Manor*

Olds Manor is a converted hotel in downtown Grand Rapids, Michigan. This eight-story facility offers supportive care and nursing care in the health center. There is an additional charge for these services. It is located on the Grand River, diagonally across from the Ford Museum.

Scottsdale Village Square*

In the shadow of Camelback Mountain is Scottsdale, Arizona. This city covers 183 square miles and has a population of 130,000 so it would be difficult to call it a suburb of Phoenix. The over-fifty group makes up 40 percent of the population and 41 percent of the households have incomes over $50,000.

Scottsdale Village Square* is located in the heart of Scottsdale. Close at hand is good shopping, (the Fifth Avenue shops have always been a favorite of ours); the Civic Center and Sky Harbor International Airport aren't too far away.

This adobe, red-tiled-roof retirement apartment village offers medical services designed to enable a person to stay in his/her own environment and live independently as long as possible. The regular services include lunch and dinner, weekly maid service, an organized activity program, van transportation, and the use of all facilities. These are the standard services found in many retirement residence facilities.

There is no nursing facility on site but there is a personal care section with twenty-four-hour professional nursing care. Optional apartment homemaker services are available. The extra health care amenities are based on the pay-as-you-use principal. These services include help in/out of showers, medicine reminder, an escort service to/from the dining room, a shopping service, and daily assurance visits. The costs could mount up but the benefits of independent living may more than offset the additional expenses.

Treemont*

In 1974 when Treemont* opened in North Dallas the ninety-acre tract was somewhat isolated. There was some open space in the vicinity. Today high-rise office buildings, hotels, and a magnificent shopping plaza with an ice skating rink have taken up the open spaces.

Treemont remains as a quiet oasis among the "progress" that has engulfed the area. The senior adult community is made up of 320 efficiency, one-, or two-bedroom apartments. A separate health care center, including a 100-bed full-care nursing facility, is located in an adjacent building. This is available on an additional cost as required basis. The knowledge that a medical staff is there to respond to a signal from the bedside and tubside emergency system has to be very comforting.

They have some interesting activities that we haven't found in many retirement communities. A local savings and loan sets up a branch office twice a week in the auditorium. One of the Dallas community colleges uses the auditorium for classes for both residents and the general public. A local drugstore chain manages the full-service pharmacy.

ASSISTED LIVING
■   ■   ■

During the last four years we have seen a dramatic increase in the building of assisted-living facilities on retirement community campuses. These are usually separate apartment buildings designed for those who can't cope with total independent living. Friendships are maintained since all that is required is a move to a different building. This should not be confused with a nursing home. Residents maintain independence except for certain assistance that they require.

Heritage Place*

Located in Memphis, Tennessee, Heritage Place refers to its health care unit as the assisted-living wing. There are private rooms, studio apartments, and one- and two-bedroom apartments. Three meals are served in their private dining room. There is an arts and crafts room, a fitness and exercise facility, and a variety of scheduled activities. A nursing assistant is on duty twenty-four hours a day, seven days a week. Assistance, if required, is available for bathing, grooming, dressing, medication maintenance, and monitoring.

Covenant Village*

Located in Turlock, California, Covenant Village is owned and operated by the Evangelical Covenant Village. They identify their personal care complex as Sequoia. It is described as a complex that is a nonmedical facility for those not yet in need of intermediate or skilled nursing care. The residents receive limited assistance in their daily needs while maintaining independence and dignity.

In the Winter 1989/90 issue of *Viewpoints*, a quarterly newsletter of

Bristol Village (see chapter 11), there is an article highlighting a slightly different use of their assisted-living complex called Bristol Court. "Last winter, Margaret and Walter Boss moved to Bristol Village from Mt. Vernon, Washington. Margaret said, 'Bristol Court was a major factor in our move to the village. We could not leave my 98-year-old mother, Ernestine Dressler, alone in Washington. But she could move into Bristol Court and we could move into the village.' " An interesting solution to the problem that many retirees face of keeping the family together.

LONG-TERM CARE INSURANCE
■ ■ ■

Complex, difficult to comprehend, expensive, mixed recommendations, frustrating. These are the range of feelings experienced by those trying to make a decision concerning long-term care insurance.

First, some definitions. Here are the major categories of long-term care taken from an AARP newsletter:

■ Skilled Nursing Home Care—For those who need intensive, twenty-four-hour-a-day care and supervision by a registered nurse under the direction of a doctor who is available in an emergency.

■ Intermediate Nursing Home Care—For those who don't require skilled care but who typically do need some nursing assistance and supervision.

■ Custodial Nursing Home Care—For those who require assistance with personal care but don't necessarily need health care services.

■ Home Health Care—This covers a wide variety of services offered at home. Sometimes under a doctor's supervision. It can include medical services, provided by trained professionals such as nurses or physical therapists, or personal care services that can be provided by home health aides.

There are other in-home services that are *nonmedical* such as: chore services; home-delivered meals; friendly visiting volunteers; emergency response systems; and telephone reassurance.

What are the chances of your requiring nursing home care? The May 1989 issue of *New Choices—for the Best Years** had a good article on the subject of nursing home insurance. The author is Marie Hodge. Statistics relative to costs and probable need of a nursing home are:

■ 1988—2.3 million Americans lived in a nursing home.

■ Average cost, $65 a day or $23,725 a year.

■ Medicare pays less than 2 percent of the nation's nursing home bill and that's primarily for skilled nursing care.

■ The average length of stay is 465 days, Medicare covers 100 days.

■ In the fifties and early sixties nursing home care is rarely required.

■ Age sixty-five to seventy-four, chances are 1 in 100 that nursing home care will be required.

■ Age seventy-five to eighty-four, chances are 7 in 100 that nursing home care will be required.

■ After age eighty-five, chances are 23 in 100 that nursing home care will be required.

Ms. Hodge has strong feelings about the need of private insurance. In her opening paragraph she says, "Nursing home insurance should be an indispensable element of your financial planning."

Further complicating this already perplexing puzzle was Congress's enactment and subsequent repeal of the Catastrophic Care Act. *Sr Texas*, a monthly magazine for Texas's most experienced generation highlighted congressional problem areas relating to seniors in their February 1990 issue.

■ Representative F.H. (Pete) Stark (Democrat-California) is pushing an effort to bring back four items from the repealed catastrophic act: mammography screening, expanded home health service, respite care, and hospice care.

■ Expected to dominate the health care agenda in 1990 is the determination of a comprehensive health care policy.

■ Other issues include a change in the way Medicare reimburses doctors, possible Medicare cutbacks, and unpaid leave time off for care of sick children or elderly parents who are sick.

The long-term care insurance puzzle remains in a constant state of upheaval. We suggest the following publications to help you determine what's best for you concerning this issue of continuing care insurance. These brochures are free for the asking:

> *The Consumers Guide to Long Term Care Insurance*
> Health Insurance Association of America
> 1001 Pennsylvania Avenue, NW
> Washington, DC 20004-2599

> *Choice Time—Thinking Ahead on Long Term Care* by Esther Peterson
> Aetna Life Insurance Annuity Company
> Choice Time
> Box 104
> Hartford, CT 06156

> *Before You Buy—A Guide to Long-Term Care Insurance* Health Advocacy Services—Program Department
> AARP
> 1909 K Street, NW
> Washington, DC 20049

In *The Wall Street Journal,* April 7, 1988, the column "Viewpoint" by Michael Gartner was entitled "The 'Golden Years' and Medicine: An Age-Old Challenge." To this we say, Amen!

18

CONTINUING CARE/ LIFE CARE COMMUNITY (CC/LCC)

· · ·

LIFESTYLE OPTION #14, PHASE TWO CARE FOR LIFE SECURITY

. . . "We average four weddings a year . . . last year we had eight . . ." said Almeta Kelso, our guide and a resident at Moosehaven* —a life care community in Orange Park, Florida.

Is a continuing care/life care community just for old folks about ready to cash in their chips? No way! It's seniors living life! It's a group of fifteen at a private luncheon singing happy birthday as an honoree opened his presents at the Village on Canyon Creek (now Temple Meridian on Canyon Creek) in Temple, Texas. It's the laughter from the dining room, and a little old man, dressed in his Sunday best, scooting along on his electric three-wheeler. His crutches are strapped to a bracket on his cart as he hurries to Sunday dinner at Pennswood Village in Newtown, Pennsylvania. It's the Spitfire, a two-seater sports car, parked in the residents' parking area at Friendship Village* in Tempe, Arizona. It's eavesdropping in the dining room at Panorama City in Lacey, Washington, on the conversation of two residents obviously having a luncheon date. At times she giggled just the way she probably giggled on her first date many, many years ago.

It's true there are old folks in a life care community. Some are very very old and forced to move a little slower. But ready to call it quits? Not from what we observed.

Even those in the health care sections had a smile and a wave of the hand. Not all of them, some were having a difficult time, but that takes place as their journey's end draws near.

The average age in a life care community is in the late seventies. This high average age doesn't mean there aren't any young old. Some folks move to a community at the time they retire from a company. Those people with a high degree of security needs find this type of community very satisfying. Some say a CC/LCC prolongs life. In newsletters that we receive from various communities there are announcements of many special parties for those who reach 100.

We have had a difficult time figuring out what to call this type of community. Most facilities refer to themselves as life care communities; however an AARP book, listing approximately 400 facilities, is entitled *National Continuing Care Directory.* The first edition was printed in 1984 and the book was revised in 1988. It can be ordered from AARP Books, 1865 Minor Street, Des Plains, IL 60016. It's a very good reference book. From here on we will refer to continuing care/life care communities as CC/LCC since they are one and the same thing. The shift to the use of continuing care has probably come about because of very bad publicity received by some life care facilities that have gone into bankruptcy. Retirees who have put most or all of their life savings into an entrance fee only to have the facility go bankrupt have raised a real howl. Court actions, headlines, magazine articles, and even jail sentences have resulted. We'll go into detail on this when we discuss the "going in" financial arrangements.

Just what is a continuing care/life care community?

We define a CC/LCC as a facility that offers housing, meals, services, and health care. There is a binding contract that guarantees and describes what is and what is not included. A fee is paid upon entry which may be called Founders Fee, capital fee, entrance fee, accommodations fee, endowment fee, or a similar name. The entry fee may or may not be fully or partially refunded upon leaving the facility. There is a monthly charge which is determined by the governing board and subject to change, usually once a year.

NOTE: Some fraternal organizations require the signing over to the organization of certain personal assets and income. These were the original truly life care communities. Residents are thereafter completely cared for. They are even given a small monthly allowance. This applies *only* to fraternal or special groups. This is not applicable to CC/LCC as described above.

We draw special attention to this because upon first hearing about a CC/LCC many people say, "I'll never sign over my estate, that's not for me."

Our definition of a CC/LCC covers the basics. We'll expand on this to give you a better understanding of the concept. The name continuing care or life care describes the basic intent—to provide a secure haven for the rest of a person's life. Take a retirement residence (Chapter 16), add a medical care facility (Chapter 17), then add an up-front fee and a contract guaranteeing care for your remaining years, and you have a true life care facility.

This has been modified in some cases through the stipulation of a certain number of days of nursing care and then it's a pay-as-you-use arrangement.

Those facilities guaranteeing lifetime care will have a large entry fee. In essence, all residents are pooling funds. Some participants may get many years of nursing care from the fund and others only a limited time. Some residents may never receive any actual health care benefits except knowing the care was available when and if they needed help. An additional benefit is the peace of mind of knowing that your surviving spouse will be cared for, regardless of how long he or she lives.

It's a form of prepaying medical care. The Internal Revenue Service ruling #76-481 allows a medical deduction for a portion of the entry fee and monthly fee that is properly allocated to medical care. Since this is an IRS ruling, it is always subject to change. Each facility will be able to explain the applicability and extent of the ruling to its complex.

Those facilities with a pay-as-you-use arrangement have smaller entry fees because their "guarantee" is less. A payback of a portion of the entry fee is becoming increasingly popular. One of the objections to life care has been the loss of assets (entry fee) when the resident leaves for whatever reason, including death. At many places formulas have been established which pay back a portion of the fee, without interest.

The study mentioned earlier that appeared in *Consumer Reports* (February 1990) gives the average fee increases for CC/LCC's according to the American Association of Homes for the Aging. Entrance fees cannot be raised retroactively but the monthly fees do change:

1985	+6.2%
1986	+5.8%
1987	+4.8%
1988	+5.8%

CONTINUING CARE ACCREDITATION
▪   ▪   ▪

The American Association of Homes for the Aging (AAHA) has established a Continuing Care Accreditation Commission (CCAC).* The primary membership of the AAHA consists of 3,300 community-based not-for-profit nursing homes, independent housing facilities, community service agencies, and continuing care retirement communities (CCRC). Approximately two thirds of all CCRC's in the United States are AAHA members.

The commission is composed of up to seventeen members, at least a third of whom are consumer representatives. In addition, a financial advisory panel of industry experts assists in financial review of CCRC's seeking accreditation.

A community applies for accreditation and an extensive self-study based on its mission and established CCAC standards is undertaken. A review team of trained volunteers evaluates the facility, with a three-day on-site study verifying the self-study report. The commission reviews all findings and makes a decision. Accreditation status is for a five-year period. As of early 1990 there were ninety-one accredited communities in twenty states. Both for-profit and not-for-profit communities can apply for accreditation. Accreditation is certainly a step in the right direction and should give those considering this lifestyle a greater feeling of security. It should be understood that this is still very new and mistakes can occur. For a list of accredited communities send a request to the commission, enclosing a self-addressed stamped envelope.

The February 1990 issue of *Consumer Reports* has a nine-page study entitled "Communities for the Elderly." An excellent article. It reports that 230,000 people, mostly over seventy-five, live in 800 CC/LCC's. This number is expected to double by the year 2000.

The article draws attention to the differentiation of continuing care and continuum of care. These continuum of care communities offer the same services as a CC/LCC but their financial arrangements are different. Occupants pay rent for their apartment, and if nursing care is required a person pays the going rate. It is inferred that this is a shady practice. We don't think so since there is no entry fee. The advantage is that if nursing care is required, when nursing beds are available the person can remain in his/her community with his/her support system nearby.

Pennswood Village

We knew we would have to visit Pennswood Village after we read an intriguing article about the facility. It is located in Newtown, Pennsylvania, about twenty-seven miles from Philadelphia. This is a Quaker-directed life care community.

The article was not a public relations pitch or a glowing story of the complex by the executive director. It was written by a resident, an experienced author. His description of the trauma that he and his wife went through as they left their home of fifty years to move to Pennswood is vivid. What happened during the first three years of their new lifestyle is written with great honesty—a better portrayal than relating what residents tell us.

Rather than describing what we saw at Pennswood it would be much more authentic to relate what these two new residents saw and experienced. What follows is a review of an article written by Gerald Carson as it appeared in the August 1983 issue of *The Country Journal* magazine.

On June 11, 1980, as he watched the movers pack up enough furniture to fill a snug three-room apartment, Gerald Carson fell off the porch. The next day he entered Pennswood via ambulance with his wife following in the family car. He was eighty and Lettie Gay was seventy-nine.

Their decision to make a major lifestyle change came about as a result of a pleasant weekend visit with friends at Crosslands,* in Kennett Square, Pennsylvania, another Quaker-directed community.

They liked what they saw. Jointly they came to the realization that their 160 acres and eleven-room house were getting too much to handle. They reasoned that there was a time for all things. The time had come to look for less responsibility and more support services. Common sense told them to face the problem now, before it became critical.

They checked out three life care facilities. What a shock! Waiting lists were for five or more years! By chance they heard that a new facility was in the planning stage and became charter members of Pennswood.

Moving from Columbia County, New York, to a new state, a new way of living among people who didn't know them, caused them emotional disarray. They arranged to leave before the tag sale ladies moved in to handle the sale of their cherished items that had to go. From eleven rooms to three rooms meant they had to sell a lot. Upon leaving, they chose a circuitous route so as not to look back on what they were leaving behind.

They felt sentimental saying farewell to the local library that Lettie had directed, to their old and valued friends, to the house with the stenciled heights of their young daughters on one of the door frames.

Pennswood was calling for compelling reasons. They answered the call but hadn't planned on such a dramatic entrance—an ambulance and a lonely driver in the family car.

Their first in-depth exposure to Quakers, they had seen an Indian but not a Quaker, was revealing. The Friends didn't say "thee" and "thou" and the picture on the Quaker Oats package didn't do them justice. The Quakers don't push their distinctive beliefs on others and are more tolerant and kind than most people. Their practice of TLC (Tender Loving Care) took Gerald Carson through the next six months of leg surgery and recuperation.

This experience with the Quakers, coupled with the investigation the Carsons had done, reinforced their initial decision to join their future with Pennswood. They had become charter members, meaning the facility was not completed. This involved some financial risk. Paying an entrance fee to a facility only partially completed and without a track record required a lot of faith. Their decision that Pennswood Village, Inc., was financially a triple-A risk proved to be right.

The 252-apartment village is located on 82 acres. It is adjacent to the 220 acres of George School, a Quaker secondary school for boarding and day students. Immediately next door is Newtown Friends School for children, kindergarten through eighth grade. There are many intergenerational programs between the Pennswood residents and the students of these two schools.

The central building is Penn Hall, containing offices, auditorium, gift shop, barbershop and coiffeur, lounges, greenhouse, and library (75 magazines, 3,000 books, and still growing). There are two dining rooms and a coffee shop. There also is a woodworking shop, a darkroom, a pharmacy, and physical therapy rooms.

One part of the community building is known as Barclay Living Area. It is for those who can't handle independent living. On the lower floor is the infirmary and rooms for those who require intensive nursing care.

There are 384 residents. Of these, 196 are singles with a ratio of women to men of 2.4 to 1, and there are 94 couples. Contact with other residents led Gerald Carson to feel that couples experience more stress on moving to Pennswood than singles. He believes that moving to smaller quarters adds significantly to the stress but there will be less problems if each partner has interests of his/her own. He feels single people are inclined to reach out more quickly than married people. Newcomers have anxiety but that will pass in three months to a year. Most people bring too many possessions, which causes the need to do more sorting out.

A demographic career picture shows ninety-seven homemakers, eighty-five educators, sixty-eight business executives, sixteen in various fields of medicine, fourteen engineers, thirteen from the literary field, ten government employees, six lawyers, and a scattering of other occupations.

The average age in 1983 was seventy-nine-plus for those in the winter of their years. There are handicaps, which are accepted and dealt with sympathetically, and borne with grace. Self-pity is conspicuously absent. (Average age in 1989 was eighty-two.)

Those who prefer to keep to themselves have that opportunity. Others who wish to reach out have seemingly unlimited options. There are forty-five standing or ad hoc committees. Outside bridges can be built through involvement in the schools or in town activities.

Volunteer work plays a prominent part in the lives of many residents. Many interest groups meet to play bridge, chess, cribbage, knit, or sew. Others meet to read books or exchange views on developments in the nation and the world. Gerald Carson wrote *The Dentist and the Empress: The Adventures of Dr. Tom Evans in Gas-Lit Paris* (Houghton Mifflin, 1983) after having settled at Pennswood.

There is an underlying spirit of optimism throughout the article. Familiar and friendly faces disappear from time to time. This is inevitable. But he feels Pennswood has undoubtedly increased his and his wife's life expectancy and has given a new dimension to their added years.

In addition to the optimism there are also many humorous explana-
tions of life at Pennswood. His views of the Quakers reflect his humor.

It is understood within the facility that there will be no smoking or
drinking of alcoholic beverages in the public areas. But the author is
thankful for the tolerance of the Quakers. He appreciates their acceptance of English common law, namely, that a resident's apartment or
room is his or her castle; and he refers to the residents taking to heart the
instructions of St. Paul to Timothy to "use a little wine for thy stomach's
sake and their other infirmities."

He reports that the manager of the local state liquor store happily told
him that business had doubled since the opening of Pennswood.

In the words of Gerald and Lettie Gay, "[We] have never regretted
the decision."

We wrote to the director at Pennswood, asked for an update on the
facility, and inquired about the well-being of the Carsons. They replied
and said the Carsons were still residents and doing quite well.

We received some copies of the *Pennswood View*, the residents' publication. Listed on the masthead as a member of the Editorial Board was
Gerald Carson. Two of the issues had stories with his byline. One of his
stories was about their visit to France in the fall of 1985. In this article
he refers to the trip as their last visit to Paris. Our calculations are that
Gerald Carson was eighty-five and Lettie was eighty-four when they
visited the museums and restaurants where "the wines were noble as well
as the prices." In another issue is a feature story about Gerald Carson's
leadership in recording the history of Pennswood.

Upon opening the Annual Report of 1984–85, there on the first page
was a picture of Mr. Carson in black tie and white coat. He and another
person served as co-chairpersons of the Pentaversary Celebration (five-
year anniversary celebration). Also included was a pictorial review of the
residents' fashion show. There was a picture of Lettie Gay modeling her
own floral print evening costume of the 1930s—slim, trim, and graceful.

There is much written about role models for younger people. Those
youngsters who have had positive role models have a much greater
chance for a good life than those without this benefit.

What about a role model for seniors? The same principle should apply
for seniors as applies to youngsters. Lettie Gay and Gerald Carson are
ideal role models for those planning retirement!

Pennswood View, Fall 1989 (quarterly newsletter).

An article titled, "I could write a book, if I had the time," written by Gerald Carson. At eighty-nine, Mr. Carson writes on. His article describes his day. Each morning he reads the *New York Times*, the *Philadelphia Inquirer*, and the local *Courier Times*. He highlights his civilizing hour before dinner with a glass of "pure limestone water of Kentucky raised to a higher form." No mention is made of Lettie Gay. Perhaps she has gone to her eternal rest. Gerald Carson continues, growing and contributing to society.

Pennswood is accredited and has a waiting list of four to ten years. All of the other Quaker-directed communities are also accredited and have extensive waiting lists.

The 1988/89 Annual Report features a report by the president of the Residents' Association. It is very obvious that open communications between the residents and management exist. A member of the association has an office that is manned one hour a day for residents to stop by and chat.

An intergeneration committee was formed to increase participation with Bucks County Community College. A course will be given at Pennswood. More quality concerts will be presented in Penn Hall—the first was a Christmas concert by the Princeton Singers. An enlarged program of aid to new residents has been initiated. Several times during the year new residents are brought together for orientation meetings.

The report compares in quality and completeness with many corporate reports. It is obvious nothing is being held back.

Since Pennswood is a life care community that offers all meals, medical services, and long-term care if required, there is an entry fee and monthly fee. Rates in effect as of January 1990:

Type of Apartment	Number Occupants	Entry Fee	Monthly Fee	Number Units
Studio, 504 square feet	1	$ 47,600	$ 1,090	24
Large one-bedroom, 728 square feet	1	78,400	1,526	66
	2	98,000	2,180	

Type of Apartment	Number Occupants	Entry Fee	Monthly Fee	Number Units
Two-bedroom, 1,064 square feet	1	$ 110,400	$ 1,744	38
	2	138,000	2,398	

Health care rates listed below are in lieu of the monthly fee for the individual concerned. (In most cases where there is permanent transfer to the nursing center the spouse will move to a smaller apartment to reduce his/her monthly costs.)

Barclay House—One person—$1,308 per month
Woolman House—One person—$1,526 per month

The entry fee is refundable during the first three months, thereafter 3 percent is deducted for each month of residence. No refund is paid in the event of death after the three-month adjustment period.

In the annual report, the associate director portrays a basic Pennswood philosophy: "While Pennswood offers many guarantees, we cannot promise you freedom from continued demands of aging. What we can do is help you to continue to adapt to life's demands."

FACILITY COMPARISON
■ ■ ■

Following are thumbnail descriptions and costs of five full and modified CC/LCC's located around the country. We will compare costs for a *one-bedroom, one-bath unit.* In most cases this would be about a 650-square-foot apartment.

John Knox Village*

John Knox Village in Lees Summit, Missouri, started in the early seventies and is an accredited community of over 2,000 residents and the largest continuing care community in the country. It is on the outskirts of Kansas City, Missouri.

Our impression of the village is that it is a city in itself. It is *big!*

Because of this, meals *are not* included in the cost. There are forty different floor plans to choose from in houses, apartments, duplexes, and garden cottages. All amenities as normally found in a retirement community are available plus many restaurants, a chapel, a fishing lake, a golf course, a library, a shopping arcade, and a thrift shop.

Adjacent to the community is the Lees Summit Community Hospital and Research Physicians Center offering professional services and specialized knowledge of geriatric care. In 1988 a 420-bed skilled nursing center was opened; it includes a 36-bed independent Alzheimer's unit.

There are nine apartment complexes. We have chosen a *one-bedroom unit* in Country Club Manor. Cost appears average for all one-bedroom apartment units. Two medical plans are available. Rates as of January 1990:

		Life Care Gold		Continuing Care	
Age		55 and over		55 and over	
Nursing Care		No cost first 90 days.		No cost first 90 days.	
		After 90 days, for unlimited time, cost is 50% of room and care fees.		After 90 days cost is 50% of room and care fees for up to 1,005 days.	
		Meals, ancillary items extra.		Meals, ancillary items extra.	

Type of Apartment	Number Occupants	Entry Fee	Monthly Charge	Entry Fee	Monthly Charge
One-bedroom	1	$ 50,323	$ 642	$ 41,953	$ 585
	2	69,743	837	53,003	724

Prorated refund of entrance fee upon death or move out	Up to 60 months 80% maximum	Up to 60 months 80% maximum

The Forum Pueblo Norte*

Located in Scottsdale, Arizona, the Forum Pueblo Norte has twenty acres and opened in the spring of 1985. Originally known as Pueblo

Norte, it was a Pacific Living Center Retirement Community in cooperation with the Adventist Health System.

In the fall of 1988 it was acquired by a nonprofit corporation sponsored by Forum Lifecare, Inc., which manages the facility. Forum Lifecare, Inc., has been involved in the development and management of life care communities since 1965 and has developed over fifty retirement communities. The parent corporation is Forum Group, headquartered in Indianapolis, Indiana, and is publicly traded on NASDAQ.

There are 174 apartments and villas housed in 20 buildings and a licensed health center. It has standard one-bedroom one-bathroom apartments, one meal a day, all utilities, weekly housekeeping, scheduled transportation, and planned activities. Use of health care facility is not included in the costs listed below. Rates as of January 1990:

TYPE OF APARTMENT: ONE-BEDROOM

Number Occupants	Plan	Entry Fee	Monthly Charge
1	Life care with equity	$ 98,500	$ 937
2	Life care with equity	98,500	+482
1	Life care estate	57,500	937
2	Life care estate	57,500	+482

The life care with equity plan has a unique feature we have not seen in other communities. A resident purchases an equity in the community which can be sold and thus shares in the benefits of any appreciation in value of the equity.

There is no additional entry fee for the second person on either plan because this is not a life care facility. The entrance fee does not pay medical expenses. If long-term care is required the cost will not be more than the monthly one-bedroom apartment fee. The life care estate plan was designed for persons who desire a lower entry fee with limited residual value for their estate. This facility can be described as Southwest desert luxury. There are 120 residents.

Covenant Shores

Located on 700 feet of Lake Washington frontage and 12 acres on Mercer Island, Washington, is Covenant Shores. A beautiful setting for the 110 residents. A fifty-boat marina juts out directly in front of the community. From its beginning in 1886 the Swedish Covenant Church, known then as the Chicago Mission Friends, has become the Evangelical Covenant Church. They have founded twelve retirement communities in six states.

Amenities include: one meal a day, scheduled transportation, an emergency call system, an activities program, craft, woodworking and a sewing room, a library, and a residence wellness clinic. Rates as of January 1990:

TYPE OF APARTMENT:
ONE-BEDROOM, 815 SQUARE FEET

Number Occupants	Entry Fee	Monthly Charge
1	$ 60,000	$ 661
2	+6,000	+275

Each person can receive nursing care benefits up to *60 days*. There is no entry fee refund program.

Golden Palms

Sponsor of Golden Palms* in the Rio Grande Valley city of Harlingen, Texas, is the Valley Baptist Medical Center. This is a major regional health care facility and is located adjacent to Golden Palms. All apartments are in a six-story building, each has a balcony. Amenities include: *one meal daily,* scheduled transportation, an activity director, an emergency call system, a heated swimming pool, craft, hobby, and woodworking rooms, a library, and a twice monthly housekeeping service and weekly flat linen service. Rates as of January 1990:

TYPE OF APARTMENT:
ONE-BEDROOM

Number Occupants	Entry Fee	Monthly Charge
1	$ 65,900	$ 1,055
2	+10,000	+475

Nursing services in a semi-private room in the health care center for an unlimited period of time are available with very little increase in the resident's monthly service fee.

Ninety percent of the admission fee is refundable.

Rappahannock Westminster-Canterbury

Located in the "northern neck" area near the Rappahannock River and the Chesapeake Bay is Rappahannock Westminster-Canterbury (RWC).* A cottage life care community on the shores of an eight-acre lake. It is located in Irvington, Virginia.

It is related to the Presbyterian and Episcopal Churches of Virginia which, according to the October 1989 newsletter, "assures residents of quality retirement living and unlimited long term care."

It is in a very fine rural setting. As we left the grounds right across the street was the entrance to the very first-class Tides Inn Golden Eagle Golf Course.

Amenities included are those found in the other communities previously listed. *One meal a day* is included. Rates as of January 1990:

TYPE OF APARTMENT:
ONE-BEDROOM

Number Occupants	Founders Fee	Monthly Charge
1	$ 105,300	$ 1,459
2	+35,000	+592

There is an additional 4 percent of the Founders Fee for each year under age sixty-five. Health care, including nursing care on the premises, is available at no extra cost for life. If death occurs within the first twenty-five months of residence the Founders Fee will be refunded less 2 percent for each month of residence.

The fee schedule had this note: ". . . [RWC] which elects to base fees on actuarial information thus assuring our residents that our future health care obligations to them will be met."

ANALYSIS
■   ■   ■

It's evident from these six CC/LCC's (including Pennswood) that pricing and benefits vary considerably. The most expensive for a one-bedroom, one-bath unit is RWC with the highest Founders Fee, followed by the Forum Pueblo Norte. Location has to have an influence on these costs. Scottsdale and the Chesapeake Bay area are top of the line addresses. The decor of both of these is first class.

Covenant Shores with a somewhat lower entry fee and monthly fee offsets this saving by limiting the "free" days in the nursing facility to 60 and offering no refund plan.

Golden Palms has an overall lower fee structure when unlimited days of nursing care are required, there is only a small increase in cost, but it is not in a campus setting. It blends in with the hospital and doctors' offices nearby.

The John Knox Village continuing care entry fee is the lowest. However, there is a medical cost and this large 2,000-person complex does not have the community atmosphere prevalent in the other complexes. Because of its size meals are not served. The daily meeting of the kindred souls at mealtimes promotes the affiliation necessary to build a support group. Here other means have to be found.

Other factors to consider are the neighborhood surrounding a facility —Pennswood excels in this category—the layout of the complex, modification restrictions, and the construction materials that are used.

Sunny Acres Villa* in Denver, Colorado, showed a great deal of wear and tear. We talked to a resident who had just added on a back porch. He was proud of his handiwork, but the carpentry didn't add much to the building and the overall beauty of the facility.

Spanish Cove Retirement Village* in Yukon, Oklahoma, is very crowded. In some cases the barracks-like buildings were within five or six feet of each other. Whereas Butterfield Trail Village* in Fayetteville, Arkansas, was spread out, well landscaped, and architecturally very attractive.

The only conclusion that can be reached is that your pocketbook and an acceptable geographic location will have the major influence on your choice of a CC/LCC.

THE CC/LCC—A NEW BUSINESS WITH GROWING PAINS
■   ■   ■

When we first started our research in the late seventies there were relatively few CC/LCC's around the country. Since that time hundreds of communities have emerged, both for profit and nonprofit. Following are some items of interest that will help you better understand this complex later-life alternative.

Mennonite Maze

We had a fascinating discussion with Earl D. Greaser, director of the Virginia Mennonite Retirement Community, Inc.* This community, located in Harrisonburg, Virginia, was building a health care center. The enthusiastic director showed us the plans and a new innovation in connection with a special wing devoted to those afflicted with Alzheimer's disease.

A large fenced-in maze will open off this wing. It will be carefully shrubbed so the fence is hidden and there will be endless shrubbed paths. We were told that people who have this disease have a great need to walk, walk, walk.

Get Up—Shut Up and Go

This Quaker-run facility located in Gwynedd, Pennsylvania, twenty miles from Philadelphia, was started in 1967. The *Foulkeway Bulletin*, the residents' publication of Foulkeways at Gwynedd, had a variance from the usual Quaker politeness code. "Get Up—Shut Up and Go" is the theme song when the fire bells jingle. A need was perceived to speed up the time necessary to evacuate the premises during a fire drill. In addition to the "move" theme two lines are to be formed. Slow walkers, those with canes or walkers to the right. Sounds like an efficient well-organized way to get the troops moving by having two lines and urging the necessity to hurry along.

John Knox Buy-Out

In the John Knox Village, Lees Summit, Missouri, 1989 annual report, the chairman's and president's message said . . . "a group of for-profit New York investors offered to purchase John Knox Village. The Board filled its fiduciary responsibilities by carefully examining the proposal and commissioning an updated actuarial report. On January 30, 1989, the Board unanimously rejected the offer."

Posh

Harbour's Edge* is the most elegant of all the CC/LCC's we have surveyed. The most expensive units overlook the inland waterway with its constant array of passing boats.

The entrance fee ranges from $225,000 to $550,000 and the membership plan provides for payback of a substantial amount of the fee. Monthly fee for the largest units on the top floors, either the fifth or sixth floors (1,860 square feet) is $1,490 for one person, $1,955 per month for two people.

A DOWN SIDE TO LIFE CARE
■ ■ ■

On Thursday, June 16, 1977, we attended an advertised Relax . . . It's Retirement meeting which featured a speaker with tremendous credentials. Over one half of the three-column fourteen-inch ad for the meeting was made up of his picture and credentials.

This was to be a unique discussion of alternate lifestyles of retirement; keeping fit and active in retirement; problems in retirement and how to avoid them; and the joys of retirement and how to find them. Refreshments, no admission charge, date, and place made up the rest of the ad. No mention was made concerning "who" was sponsoring the meeting.

The presentation was entertaining, interesting, and informative. The talk built up to a very positive and exciting description of living care retirement which later was called life care. A low-key reference to the eventual building of a John Knox Retirement Community in a town thirty miles north was also made. We, along with about 200 other people, signed up to be put on the mailing list and then we had punch and cookies.

There were many staff people standing around and a lot of books were for sale. We met a gentleman from Group Communication Company, a subsidiary of Christian Services, Inc. The speaker had referred to Dr. Berg a few times so we bought his book entitled *Affordable Retirement Living.* It cost $1.95.

This was at the time that we were searching out everything we could find on retirement. There wasn't much in those days.

We found Dr. Berg's thoughts and accomplishments extremely helpful. Dr. Berg had received his Doctor of Ministry Degree and was a Presbyterian pastor as well as founder and chairman of the board of Christian Services, Inc.

The meeting speaker had directed Dr. Berg's research and guided him in his dissertation while Berg was at the University of Southern California. The book contained a list of twenty-seven living care projects developed with Dr. Berg's leadership. Four John Knox villages were included in the list.

The book contained many testimonials starting with one from former President Richard M. Nixon, moving onto statements from ministers, doctors, business executives, politicians, and residents of John Knox Villages. There was a great deal of "God's Word" in the book as well as old-fashioned sell for the living care concept and Christian Services, Inc.

The John Knox Village of Denton, Texas, became a partial reality. Financial troubles plagued the facility and it later became Lake Forest Village, owned and operated by Lake Forest Corporation, a nonprofit board. They filed for protection under Chapter 11 of the U.S. Bankruptcy Code in 1984. Today it is known as Lake Forest Good Samaritan Village,* Denton, Texas—a ministry of the Evangelical Lutheran Good Samaritan Society.

We met with the director and progress is being made. A health care unit has been built and there is a general "sprucing up" of the facility. The original members of the John Knox concept lost their life care guarantee. The reality of their situation is that they never had a life care guarantee. They paid a Founders Fee but medical facilities were never built. Today it is not a CC/LCC. Medical facilities will be available on a pay-as-you-use basis.

There is a resident morale problem. This is to be expected because of the financial beating the old-timers received. The director had a positive view but readily acknowledged they have a long way to go.

A picture in the April 1985 issue of *Money* Magazine looked familiar. It was a mug shot of Reverend Kenneth Berg, jailed in 1984 for securities fraud in Alabama. The magazine article is entitled "The Broken Promise of Lifecare Communities." It is a disturbing report on an industry that is failing the nation's elderly. In three months of investigation reporters identified forty continuing care/life care communities that since the mid-seventies have gone bankrupt or experienced severe financial difficulties.

The article doesn't pull punches. It names many places where promises were not kept, where elderly hearts were broken. We feel the life care concept is a great approach for many people. We do not want to deter anyone from this lifestyle by including this negative aspect. However, we would not be fair to our readers if we didn't point out these problems. Prudent investigation and analysis will greatly reduce the chances of buying into a failure.

Some failures or near failures can come about because of poor management decisions or in some cases inexperience because of the newness of the CC/LCC concept.

We talked to the chairman of the board of a not-for-profit CC/LCC who told us that the life expectancy of their residents doubled. Their residents lived twice as long as the actuarial tables for their age had projected. He said it took some careful budgeting and expense control until they could get income and expenses in line. That meant some tough decisions had to be made. Needless to say, all residents weren't completely happy with these decisions. Fortunately a solid business approach was taken.

A similar problem was met head on at Sunny Acres Villa in Colorado. An executive director's report stated that their residents are living between twelve to thirteen years. Their financial calculations were based on a longevity of ten years and they had to make major cost adjustments.

In the report an interesting comparison was made concerning length of stay in the nursing center. A study of twenty-six life care communities showed that the average time spent in a skilled nursing center was four years. At Sunny Acres Villa it was less than two years. They attributed this difference to providing more and better in-apartment nursing and other support care. This allows residents to stay in their own apartments longer.

Understandably, many financial problems have come about because of an oversensitivity to the concerns of the residents. By this we don't mean that resident concerns shouldn't matter, they do. However, if price adjustments are not made and the facility goes into bankruptcy, everyone suffers. Making a tough decision may well enable the community to survive.

The question of who is responsible for the successful operation of a CC/LCC facility is extremely important. This question has to be followed by, "Who is liable in case of a closing?" A resident's agreement doesn't give the resident any ownership for his/her entrance fee. In essence, it's a blind faith arrangement with the entity owners. In the case of Pacific Homes, the statement "a non-profit corporation of the United Methodist Church" would lead many people to feel that their money was in good hands, but they ended up in bankruptcy.

We have found these same kinds of statements on numerous brochures. For example: Sponsored by Valley Baptist Medical Development Corp. . . . Chartered by the Episcopal and Presbyterian Churches in Virginia . . . Ministry of the Christian and Ministry Alliance Foundation . . . and Nonprofit communities for older people governed by a board composed of members of the Religious Society of Friends (Quakers). It's vitally important that anyone considering a CC/LCC know exactly what these statements really mean! We found one that spells out the conditions in no uncertain terms. A brochure entitled, *Southern California Presbyterian Homes* describes a variety of facilities governed by twenty-four trustees. There is a note that reads: SCPH has neither a legal nor financial relationship to the Presbyterian Church— (U.S.A.).

We had a very unique experience while surveying the Village on Canyon Creek, a CC/LCC in Temple, Texas. Our purpose of gathering material for a book was explained to a host who said his wife would be back in a minute.

Soon she appeared with an older couple. They had just looked at an apartment that they wanted and had agreed to sign a reservation agreement. They had not seen the rest of the facility! We joined them for the remainder of the tour, stopping off to see the apartment they chose. It was explained that the reservation fee would be refunded if they changed their minds. Refunded, when that particular unit was sold!

This couple was very congenial. They were from a small town about 100 miles north and were on their way to the Rio Grande Valley to tour a John Knox Village. Their questions were minimal. We had a general discussion at the end of the tour. No questions were asked nor was information given about the financial condition of the village or who the owners were. Our guide told us that quite a few people have moved to the village without having previously visited the facility.

On the back of one of the brochures there was the following notation: ". . . is owned and operated by Temple Retirement Community, Inc., a not-for-profit corporation made up of local leaders concerned about the quality of housing for older persons in our community."

They went bankrupt! LeGan Company* became the new owners. This Denver-based company has been involved in the ownership and operation of fifteen retirement communities throughout the States. Temple Meridian on Canyon Creek* is its new name.

What about residents who paid the original entrance fee? Mr. Michael Garner, marketing director of Temple Meridian, told us that they would not lose any money. The "old" residents wouldn't suffer in any way, other than through the high stress which they experienced worrying about their future as the facility went downhill.

Today there are two plans: (1) a straight rental plan, or (2) a trust deposit program that lowers monthly costs. FDIC insurance guarantees the trust deposit program.

The "new image" has a great deal of flexibility. Included in the monthly fee are fifteen meals, twice-a-month housekeeping, and weekly flat linen service. If these services are not wanted, they are deducted from the monthly fee. Health care is on a pay-as-you-use basis. A cap on the monthly fee based on the consumer price index protects residents from any future hidden surprises.

Building credibility has to be extremely difficult. Even though there are new owners, the past stigma of bankruptcy, especially in a small town of 50,000, will carry over for quite a while. This undoubtedly had a bearing on the promise that the "old" residents would not lose their money. We know of other cases where this didn't happen and many who had put most of their savings in the entrance fee were hurt very badly.

The new management should be congratulated on honoring the past commitments.

For those considering CC/LCC we urge you to do your homework concerning this lifestyle. Here are some publications that we have read which will help you understand the complexities of CC/LCC. Your local library may have these.

The Older American Guide to Housing and Living Arrangements by Margaret Gold. Published by the Institute for Consumers Policy Research; Consumer's Union, 256 Washington Street, Mount Vernon, NY 10553.
The Continuing Care Retirement Community
The American Association of Homes for the Aging
1050 Seventeenth Street, NW
Washington, DC 20036
A Consumer Guide to Life Care Communities
National Consumer League
815 Fifteenth Street, NW
Suite 516
Washington, DC 20005

FRATERNAL/OTHER LIFE CARE
▪ ▪ ▪

Many of the large fraternal orders have homes for their aged members. In our younger years there were references by our parents that someday they might end up in "the home." In both cases, this was in reference to the Masonic Home. These types of facilities are nice and provide a haven for a lot of people. We found one that is quite unique—the closest to a true extended family that we discovered in all our travels— Moosehaven. Known as the City of Contentment, this sixty-one-acre campus is located on the St. Johns River, fifteen miles from Jacksonville, Florida, one of three rivers in the world that flow northward.

Begun in 1922 by the Loyal Order of Moose, this complex is restricted to members of the order and their wives. A member must be sixty-five, in reasonably good health, and in good standing for at least fifteen years immediately preceding his application. It is for those members who are in financial need.

Since its beginning more than 2,000 members and their wives have lived at Moosehaven. When we visited there were 257 men and 257 women in residence. This is the first time in their history that there were as many men as women. There were 87 couples and 340 singles. The average age is eighty for men and seventy-eight for women.

Whatever income or estate a person has is signed over to Moosehaven. Everything a person needs is supplied, including a monthly allowance of $25. Everything means food, clothing, personal needs, a room in one of the twelve residence halls, all medical care, including skilled nursing, in the 150-bed health center, transportation (private cars are not allowed), recreation, a special allowance for a yearly vacation, and burial in Moosehaven Cemetery. Needless to say, this is supported by the brethren throughout the country. A portion of each member's dues is allocated to Moosehaven.

The location in the city of Orange Park is ideal. A long concrete fishing pier juts out into the river. The grounds are well kept. There are arts and crafts rooms, a chapel, woodworking, a model railroad layout and a real caboose, a large meeting hall where the on-site lodge meets, an administration building, and a large snack bar, gift shop, and common room.

The entire atmosphere was one of contentment. There are canes and wheelchairs but they don't stop the smiles. We reflected on the comparison of these folks and the invisible elderly. Much has been written about doing everything to keep people in their own home. The familiarity of one's home and possessions is undoubtedly a plus. But when loneliness settles in, when there is no support group available, we wonder if that doesn't negate the plus of being at home.

CC/LCC CHECKLIST
■   ■   ■

Investigate this lifestyle long before you need it! Waiting until health impairments have taken place may make you ineligible. Rushing to find a place because of a forthcoming possible impairment will put you in a crisis mode, jeopardizing rational decision making. You should keep in mind that many places have long waiting lists.

Questions and Information Needed for Later Evaluation

Be interested, courteous, businesslike, and firm when visiting CC/LCC's, not submissive or humble. If it makes you feel more comfortable take a close friend or adviser with you.

Is the community accredited by the AAHA? If not, why not? Who are the legal owners? Is it a not-for-profit or for-profit community? If affiliated with, sponsored by, or if similar phrases are used, ask exactly what that means. Who is ultimately responsible? Has the community ever changed ownership? A positive answer is a warning sign. Get the details.

Obtain a copy of the annual report and a current financial statement. If you are denied this, walk away from this type of community. What is the history of increase in the monthly fee? Get specific amounts. The annual report will probably list the board of directors. If not, obtain a list with their affiliations. Go over the list of services provided. Ask for clarification of each item. Take notes. Obtain a copy of all forms and the contract to be signed. Ask for a run-down of each item and take copious notes. Are any residents on the board of directors? Who? Talk with them. Is there a residents' council? If not, why not? If so, get a listing with addresses and phone numbers. Talk with some of them.

Is the nursing facility licensed? Medicare/Medicaid-approved? Is space in the nursing center guaranteed? Or, if available, can a substitute nursing center be used? Beware of this. Exactly who makes the decision as to when a person is transferred to the nursing center? Will your physician and your family be consulted?

Talk with residents other than your official host. Wander around on your own. Join in on activities, become one of the group, then ask resident opinion type questions. Admire the grounds and get to know a maintenance person. Ask what really goes on. Where available, stay overnight a couple of times. Have meals on different days. Drop in unannounced.

Does an outside firm manage the community? Who? Get background information. How long has the current director been in office? The previous director?

Visit with a couple of people in the nursing center—someone who has been in the center for a while and also a newcomer.

Have a cup of coffee or ice cream with residents in an informal setting —ask questions. Some communities have happy hours—join them—be restrained in your indulgence, circulate, and ask questions especially toward the end of the happy time!

Up to this point, we have suggested opinion and fact finding. Now it's analysis time. Seek professional assistance—your lawyer, accountant, banker, physician, minister, priest or rabbi. Do not discuss whether you should move or if this is the lifestyle for you—that is exclusively your decision. What you want is help in analyzing the financial condition of the complex, the legalities of the contracts, and the adequacy of the medical facilities and total complex.

Then it's decision time—not a vote of all concerned. There is only one vote—*yours!*

Entrance Paperwork

There are basically four documents to be completed when seeking to gain admittance to a CC/LCC:

1. Waiting list agreement
2. Application/financial data
3. Medical history/physician's statement
4. Occupancy agreement

The *waiting list agreement* specifies the amount received in order to be put on the waiting list and the type of residence requested. The agreement states that there is no guarantee as to when an appropriate residence will be available and that the entrance fee and monthly fee in effect at that time will be charged. The waiting list fee is usually applied to the entrance fee if you become a resident, but it is nonrefundable if you do not become a resident.

Application/financial data include: personal data, family, references; listing of all assets; listing of all liabilities; monthly income from all sources; and additional data if income is insufficient.

The *medical history/physician's statement* is a requirement that seems to vary. Some places require only a statement that all is well. Others want a physical exam, including the doctor's evaluation as to the person's mental condition: clear, partially confused, badly confused.

One facility requires a signed statement that the person is handling his/her own finances. If a power of attorney has been given it must be substantiated that it is for convenience, not a necessity. It also includes a statement that the person must fill out the application independently and alone.

The *occupancy agreement* is fairly uniform. The language is legal in nature with the hereto's, the hereof's, and the hereinafter's. Several items are contained in the agreement. The entrance fee and terms of payment are specified. It is spelled out that the occupant has no lease or any interest in the real estate and property. The occupancy privilege does not pass on to the heirs, assignees, or representatives of the resident. The monthly fee is to be paid on the first of the month in such amount as determined by the board of directors. For this the entity will provide a list of things such as number of meals a day, utilities, maintenance, medical, and other services provided, etc. These are usually short phrases not detailed descriptions. Furnishings within the living unit will be provided by the resident. Nonprofit organizations clarify the intent of the facility to operate as a nonprofit entity. In some cases they clarify their intent not to force a person to leave if he/she can't make the complete monthly payment. They would allow the resident to remain and accept a partial payment as full payment. There are usually three or four detailed paragraphs specifying how and when a person is transferred to the medical complex. The decision is usually made by the facility administration. If there is a return of the entry fee, the terms are specified. The payback feature is usually highlighted in a special brochure as being a major advantage. However, in many occupancy agreements there is a statement similar to the following: In the event residency is terminated . . . the sponsor will attempt to locate a new occupant . . . from the entry fee made by such a new occupant to the extent such sum is sufficient, the departing occupant will be reimbursed for the amount of his entry fee previously made less an appropriate charge for the period of occupancy and the period until the new occupant assumes residency, *provided that such repayment, in the sole opinion of the Board of Directors of the sponsor, does not jeopardize the sound financial structure of the sponsor.* The resident's rights under the agreement will be subordinated and junior to the rights of the mortgage.

We do not want to scare anyone away from a CC/LCC by highlighting some of the provisions of the occupancy agreement. It is our intent to show that a great deal of care needs to be taken when considering this type of arrangement. There is a lot of money involved, in some cases the majority of a person's life savings. We would urge everyone to get professional legal and financial help before signing anything. It's just good common sense to get objective third-party assistance.

Security

There have been some ups and downs in the development of the CC/LCC concept. Some people have been hurt. Painfully hurt, at a time in their lives when there should be a fair degree of contentment. The failure of some facilities to live up to their commitments can't be whitewashed. A very few have been due to fraud; the majority have been due to inept management.

Companies have emerged that will manage a facility using sound business principles. Emotional considerations are not ignored, but when tough decisions such as a monthly rate increase need to be made, the determination is made based primarily on the financial condition of the facility.

One company in the CC/LCC business is Life Care Services Corporation.* The parent company is the Weitz Corporation, founded in 1855. This company is engaged in three main businesses: general contracting primarily for building construction, real estate development, and management of retirement homes developed by Weitz and other companies.

In a newsletter put out by Life Care Services Corporation, Fred Weitz, chairman, president, and CEO, stated, "Life Care Services has one ultimate aim. That goal is to utilize all of our resources to assist in the development and management of quality adult communities which are fiscally responsible and genuinely responsive to human needs. The standard we impose upon ourselves is excellence."

Since 1961 this company has been involved in the development and management of more than fifty life care retirement communities.

Another success story is the Evangelical Lutheran Good Samaritan Society.* This society is a Christian, nonprofit corporation which has been recognized as a sound leader in the health care and management field since 1922. They operate more than 200 successful nursing homes and retirement centers from coast to coast. Their goal is to provide each of their 23,000 residents with the best possible service at the least possible cost.

Earlier in this chapter we commented about the Society of Friends (Quakers) and their involvement in many successful CC/LCC facilities.

The emergence of the Marriott Corporation in the CC/LCC field is being watched very carefully. There is no denying they have management expertise.

Life Care at Its Best—True Life

Twenty-two years ago Rosetta Bell and her husband Bill looked at swampland that later became Shell Point Village,* a CC/LCC located near Fort Myers, Florida—a ministry of the Christian and Missionary Alliance Foundation.

They had just retired as lifelong missionaries and wanted to establish roots in a community of folks with similar beliefs. This community is on an island along the Caloosahatchee River and has been home to Rosetta for twenty-one years. She is approaching her ninety-sixth birthday. Her husband passed on years ago.

She has progressed from a regular apartment—to the Kings Crown 120-apartment assisted-living unit—to the nursing pavilion due to a bout with the flu. Her weight is down to seventy-six pounds. She told us:

> I've lived on three continents—North America, Asia, and Europe. I've slept at the base of the Rockies, Himalayas, and Alps. I have three wonderful children. If the Good Lord will let me live ten more years I will have lived in three centuries! In a few days I hope to be back in my apartment in Kings Crown.

Her greatest joy is that she is not a burden on her children.

For those granted the privilege of aging, Rosetta Bell leads the way in a truly inspiring manner.

IS A CC/LCC FOR YOU?
■ ■ ■

Some people will react negatively to the money involved in the entry fee. They will feel interest should be paid when a refund is made. Others will visualize a CC/LCC as a nursing home or associate it with the "old folks home" that their parents whispered about when they were children.

A few who have had personal experience with dependent, aged parents or have been associated with the "hidden elderly" will have more positive thoughts.

"No way would I be cooped up with a bunch of old people," a few will say.

"Maybe at a later time," would be a common answer.

Our perception of those enjoying this lifestyle is that they are content, secure, and worry-free as far as their future is concerned. They feel independent knowing they will not be a burden on their kids, spouse, friends, or society in general.

They have little concern about whether or not the expenditure is a good financial move. Of prime importance is their sense of well-being knowing that when the time comes when they will need assistance, it will be there.

They reason that they have no other use for the money. Therefore, this "last expenditure," even if it uses up most of their funds, is a very good investment. The return on the investment is peace of mind through dignity in old age.

We suggest that as you consider this lifestyle option you project ahead to the time when slowing down becomes more pronounced—to the time when friends are more frequently listed in the obituary column.

There is a great deal of truth to the old saying: If you don't continue to make new friends, you will eventually be all alone.

Is this lifestyle for us? Our answer is most likely either a retirement complex with adjacent health care or a CC/LCC—but not today. Sometime in the future. We will try very diligently to make the decision before we are forced into making a decision. The waiting-list time requires this action. We hope that we will have the same good sense that the Carsons had when they moved to Pennswood.

In our less physical years, we have the same choice we have always had —to live life to the fullest or sit back and let life pass us by.

As we progress through our life passages, the slowing-down time can be one of disillusionment or challenge; negativism or positive acceptance of reality; becoming a member of the invisible elderly or the active involved seniors; making opportunities or waiting to see what happens. Regardless of age we can greatly influence our own well-being.

The passage into Phase Two is just another segment of the life cycle. No tougher, no more distressing than any of our other life transitions. True, there can be some inconveniences that we haven't experienced before. Perhaps we don't move as fast, see or hear as well, or must adhere to a special diet. But thinking back through one's life there have always been inconveniences that caused concern.

Those evenings when our parents said we had to study—we wanted to be with the gang; the separation from family caused by World War II or the Korean conflict; career disruption or setback; a divorce in the family; the loss of a loved one.

Regardless of age, there is a need for meaningful purpose. Without it, what is there to dream about? The excitement of anticipation and the satisfaction of accomplishment make it all worthwhile.

In the golden years our goals don't need to be as lofty as in our younger years. But having goals is vitally important. It's what makes it worthwhile to get up in the morning. Granted, getting up may be a little tougher, a little more cumbersome, but the desire to accomplish and the thrill of a goal completed make the extra effort worthwhile.

The very last paragraph of the book *Passages* by Gail Sheehy (Bantam Books, 1977) captures the essence of our movement through life: "The courage to take new steps, which allows us to let go of the past, gives us the opportunity to find the richness of the future."

The richness of the golden years!

Don't waste any portion of the only life you have here on earth. Live it to the absolute fullest!

19

YOUR LIFESTYLE
PREFERENCE

· · ·

Lucky you if you know exactly how you are going to handle retirement. Assuming your spouse concurs, you're both on the way to a great retirement. Congratulations!

We would be willing to bet that the vast majority of readers aren't so lucky. However, the very fact that this book is being read shows a sincere desire to try and work out this difficult choice.

It's time to narrow the lifestyle choices. Time to make some initial decisions about which lifestyle best satisfies your needs. If there is a spouse, he or she also needs to narrow the choices. Problems may result. We recognize that there might not be agreement. Each person may have widely different choices. That's a problem, but it can be solved. Surfacing a difference is the only way an acceptable middle ground can eventually be determined.

If a resolution is needed, it's the time to be sure that there is attentive, responsive listening and open two-way communications.

We will review some of the important personal considerations in Chapter 1 and then ask you and your spouse independently to rate the different lifestyles. There will be three choices for each lifestyle: (1) Yes, Interested, (2) Maybe, (3) No Interest.

The next chapter has guidelines for developing a retirement plan. Your lifestyle ratings will be used in developing your unique plan.

REVIEW CHAPTER 1—FIVE KEY QUESTIONS
■ ■ ■

Self-understanding—we all have needs that influence our behavior. The fulfillment or lack of fulfillment of these needs affects us greatly. It influences how we feel about ourselves. Being aware of our needs and knowing the level of satisfaction each of us requires will be helpful in rating lifestyles.

Retirement doesn't change who and what we are. It's been established that the older we get the more we become what we were. Another way of saying this is, when we get older, whatever we are we become more so. Those statements need some explanation.

The phrase "he is set in his ways" is illustrative of this concept. Many years of life's experiences give us a grounding in what we believe. Add to that those things with which we were born: personality, intelligence, and many other attributes, and the mold is pretty well established.

For example, a person who always finds ways to be in the limelight will continue to need the spotlight. The conservative who has taken very few risks will probably take even fewer risks in retirement. Drastic changes are not likely. We will remain in the mold that we are familiar with and in which we feel comfortable.

In some cases where there have been restraints which have produced an artificial mode, the opportunity for a breakout may foster a major change. This happens occasionally. It's the exception rather than the rule.

What is your comfort level—high, average, low—for these needs:

- *Security*—Safety, predictability, orderliness, structure, risk avoidance.

- *Affiliation*—Belonging, group identification, and acceptance.

- *Ego Satisfaction*—Recognition, status, prestige.

Consider your answers when rating each lifestyle.

What were your answers and your spouse's answers to the following:

1. Do you know what your retirement income will be?
2. Are you going to retire or change jobs?

Assuming Retirement:

3. How great a change do you want to make to your lifestyle?
4. How much provision for "old age" (when there are health impairments) do you want to include?
5. What will you do with your free time?

Here again, there may be differences of opinions between yourself and your spouse. Difficult as the resolution may be, now is the time to clear the air.

When rating the fourteen lifestyles, do so with a great deal of careful thought. There is a good probability that you will have close to a third of your life ahead of you.

Where a husband and wife are concerned, there should be no collaboration. Let your true feelings dictate your rating. At this point don't concern yourself about what others, including your spouse, think or believe.

One way of approaching this rating is first to review and think through all of the lifestyle choices. Secondly, rate those that are very definitely of no interest to you. Then take those that are left and determine between a definite interest and "maybe." Consider a "maybe" as a need for more information, further exploration, or of possible interest in the future.

The comments section on the rating sheet is where you list a concern or qualifier. If one lifestyle is of prime importance, but is dependent upon "certain things happening," then this qualifier should be noted under "comments." A lifestyle that might be of interest in the future should be noted. Include an explanation and a time frame.

We have added a #15 lifestyle choice, "Additional Lifestyle." You may have one that we didn't come across; or you may have a combination of various lifestyles that fulfill your needs. This is the place to list this unique lifestyle along with an explanation.

We suggest you use a separate sheet of paper for your answers. A pencil with a good eraser will be useful. As one lifestyle is rated against another there may be several changes in ratings.

Following #15 is an open-ended question that will require some soul searching: I'll spend my time doing—? How will you utilize 2,500 + newfound hours a year? If the answer is a second career, what will it be?

Full or part time? What will keep you active and alert during Phase Two days when work may not be feasible?

Have any of the ideas in Chapter 3, "Seventy-five Activity Idea Generators," sparked an interest?

Remember, retirement is opportunity time; don't be inhibited about what you would like to do—let the child loose!

Don't leave a question blank. If you're in a quandary and don't know, then that's the answer to the question.

YOUR PREFERENCE

Lifestyle Option	Yes, Interested	Maybe	No Interest
# 1. Stay put in community			
A. The same house	_____	_____	_____
B. Another residence	_____	_____	_____
Comments:			
# 2. Snowbirds	_____	_____	_____
Comments:			
# 3. RV'ing	_____	_____	_____
Comments:			
# 4. Retirement area living	_____	_____	_____
Comments:			
# 5. Leisure/Social-centered (Club/Resort/Vacation Community)	_____	_____	_____
Comments:			
# 6. Retiree-dominated (Large Retirement Village/ City)	_____	_____	_____
Comments:			
# 7. Intergenerational Planned Community	_____	_____	_____
Comments:			
# 8. Partial Retiree-dominated (Small Retirement Community)	_____	_____	_____
Comments:			
# 9. Hawaiian Living	_____	_____	_____
Comments:			

Lifestyle Option	Yes, Interested	Maybe	No Interest
#10. Foreign Living	_____	_____	_____
Comments:			
#11. Special Interests	_____	_____	_____
Comments:			
#12. Phase Two Carefree Living (Retirement Residence)	_____	_____	_____
Comments:			
#13. Phase Two Health Care When Needed	_____	_____	_____
Comments:			
#14. Phase Two Care for Life Security	_____	_____	_____
Comments:			
#15. Additional Lifestyle	_____	_____	_____
Comments:			

I'll spend my time doing—?

Now is the time to compare answers with your spouse. Differences of opinion will surface. They need to be resolved, not by dominance but by clear thinking and a meeting of the minds. Where there's a will, there's a way.

Singles should use a confidant as a sounding board to make sure they are thinking rationally. A kind of reality check.

The foundation of planning is determining a goal. Undoubtedly everyone's goal is Having a Great Retirement! The question is—how? The answer has four parts:

1. Having a positive attitude about retirement.
2. Your choice of lifestyle and activity.
3. Determining an action plan before retirement.
4. Taking action.

2 0

YOU ARE UNIQUE—
YOUR PLAN IS
UNIQUE

▪ ▪ ▪

"Let the Child Loose." That was the title of a Sunday sermon. We sat in our pew expecting some words of advice on letting go of our children. Not to meddle or closely lead them along life's rocky roads.

Our pastor, Dr. Bruce Weaver, started by vividly relating a recent personal experience. His grandchild was in the pool urging him to "come on in." A scorching August day in Texas made such an invitation extremely attractive. He replied, "I don't have a swimsuit with me." There was more impish-type urging: "So what—water won't hurt you, come on in."

He described his feelings: It was hot, blistering hot and the water looked cool, inviting. It couldn't really hurt these slacks, but no, grandpas don't do that and certainly not a Methodist man of the cloth. That sun is getting hotter by the minute . . . maybe . . . of course not . . . what would people think . . . why not . . . again . . . why not . . . and with a boisterous laugh he flung himself into the pool, clothes and all.

There was the title of the sermon: "Let the Child Loose." For one fleeting moment the child won out. He said it was great. Exhilarating. A wonderful grandchild/grandpa experience. Why not let the child loose more often? A good question.

Retirement gives us freedom. No need to worry about what the boss thinks! Who cares about what you do? The neighbors, your kids, your relatives, your friends? They are interested and concerned about your well-being. But they don't have a dominant influence on your behavior in the same manner as your company, your department, your boss, and your boss's boss.

With retirement you're free—within certain limits. We are not suggesting you go hog wild. Just apply some good old common sense, but don't feel you have to "act your age."

Think back. Back to your teens or even before adolescence. Was there something you dreamed about doing, but couldn't afford? As a young adult and on into middle life, was there something you wanted to do but never had the time? Now in later life, retirement time, you probably have some money to work with and you have the time. Why not go after your dream?

What is that dream . . . a motorcycle . . . an RV . . . see the U.S.A. . . . world travel . . . a private pilot's license . . . a quarter horse . . . a convertible . . . a gift shop . . . a skill to learn . . . a degree to earn . . . a cause to espouse . . . a helpful hand to others . . . Is there some hidden adventure in your soul waiting to be released?

You are unique. Your dreams are unique. No one can tell you what's right for you. What others have done can help you evaluate alternatives. You can visit localities, observe lifestyles, and study the myriad of opportunities. You should become well informed. But when push comes to shove, it's your decision, your retirement.

Retirement is a new beginning. Will it be just putting in time? Of course not. That's not fulfilling. That's retiring *out* of life. Stay *in* the mainstream of life and you will be vibrant, full of zest. When Phase Two retirement comes about, maintain that involvement in life. These can be the XYZ years—*X*tra *Y*ears of *Z*est.

What's needed is a plan, your unique plan to fit the unique you. A qualifier—where there are two persons concerned, it's a plan for the "unique we."

PREPARING YOUR UNIQUE PLAN
■ ■ ■

One of the axioms in business planning is—if it's not in writing, it's not a plan; it's just an idea that can be altered at any time without rational thinking or discussion. A plan must have a goal, be definitive, and have action steps so the goal can be accomplished. On that basis, we would like to help you develop your retirement plan. Based on one assumption—you are an action person and not an "un-til-er" or a "should've" person.

Goal—Have a Great Retirement
Step One—Dates and Money

Today's Date _____ Projected Retirement Date _____
Projected yearly retirement income will be about $_____
If unable to complete, who will make the determination? _____
When will this be completed? _____

Step Two—Lifestyle Preference

Rank order lifestyle preferences that were answered *Yes, Interested* in the preceding chapter.

SELF	SPOUSE
1. _____	1. _____
2. _____	2. _____
3. _____	3. _____

Questions or additional
information needed

Who will
investigate?

When
completed?

Self _____ _____ _____

_____ _____ _____

_____ _____ _____

Spouse _____ _____ _____

_____ _____ _____

_____ _____ _____

List lifestyle preferences that were answered *Maybe* in the preceding chapter.

SELF   SPOUSE

1. _____   1. _____
2. _____   2. _____
3. _____   3. _____

Questions or additional   Who will   When
information needed   investigate?   completed?
Self _____   _____   _____
     _____   _____   _____
     _____   _____   _____

Spouse _____   _____   _____
       _____   _____   _____
       _____   _____   _____

Step Three—Time Utilization

Answer: How will I effectively utilize 2,500+ newfound hours each year?
Self _____
_____

Questions or additional information needed _____
_____

What are the action steps and timetable required to answer questions, obtain information, make a decision? _____
_____

Spouse _____
_____

Questions or additional information needed _____
_____

What are the action steps and timetable required to answer questions, obtain information, make a decision? _____
_____
_____

Step Four—Follow-Up

Make up a master list of all action steps.

    Action   *Assigned to*   *Target Completion*

Put this list along with the following review dates in a conspicious place.

3-Month Follow-Up 6-Month Follow-Up 12-Month Follow-Up
Review Date _____   Review Date _____   Review Date _____

Step Five—Analysis

Here are ten questions that should be considered:

■ Will the projected retirement income be sufficient to support the lifestyle?

■ Have you taken into consideration an inflation factor?

■ Could present living expenses be adjusted in order to have a larger retirement nest egg?

■ What preparation is needed if you choose a second career? Or a business of your own?

■ Will your activities include just yourself or others? Indoor or outdoor activities? Will they offer both mental and physical stimulation?

■ If you choose to move, will your lifestyle and activity preferences be practical in the new surroundings?

■ Have you taken Phase Two of retirement into consideration? What if you live to be ninety?

■ Is the plan acceptable to all concerned or is it a one-sided "me" plan?

■ Will the plan enable you to live all your life to the fullest?

■ Have you "let the child loose"?

Step Six—The End Result

From all of the information accumulated and the decision made, answer: Here's how I/we are going to Have a Great Retirement.

The essence of time management is self-discipline. Will you follow through? This requires a determination on your part along with self-discipline. The final editing of your unique plan is in your hands.

THE FINALE
■   ■   ■

When we were children each of us had a most wonderful gift. It was the splendid gift of curiosity and discovery along with a mind that knew no limits. As we progressed through life we constantly filled our mind with insights of the world around us.

Each of us, to varying degrees, set aside the curiosity and discovery in favor of the materialistic need for making a living. Now as we pass from adulthood to maturity, we are offered a rare opportunity to again experience curiosity, discovery, and a mind that knows no limits.

The young have a strong need to conform and imitate their peers. They don't want to be "different." They want to be accepted, not unpopular.

Maturity gives us the opportunity and the right to be individualistic. Our responsibilities are fewer, we can pursue our happiness without any apology. We can be unique!

It is our hope that this book has helped you prepare for the exciting senior years. You can make them exciting. Your future is in your hands. Whether you are single or married, it makes no difference—go for it!

It's been a lot of fun writing this book. In addition, we have achieved a deep sense of fulfillment. It's a warm feeling. Maybe, just maybe, we have added a little light to help you along life's way.

Have a Great Retirement! By living your total life to the fullest!

EPILOGUE

. . .

Years of research, our seminars, writing this book, then updating and revising, have caused us to spend many hours contemplating our forth-coming sunset years.

Phase Two is somewhere over the horizon, hopefully not tomorrow, but sooner or later it will arrive.

How will we handle this new challenge?

Our Mission in the Winter of Our Lives

Until we're forced to permanently hang up our boots, we'll continue to contribute to the world around us. Sitting back and finding ways to fill each day with busy work will be guarded against with great vigor.

Our contribution will not be in an environment of great pressure. The pace will be moderate with sufficient time allocated for leisure.

Knowing that we're still an integral part of society will keep our self-esteem high. We will have mental stimulation and meaningful purpose in our lives and feel good about ourselves.

A concentrated effort will be made to sustain our love for each other with the same intensity as in the past forty-seven years; maintain good health: every day must have a measure of physical stimulation; and continually make new friends since old friends will fade away for a variety of reasons.

Whatever losses are sent our way will be accepted. We'll rally and with God's help continue on regardless of how severe the loss.

We're not going to grow old gracefully. We're going to fight it all the way. But we will grow old with dignity—our heads held high—living our entire life to the very fullest extent possible.

We will work diligently to have this mission statement undergird our actions.

Alice and Fred Lee
1990

APPENDIX
WHERE TO WRITE

■ ■ ■

Air Force Enlisted Widows Home
Foundation, Inc.
571 Mooney Road
Fort Walton Beach, FL 32548

Air Force Village I
4917 Ravenswood Drive
San Antonio, TX 78227

Air Force Village II
5100 John D. Ryan Boulevard
San Antonio, TX 78245

Air Force Village West
100 Village West Drive
Riverside, CA 92508

Alamo Chamber of Commerce
Alamo, TX 78516

Aldersly
326 Mission Avenue
San Rafael, CA 94901

Alexian Village of Tennessee
100 James Blvd.
Signal Mountain, TN 37377

American Association of Retired
Persons
1909 K Street NW
Washington, DC 20049

Arcadia Retirement Residence
1434 Punahou Street
Honolulu, HI 96822

Athens Chamber of Commerce
Box 608
Athens, TX 75751

Austin Chamber of Commerce
Box 1976
Austin, TX 78767

Austin Manor
95 Elizabeth Street
Delaware, OH 43015

Avion Travelcade Club
Box 236
DeBary, FL 32713

Balboan
2340 Fourth Avenue
San Diego, CA 92101

Bella Vista Village
Village Hall
Bella Vista, AR 72714

Bentonville Chamber of Commerce
412 South Main Street
Bentonville, AR 72712

Berryville Chamber of Commerce
Berryville, AR 72616

Bob Hope Village
30 Holly Avenue
Shalimar, FL 32579

Bristol Village
111 Wendy Lane
Waverly, OH 45690

Brownsville Chamber of Commerce
Brownsville, TX 78520

Burgundy Place
8887 South Lewis
Tulsa, OK 74137

Butterfield Trail Village
1923 East Joyce
Fayetteville, AR 72703

Camp Coast to Coast
64 Inverness Drive East
Engelwood, CO 80112

Cape Cod Chamber of Commerce
Hyannis, MA 02601

Carefree Chamber of Commerce
Box 734
Carefree, AZ 85377

Carlyle on the Bay
1900 North Bayshore Drive
Miami, FL 33132

Carriage/Royals International
Travel Club
Box 246
Millersburg, IN 46543

Castle Ridge
635 Prairie Center Drive
Eden Prairie, MN 55344

Champion Fleet Owners
Association
Dryden, MI 48428

Chandler Chamber of Commerce
Chandler, AZ 85224

Château La Jolla
233 Prospect
La Jolla, CA 92037

Chautauqua Institution
Program Center for Older Adults
Chautauqua, NY 14722

Cherokee Village
P.O. Box 720
Cherokee Village, AR 72525

Clearbrook
128 Sussex Way
Jamesburg, NJ 08831

Clemson Chamber of Commerce
P.O. Box 202
Clemson, SC 29631

Clemson Downs
337 Summer Walk
Clemson, SC 29631

Clerbrook RV Resort
US 27 at Florida Turnpike
Clermont, FL 32711

Coachman Caravan Travel Club
Box 30
Middlebury, IN 46540

College Harbor
4600 Fifty-fourth Avenue South
St. Petersburg, FL 33711

College Walk
Neely Road
P.O. Box 1117
Brevard, NC 28712

The Colonnades
c/o Alumni Hall
211 Emmet Street
Charlottesville, VA 22903

Concordia at Bella Vista
1 Concordia Drive
Bella Vista, AR 72714

Continuing Care Accreditation
Commission
Suite 400
1129 Twentieth Street NW
Washington, DC 20036-3489

Cooper Industries
1801 Forest Hills Boulevard
Bella Vista, AR 72714-2399

Costa Rica Tourist Board
200 South East First Street, #402
Miami, FL 33131

Covenant Shores
9150 North Mercer Way
Mercer Island, WA 98040

Covenant Village
2125 North Olive Avenue
Turlock, CA 95380

Creative World Rallies & Caravans
606 North Carrollton Avenue
New Orleans, LA 70119

Crestwood
Route 530, Box 165
Whiting, NJ 08759

Cross Keys Village
Box 128
New Oxford, PA 17350

Crosslands
Box 100
Kennett Square, PA 19348

Cruise America
5959 Blue Lagoon Drive #250
Miami, FL 33126

Cruise Canada
5959 Blue Lagoon Drive #250
Miami, FL 33126

Dallas Christian Counseling Service
1801 Gateway, #205
Richardson, TX 75080

Desert Hot Springs Chamber of
Commerce
Box 848
Desert Hot Springs, CA 92240

Donna Chamber of Commerce
Donna, TX 78537

Dunwoody Village
3500 West Chester Pike
Newtown Square, PA 19073

Eagle Towers
77 Third Street
Stamford, CT 06905

Eckerd College
4200 Fifty-fourth Avenue South
St. Petersburg, FL 33711

Edinburg Chamber of Commerce
Edinburg, TX 78539

El Castillo
205 East Alameda
Santa Fe, NM 87504

Elderhostel
80 Boylston Street, #400
Boston, MA 02116

Escapees, Inc.
Route 5, Box 310
Livingston, TX 77351

Escondido Chamber of Commerce
720 North Broadway
Escondido, CA 92025

Eureka Springs Chamber of
Commerce
Box 551
Eureka Springs, AR 72632

Evangelical Lutheran Good
Samaritan Society
1000 West Avenue North
Sioux Falls, SD 57117-5038

The Fairfax
9140 Belvoir Woods Parkway
Fort Belvoir, VA 22060

Falcons Landing
Box 44709
Fort Washington, MD 20744

Family Motor Coach Association
8291 Clough Pike
Cincinnati, OH 45244

Fayetteville Chamber of Commerce
Fayetteville, AR 72701

Fayetteville Chamber of Commerce
P.O. Drawer 9
Fayetteville, NC 28302-0009

Flagstaff Chamber of Commerce
101 West Santa Fe Avenue
Flagstaff, AZ 86001

Flippen Chamber of Commerce
P.O. Box 118
Flippen, AR 72634

Fort Myers Chamber of Commerce
Fort Myers, FL 33902

Fort Washington Estates
Fort Washington and Susquehanna
Avenues
Fort Washington, PA 19034

Forum Pueblo Norte
7090 East Mescal Street
Scottsdale, AZ 85254

Foulkeways at Gwynedd
Gwynedd, PA 19436

Fountain of the Sun
8001 East Broadway
Mesa, AZ 85208

Fredericksburg Chamber of
Commerce
Box 506
Fredericksburg, TX 78624

French Embassy
4101 Reservoir Road NW
Washington, DC 20007

Friendship Village
2645 East Southern Avenue
Tempe, AZ 85282

Gardens
1050 Pine Street
Silver City, NM 88061

Georgetown
2512 Q Street
Washington, DC 20007

Glendale Chamber of Commerce
Glendale, AZ 85301

Global Home Exchange and Travel
Service
P.O. Box 2015
South Burlington, VT 05403

Golden Palms
2101 Treasure Hills Boulevard
Harlingen, TX 78550

Good Samaritan Cedar Lodge
5 Cortez Road
Hot Springs Village, AR 71909

Good Sam RV Owners Club
29901 Agoura Road
Agoura, CA 91301

Go Vacations, Inc.
24701 Frampton Avenue
Harbor City, CA 90710

Go Vacations, Inc.
129 Carlingview Drive
Rexdale, ON Canada M9W5E7

Grace Graham Vacation College
Housing Office, University of
Oregon
Eugene, OR 97403

Gray Panthers Project Fund
1424 16th Street NW
Suite 602
Washington, DC 20036

Greek Embassy
2211 Massachusetts Avenue NW
Washington, DC 20008

Green Valley
Box 587
Green Valley, AZ 85614

Greenville Chamber of Commerce
P.O. Box 10048
Greenville, SC 29603

Guide Dog Foundation for the
Blind, Inc.
371 East Jerico Turnpike
Smithtown, NY 11787

Gwynedd Estates
Norristown Road and Tennis
Avenue
Spring House, PA 19477

Harbour's Edge
401 Linden Boulevard
Delray Beach, FL 33483

Harlingen Chamber of Commerce
Box 189
Harlingen, TX 78551

Harrison Chamber of Commerce
Harrison, AR 72601

Heartmeadow
134 Flagg Road
West Hartford, CT 06117

Hemet Chamber of Commerce
395 East Latham Avenue
Hemet, CA 92343

Henton at Elon
Elon College, NC 27244

Heritage
2015 Fredericka Road
St. Simons Island, GA 31522

Heritage Hills of Westchester
Heritage Development Group, Inc.
Box 304
Somers, NY 10589

Heritage Place
2990 Hickory Hill Road
Memphis, TN 38115

Heritage Village
Heritage Development Group, Inc.
Southbury, CT 06488

Hideaways International
P.O. Box 1464
Littleton, ME 01460

Hilton Head Chamber of
Commerce
1 Chamber of Commerce Drive
Hilton Head Island, SC 29938

Holiday City
24 Weybridge Court
Toms River, NJ 08757

Home Exchange International
185 Park Row, #14D
New York, NY 10038

Hot Springs Village
Highway 7 and Desota Boulevard
Hot Springs Village, AR 71909

Huntington Terrace
18800 Florida Street
Huntington Beach, CA 92648

Innisbrook
P.O. Drawer 1088
Tarpon Springs, FL 33589

Interhostel Program
University of New Hampshire
6 Garrison Avenue
Durham, NH 03824

International Executive Service
Corps
622 Third Avenue
New York, NY 10017

International Home Exchange
Service
P.O. Box 3975
San Francisco, CA 94119

International Living
824 East Baltimore Street
Baltimore, MD 21202

Irish Embassy
2234 Massachusetts Avenue NW
Washington, DC 20008

Island on Lake Travis
3404 American Drive
Logo Vista, TX 78645

Italian Embassy
1601 Fuller Street NW
Washington, DC 20009

Joan Maehr, Inc.
P.O. Box 553
Addison, TX 75001

John Knox Village
500 North Murray Road
Lees Summit, MO 64063

Kendal at Longwood
Box 100
Kennett Square, PA 19348

Keowee Key
Route 2
Salem, SC 29676

Kerrville Chamber of Commerce
1200 Sidney Baker
Kerrville, TX 78028

Kingdom of the Sun
800 West Buckeye
Deming, NM 88030

Kingman Chamber of Commerce
P.O. Box 1150
Kingman, AZ 86401-1150

Kings Row
1800 Highway 35
Middletown, NJ 07748

LaFeria Chamber of Commerce
LaFeria, TX 78559

Lake Fairways
Box 4535
North Fort Myers, FL 33903

Lake Forest Good Samaritan
Village
3904 Montecito Drive
Denton, TX 76205

Lake Park Santa Ana North
15010 East Fairhaven Avenue
Santa Ana, CA 92701

Lakeway
2201 World of Tennis Boulevard
Austin, TX 78734

Laniolu Good Samaritan Center
333 Lewers Street
Honolulu, HI 96815

La Vida Llena
10501 Lagrima de Oro NE
Albuquerque, NM 87111

Lawrence Welk Resort
8860 Lawrence Welk Drive
Escondido, CA 92026

LeGan, Inc.
One Tabor Center
1200 Seventeenth Street
Denver, CO 80202

Leisure Care
275 118th Avenue, #220
Bellevue, WA 98005

Leisure Knoll
4 Buckingham Drive, North
Lakehurst, NJ 08733

Leisure Towne
1 Plymouth Court
Vincentown, NJ 08088

Leisure Village
4701 Leisure Village Way
Ocean Hills, CA 92054

Leisure Village West
959 Buckingham Drive
Lakehurst, NJ 08733

Leisure World
908 South Power Road
Mesa, AZ 85206

Leisure World-Laguna Hills
23522 Paseo de Valencia
Laguna Hills, CA 92653

Leisure World-Seal Beach
1901 Golden Rain Road
Seal Beach, CA 90740

Life Care Services Corporation
800 Second Avenue
Des Moines, Iowa 50309

Lifestyle Explorations
P.O. Box 57-6487
Modesto, CA 95355

Loners on Wheels, Inc.
P.O. Box 1355
Poplar Bluff, MO 63901

Los Angeles Chamber of
Commerce
505 South Flower Street
Los Angeles, CA 90071

Luther Crest
800 Hausman Road
Allentown, PA 18103

Madison House/Edmunds
2150 Seventy-second Avenue West
Edmunds, WA 98020

Madison House/Medford
2979 Barnett Road
Medford, OR 97501

Madison House/North
East 100 Dalke
Spokane, WA 99207

Madison House/San Antonio
8645 Fredericksburg Road
San Antonio, TX 78229

Madison House/Totem Lake
12215 North East 128th Street
Kirkland, WA 98034

Madison House/Yakima
3300 Englewood Avenue
Yakima, WA 98902

Martins Run
11 Martins Run
Media, PA 19063

Mature Outlook
Box 1205
Glenview, IL 60025

McAllen Chamber of Commerce
Box 790
McAllen, TX 78501

McAuley
Box 745
West Hartford, CT 06107

Meadow Lakes
Box 695
Marble Falls, TX 78654

Meadowood
2455 Tamarack Trail
Bloomington, IN 47401

Meadowstone Place
10410 Stone Canyon Road
Dallas, TX 75230

Mercedes Chamber of Commerce
P.O. Box 37
Mercedes, TX 78570

Mesa Chamber of Commerce
Mesa, AZ 85201

Mission Chamber of Commerce
Box 431
Mission, TX 78572-0431

Moosehaven
Orange Park, FL 32073

Mountain Home Chamber of
Commerce
Mountain Home, AR 72653

National Association of Partners in
Education, Inc.
601 Wythe Street, #200
Alexandria, VA 22314

National Church Residences
2335 North Bank Drive
Columbus, OH 43220

National Council of Senior Citizens
925 Fifteenth Street NW
Washington, DC 20005

National Mental Health Association
1021 Prince Street
Alexandria, VA 22314

New Choices for the Best Years
P.O. Box 1945
Marion, OH 43305-1945

Olds Manor
201 Michigan Street, NW
Grand Rapids, MI 49503

Outdoor Resorts of America
Box 2093
South Padre Island, TX 78597

Outdoor Resorts Palm Springs RV
Resort and Country Club
69-411 Ramon Road
Palm Springs, CA 92234

Pacific Regent
919 109th Avenue NE
Bellevue, WA 98004

Palm Springs Chamber of
Commerce
Municipal Airport Terminal
Palm Springs, CA 92262

Panorama City
150 Circle Drive
Lacey, WA 98503

Pathfinder Vacations, Inc.
8120A Westminster Highway
Richmond, BC Canada V6X1A6

Peace Corps
P-301
Washington, DC 20526

Pennswood Village
Newtown, PA 18940

Peter Becker Community
Maple Avenue and Yoder Road
Harleysville, PA 19438

Pharr Chamber of Commerce
P.O. Box 1341
Pharr, TX 78577

Phoenix Chamber of Commerce
Box 10
Phoenix, AZ 85001

Pinehurst
Box 2270
Southern Pines, NC 28387

Pine Lakes Country Club
P.O. Box 3494
North Fort Myers, FL 33918

Pine to Palm Resort
Route 2 FM 1015
Weslaco, TX 78596

Pine Run Community
Ferry and Iron Hill Roads
Doylestown, PA 18901

Pohai Nani Good Samaritan
Kauhale
45-090 Namoku Street
Kanoehe, HI 96744

Port Isabel Chamber of Commerce
213 Yturria
Port Isabel, TX 78578

Portuguese Embassy
2125 Kalorama Road NW
Washington, DC 20008

Prescott Chamber of Commerce
Prescott, AZ 86301

Providence Point
4135 Providence Point Drive, SE
Issaquah, WA 98027

Rancho Bernardo
(San Diego Chamber of
Commerce)
P.O. Box 28517
San Diego, CA 92128

Rappahannock Westminister-
Canterbury
10 Lancaster Drive
Irvington, VA 22480

Recreational Vehicle Industry
Association
Box 2999
Reston, VA 22090

Recreational Vehicle Rental
Association
3251 Old Lee Highway, #500
Fairfax, VA 22030

Remington Club
16925 Hiebra Drive
San Diego, CA 92128

Rental Management Systems
1201 Baldwin Park Boulevard
Baldwin Park, CA 91706

Retirement Inn/Forest Lane
2920 Forest Lane
Dallas, TX 75234

Retirement Inn/Quail Run
12401 Trail Oaks Drive
Oklahoma City, OK 73120

Retirement Newsletter
7811 Montrose Road
Potomac, MD 20854

Rio Grande Valley Chamber of
Commerce
P.O. Box 1499
Weslaco, TX 78596

Rockport Chamber of Commerce
Rockport, TX 78382

Rogue Valley Manor
1200 Mira Mar Avenue
Medford, OR 97504

Rossmoor
Box 93
Cranbury, NJ 08512

Rydal Park on the Fairway
Rydal, PA 19046

St. Petersburg Chamber of
Commerce
Box 1371
St. Petersburg, FL 33721

Sandestin Beach Hilton
554 Highway 98 East
Destin, FL 32541

Sand Hills Chamber of Commerce
P.O. Box 458
Southern Pines, NC 28387

San Diego Chamber of Commerce
110 West C Street, #1600
San Diego, CA 92101

San Juan Chamber of Commerce
San Juan, TX 78589

Santa Fe Chamber of Commerce
Box 1928
Santa Fe, NM 87504-1928

Saugatuck Chamber of Commerce
Saugatuck, MI 49453

Savannah Lakes Village
P.O. Box 1469
McCormick, SC 29835

Scottsdale Chamber of Commerce
7333 Scottsdale Mall
Scottsdale, AZ 85251-4498

Scottsdale Village Square
2620 North Sixty-eighth Street
Scottsdale, AZ 85257

Sedona Chamber of Commerce
P.O. Box 478
Sedona, AZ 86336

Senior Citizens Services
City Administration Building
202 C Street
San Diego, CA 92101

Service Corps of Retired Executives
1825 Connecticut Avenue NW
Suite 503
Washington, DC 20009

Shell Point Village
R.R. 12 Shell Point Boulevard
Fort Myers, FL 33908

Sierra Club
730 Polk Street
San Francisco, CA 94109

Silver City Retirement Community
1103 North Hudson
Silver City, NM 88061

Southampton Estates
238th Street
Southampton, PA 18966

South Padre Island Chamber of
Commerce
South Padre Island, TX 78578

Spanish Cove Retirement Village
1401 Cornwell
Yukon, OK 73099

Spanish Embassy
2700 Fifteenth Street NW
Washington, DC 20009

Sportscoach Owners International
3550 Foothill Boulevard
Glendale, CA 91214

SR Texas
11551 Forest Central Drive
Suite 305
Dallas, TX 75243-3916

Stillwaters Estates
2800 Cooks Hill Road
Centralia, WA 98531

Sugarmill Woods
92 Cypress Boulevard West
Homosassa, FL 32646

Sun City Center
Box 5698
Sun City Center, FL 33571

Sun City Chamber of Commerce
Phoenix, AZ 85351

Sun City Chamber of Commerce
Box 37
Sun City, CA 92381

Sun City Summerlin
Box 80180
Las Vegas, NV 89180

Sun City Vistoso
P.O. Box 73230
Tucson, AZ 85740

Sun City West
Box 1705
Sun City, AZ 85372

Sunflower Resort
16501 El Mirage Road
Surprise, AZ 85374

Sun Lakes
25612 E. J. Robson Boulevard
Sun Lakes, AZ 85248

Sun 'N Lake
4101 Sun 'N Lake Boulevard
Sebring, FL 33872

Sunny Acres Villa
2501 East 104th Avenue
Denver, CO 80233

Sun Village
3252 Kuhio Highway
Lihue, Kauai, HI 96766

Swansgate
Box 6725
Greenville, SC 29601

Tamarron
P.O. Drawer 3131
Durango, CO 81301

Tellico Village
112 Chota Center
Louden, TN 37774

Tempe Chamber of Commerce
60 East Fifth Street, #3
Tempe, AZ 85281

Temple Meridian on Canyon Creek
4312 South Thirty-first Street
Temple, TX 76502

Tennis Club of Palm Beach
2800 Haverhill Road North
West Palm Beach, FL 33409

Teresa Village
354 Woodrow Street
Fort Walton Beach, FL 32548

Thousand Trails
12301 North East Tenth Street
Bellevue, WA 98009